AMERICAN
ASSOCIATION
OF MUSEUMS

Technical

Information

Service

Public institutions for Personal Learning

Establishing A Research Agenda

John H. Falk, Ph.D.
and Lynn D. Dierking, Ph.D.,
Editors

1995

Public Institutions for Personal Learning: Establishing a Research Agenda
John H. Falk and Lynn D. Dierking, editors.
Includes bibliographic references.
ISBN 0-931201-24-1 (paper)

Public Institutions for Personal Learning

Contents

Foreword

The American Association of Museums is dedicated to promoting excellence within the museum community and to providing services to the nation's museums and their staffs. This publication represents one of AAM's many efforts to advance understanding and provide the profession with the knowledge and skills necessary to examine its own practices and standards.

This publication is divided into two distinct parts. The first describes the events of the 1994 National Science Foundation-funded conference "Public Institutions for Personal Learning: Understanding the Long-Term Impact of Museums," which sought to explore how and what people learn in the wide range of educational institutions called museums. A synthesis of conference discussions precedes two sections of analytical background papers. Reflection on the conversations from the conference will reward the reader with insights into a variety of ideas about museum learning as well as with some very concrete recommendations for future study. This section offers useful resources for defining questions crucial to establishing a research agenda for investigating learning in museums.

The second section of the publication includes academic papers that provided the basis for the group discussions. These papers should satisfy casual readers as well as practitioners and contribute to the idea of building a research framework. Additionally, the benefits realized from this volume in its entirety present a convincing case for replication of this exercise in order to contribute to the development of the discipline of museum learning. Drs. Falk and Dierking are willing to share their conference experiences, observations and notes with anyone interested in exploring issues of museum learning at their institution.

Acknowledgements

As with any endeavor, this conference and resulting book were not the product of just one or two individuals. We would like to thank Barbara Butler, Hyman Field and Robert Russell of the National Science Foundation for supporting this project. We also are grateful to the American Association of Museums for their efforts to ensure that these ideas reach a broader audience; in particular, we would like to thank Kim Igoe, Sara Dubberly, Roxana Adams, and Sarah Jepsen.

We are indebted to all of the individuals who participated in the Annapolis conference, who gave of their time and intellect to help make this a very special and important event. In particular, we thank our seven "domain experts," Mike Czikszentmihalyi, Gary Evans, Alan Hedge, Doug Herrmann, John Ogbu, Barbara Rogoff and Jeremy Roschelle for taking time out of their busy schedules to invest in the future of the museum community. We are especially grateful to John Balling, Valerie Crane, Jeff Hayward, George Hein and Mary Ellen Munley—who not only helped us facilitate the small group sessions at the Conference, but also helped to profoundly shape the discourse and thought-processes of the participants—including ours. And of course, we want to thank all of the participants who attended the conference and brought their own unique ideas, perspectives and agendas to the discussions that ensued. As it should be, the resulting product is a blending of all of these diverse perspectives.

We also owe a debt of gratitude to those who helped to consolidate the "process" of a conference into a single "product"; this book. We are sincerely appreciative of the efforts of Courtney Abrams, Dana Holland and Rebecca Fye for their assistance in helping pull together the many pieces. Special thanks are due to Jeff Hayward, George Hein, Ellen Hirzy, Tom Krakauer, Mary Ellen Munley and Dennis Schatz for reviewing a draft of this book and providing invaluable comments and Ann Grogg for her copyediting. Their insights and perspectives have helped us to capture the spirit and flavor of the conference.

Finally, we would especially like to thank Ursula Marcum, now of Threshold Studios, Alexandria, Virginia, who selflessly toiled for over a year to help make this conference and book a reality. Without Ursula's efforts, the Annapolis conference would not have been the success that it was.

John H. Falk
Lynn D. Dierking
Science Learning, inc.
November 1, 1995

Introduction

A Case for Conducting Long-Term Learning Research in Museums

John H. Falk
Lynn D. Dierking

Even though museums have increased in variety and exploded in popularity over the last few decades, their value to society seems to be in question as never before. While museums are aggressively characterizing themselves as institutions of public learning, diminishing resources and a political climate of public accountability are requiring that they demonstrate their educational value to society and justify their very existence.

In response to these trends, understanding learning in museums has become a high priority within the museum community (AAM 1984; 1992). The American Association of Museums' document *Excellence and Equity* (1992) states that the commitment to education is central to a museum's public service and must be "clearly expressed in every museum's mission and pivotal to every museum's activities" (p. 3). The document goes on to suggest that museums must not only develop and expand their educational functions, but they should also seek to understand the learning opportunities that museums afford the public. In the last five years, at least four professional meetings have addressed learning in museums generally, and sessions on learning have been held at virtually every meeting of the American Association of Museums, American Association for State and Local History, Association of Science-Technology Centers, and Museum Education Roundtable, including a number of ad hoc sessions.

This heightened interest in museum learning has directed the profession to a museum research literature covering more than seventy years of investigations. Unfortunately, much of the previous museum-based learning research focused on short-term studies assessing the in-museum behavior or exit knowledge of visitors. Although useful in providing a suggestion of what kinds of learning might take place within museums, most museum professionals believe that these studies do not fully encompass the breadth of museum-based learning. In addition, previous attempts to define and measure learning in museums have lacked both a clear focus and a well-formulated theoretical underpinning. Consequently, understanding of even the most fundamental questions about learning in museums remains elusive. The net result has been an inability on the part of museum professionals to state clearly, succinctly, and persuasively how museums meaningfully affect people's lives, at the very time that the articulation of this connection seems essential to museums' continued existence and prosperity.

It is our feeling that until professionals in the museum field can develop a significantly better understanding of the long-term impact of museum experiences on visitor knowledge, attitudes, and behaviors, it will be difficult for museum professionals to be specific about the extent of the museum's benefits. What is required is a concerted, conceptually consistent effort to conduct basic, long-term research that answers the following general questions:

1. What do people who visit museums learn?

2. How does this learning enrich the lives of visitors? For example, in the case of a science-oriented museum, does a visitor's experience influence his or her "acculturation" into the scientific and technological world?

3. How does the learning that occurs in a museum setting connect with the learning that occurs in other settings? Under what circumstances are connections facilitated, and under what circumstances are connections inhibited?

4. What is the process by which learning occurs in museums? Is it similar to, or fundamentally different from, the process of learning in other settings, such as schools?

5. And finally, what role do museums, and the learning that occurs in museums, play in the larger cultural and learning experiences of Americans?

These are fundamental questions that can be answered only through systematic, basic research. Saying this, it is essential that we differentiate systematic, basic research from evaluation. Over the past decade, museums of all kinds have implemented hundreds of evaluation studies. Most of these studies, appropriately, have been formative evaluations, designed to facilitate the ongoing design and implementation of exhibits and educational programs and materials. But while evaluation, whether front-end, formative, or summative, uses methodologies similar to those of basic research, it is inherently ill-suited to answering fundamental questions such as the ones listed above. The essence of evaluation, as opposed to basic research, is assessment of whether something is working or not. It is designed, in the terminology of Levins (1968), to maximize realism and precision at the expense of generalizability. A good evaluation study will very definitively answer very specific questions, for a very specific context; these findings normally cannot be generalized beyond those specific questions or context.

High-quality basic research, by contrast, always strives to maximize generalizability, sometimes at the expense of precision. Whether it is hypothesis-testing or hypothesis-generating research, basic research seeks to understand fundamental issues and to answer fundamental questions in ways that permit generalization. In other words, the study findings not only relate to the real world of one exhibit in one museum but to the larger world of exhibits in museums. Because the questions on museum learning we have posed are fundamental, and because we hope to generate generalizable answers, basic research is the tool we must utilize.

Museums and Learning

It is not that the field knows nothing about museum visitors and museum visitor learning. A growing body of visitor research provides insights about who museum visitors are and what they do in museums (Falk and Dierking 1992; Bitgood, Serrell, and Thompson 1994; Screven and Shettel 1993). Much less well understood, however, is what sense visitors make of museums and what messages they take with them when they leave. After nearly three-quarters of a century of inquiry, understanding the long-term impact of the museum experience continues to be the most difficult aspect of visitor research.

There are reasons for this difficulty, reasons related to the diversity of individuals who visit museums, the inherent complexity of the museum environment, and the rapidly evolving expectations among museum staffs as to what can be communicated during a museum visit. Museums are public spaces that people of all ages and types independently choose to visit. Visitors have many different backgrounds and invest differing amounts of time and interest in their visits. Within the museum, visitors continue to act independently, choosing what to look at, what to skim, and what to study. In contemporary museums there are additional options. Vistors can listen, watch, touch, and use computer terminals to manipulate the objects and information.

The content of what museums present to the public has changed dramatically in recent years. Although static survey-style exhibitions can still be found, the trend is clearly away from these types of exhibits. Subjects are focused and topical: HIV and AIDS, deforestation, art censorship. The goals of these exhibitions include not only conveying content but influencing beliefs. At a recent meeting of the Association of Science-Technology Centers, a group of science museum professionals listed more than thirty possible learning outcomes for a museum visit. Most of the outcomes generated during this brainstorming session had little to do with learning science facts. Rather, this group of museum professionals felt that exhibitions and programs should be developed and presented to enhance curiosity, encourage positive attitudes toward science, and increase the ability to ask good questions (*ASTC Newsletter* 1994).

Although much of what the museum visitor encounters is subject-specific information related to science, history, or art, much is not (Falk and Dierking 1992). Visitors also perceive, and subsequently remember, other facets of the rich social, physical, or personal context museums afford. Various studies have documented that beyond "content," museums afford opportunities for social interaction (Dierking and Falk 1994), for escape from the humdrum of the work-a-day world (Graburn 1984; Yellis 1985), and for access to interesting and unusual built or natural environments (Kimmel and Maves 1972; Falk 1988).

Are people learning in museums? This question is easy to frame and hard to answer. In part, the difficulty lies in defining the term *"learning"* which, in recent years, has generated considerable debate within the museum community. Learning is both a verb and a noun, a process and a product.

Learning as Process

Let us first discuss learning as a process. We propose organizing our thinking about the learning process around a series of key features of the learning experience, using what we currently know about learning in general to approach museum learning in particular.

Learning involves a multitude of processes. At the very least, it involves perception and memory. Perception is strongly influenced by prior experiences. The ability to see a group of trees and perceive this as a forest is directly related to our past experience with trees and forests. In the absence of prior experience, real and/or conceptual, we could not reach this conclusion. Research has shown that no two individuals perceive the world in exactly the same way, in large part because no two individuals share the same prior experiences. In addition to experience, though, there are genetic components to perception. Even individuals who ostensibly experience the same event may, because of different preferred modes of acquiring information (e.g., kinesthetic versus linguistic), end up with very different perceptions of the event.

Learning is an active process of collecting information, a process of utilizing this information to build complex, internal knowledge structures called *schemata*. Every individual's schemata are unique and appear to have a physical reality represented by many branching connections of neurons within the brain. Schemata are accessed both as places in which to store new information and as places from which to retrieve old information. By virtue of differences in both genes and experience, every individual uniquely acquires, processes, and stores information.

A review of the literature suggests that the process of learning can be conceptualized as involving seven major factors. These are the influences of:
- prior knowledge and experience
- subsequent, reinforcing experiences
- motivation and attitudes
- culture and background
- social mediation
- design and presentation
- the physical setting

To fully understand the nature of the museum learning process requires an understanding of the role, independently and collectively, of these seven influences.

Prior Knowledge and Experience
Learning is the cumulative process of using current experiences to reinforce and extend prior remembered experiences. Thus to understand the nature of someone's museum learning requires understanding the complete range of experiences that helped to create that learning. That means examining the knowledge a visitor brings with him or her to the museum and the knowledge gained while there.

Subsequent, Reinforcing Experiences
Prior knowledge and experience are not the only determinants of learning and memory. Often what happens subsequent to an experience can be vital to learning. Future reinforcing experiences are extremely important. Assessing the impact of a museum experience will require determining how and when relevant knowledge was added subsequent to the museum experience.

Motivation and Attitudes
Although visitors are exposed to a wide range of information when they visit a museum, most seem to focus on only a subset of available information. Part of this self-selection is related to information overload, but much appears to be deliberate. Under normal conditions, individuals pay more attention to the things in which they have more interest. Interests are predictably based upon prior experiences, knowledge, and feelings—a classic feedback loop. People learn best those things about which they already have some knowledge and in which they are interested. In other words, people learn best those things that they are motivated to learn. The informationally rich, free-choice nature of museums both facilitates and necessitates choice.

Culture and Background
Different people perceive the world in different ways. One dimension of this difference can be attributed to culture and socialization. People from different cultural backgrounds approach ideas and even objects very differently; these differences influence how information is perceived and, ultimately, how information is encoded in memory.

Social Mediation
Learning is almost always a process that is socially mediated. This social mediation is normally overt, though occasionally subtle and indirect. Because humans are social organisms, information is rarely acquired in a social vacuum. People learn while talking to, listening to, and watching others. The interpretations provided by companions become fused with one's own interpretations. Ideas, feelings, and even physical actions are normally amalgamations forged during social contacts.

Design and Presentation
Museums, like many other settings, are physical environments designed to influence learning and behavior. Museums develop exhibitions and displays, present films, and provide interactive devices to affect visitor learning. Sometimes the design of these educational media are exceedingly effective at channeling visitor experience and attention; other times they are woefully inadequate. The more that is understood about the specifics of how design influences visitor behavior and learning, the more likely researchers will be able to understand how museums in general affect visitor learning.

Physical Setting
What people learn from settings, however, is not always a consequence of premeditated design. Settings are at once physical and psychological constructs. The light, the ambience, the "feel," and even the smell of an environment influence learning. Often these influences are at once the most subconscious and the most powerful, the hardest to verbalize but the easiest to recall. For this reason, the role of the physical context upon learning has been one of the least-studied, most-neglected aspects of learning.

Learning as Product

The previous section outlines some general issues related to the process of learning—the when, where, why, and for whom of learning, in short the how of learning. The question most frequently asked of, and by, museum professionals, though, is the what of learning. What kinds of learning occur within the context of a museum visit? In what ways do these learnings enrich the lives of visitors? What are the learning outcomes of a museum experience? We know less about the products of museum learning than we do about the processes.

To assess the long-term learning outcomes of museum experiences it will be important to think very broadly, to encompass all the richness of experience that occurs within museums. It will therefore be important to free ourselves from the traditional information acquisition biases about learning, biases that tend to equate learning with acquiring facts and concepts only and that separate cognitive learning, affective learning, and psychomotor learning. The products of learning such as ideas, feelings, and sensations, are rarely clearly delineated or separable.

The strongly contextual nature of learning is one reason the learning that occurs in museums is so difficult both to predict and to assess. No two individuals have the same experience. As visitors make their way through the museum, they pay attention to different exhibits and objects, even understanding the words in a label differently. As a result, learning outcomes are always relative to the individual and the unique circumstances in which they occur.

The learning outcomes we should focus on are both useful and long-term. Ausubel defined this type of learning as "meaningful learning" (Ausubel, Novak, and Hanesian 1978). Meaningful learning implies that new information, be it new facts, attitudes, or feelings, is linked to existing information in a learner's knowledge structure in such a way that the learner is able to recall this information after extended periods of time and to apply these ideas to new situations or problems. In other words, within a museum context, meaningful learning for a visitor might involve observing objects, reading labels, manipulating a device, role-playing, or simply talking with friends and family. The new ideas, attitudes, information, or skills acquired become part of the visitor's permanent store of knowledge, available for his or her use long after the museum visit has ended.

The Annapolis Conference

In August 1993 Science Learning, inc., received support from the National Science Foundation to organize and convene a small working conference to consider the question of conducting long-term, basic research on the how and what of museum learning. Additional support was provided by the American Association of Museums, which agreed to publish the outcomes of this effort as a part of its Technical Information Service. On August 26 and 27, 1994, forty-eight individuals from diverse backgrounds and institutions assembled in Annapolis, Maryland, to participate in a conference, "Public Institutions for Personal Learning: Understanding the Long-Term Impact of Museums."

The purpose of the conference was to move beyond the rhetoric about learning that has dominated the museum field and catalyze actual efforts at defining and answering fundamental questions related to the long-term impact of museum experiences on individuals and society. Conference attendees were told on the first day of the meeting: "We are not here just to talk, we are here to develop a plan of action." The conference was designed to clarify the issues that underlie research on learning in museums, develop some consensus on what needs to be done, and define some appropriate research questions and methodologies for actually conducting such research.

To accomplish this task we brought together a diverse cross-section of individuals interested in long-term museum learning. Included were prominent social science researchers, museum learning researchers, museum professionals, representatives of museum professional associations, and representatives of funding agencies. There were no formal presentations, only large and small group discussions. There was no firmly fixed agenda, only a plan for using the two days of meetings to define museum learning outcomes and begin to develop research strategies for assessing those outcomes. The intent of the meeting was to provide a forum in which this diverse group of individuals could arrive at some broadly acceptable consensus and develop a research agenda that could be presented to the museum community and the museum funding community. First a few words about the participants.

Key to the concept of the conference was the contribution of social scientists. Our review of the literature had identified seven major factors as influencing the process of learning. Accordingly, with the recommendations of peers, we selected an eminent social scientist to represent each factor. These academics were invited to participate in the two-day conference so that they could contribute their perspectives and expertise to the deliberations. Each was also commissioned to write a background paper that would review the literature in their area of expertise and, to the extent possible, relate that literature to the question of investigating learning in museums.

Also invited to participate in the conference were seven individuals with strong backgrounds in the social sciences and experience in investigating learning in museums. Each was paired with one of the seven social scientists and also served as a discussion group facilitator. These individuals were chosen because of their ability to "speak" both "social science research" and "museum" and because of their ability to help facilitate small group discussions.

The majority in attendance, twenty-four individuals, came from the ranks of the museum profession—people with experience in the day-to-day operation of museums but also with a deep and abiding concern for understanding the impact of museums on visitors' lives. These two dozen individuals included museum directors, educators, curators, and designers from large and small institutions; they represented aquariums, art museums, botanical gardens, children's museums, history museums, natural history museums, and science centers. Announcements about the conference were made at Association of Science-Technology Centers and Visitor Studies Association meetings during the summer and fall of 1993, and a flyer announcing the conference was widely circulated. Participants were selected primarily on a first-come, first-served basis; some discretion was used to ensure a broad representation of museum types and professional roles.

A final group of participants represented funding agencies, public and private, that are currently supporting museum-related programs and projects. Invitations to participate in the conference were mailed to seventeen foundations, and seven chose to send representatives. In addition, representatives from two national associations dedicated to supporting museums as cultural institutions were included: the American Association of Museums and the Association of Science-Technology Centers. Also present was a representative from *Informal Science Review,* who reported on the conference (Russell and West 1994).

These forty-eight conference participants, although representative of the museum community, were not "representatives." They came as individuals, with their own agendas, interests, and personal biases. Prior to arriving, each participant read draft versions of the background papers so that there would be some common vocabulary and frames of intellectual reference. Additionally, each museum-based participant was asked to consider three questions before arriving:

1. What does your institution expect visitors to learn?
2. Why are these outcomes important?
3. How can we assess these outcomes?

Public Institutions for Personal Learning

This book, then, is an outgrowth of the efforts of these four dozen individuals to move beyond rhetoric toward a plan of action for better understanding the impact of museums on people's lives. It is not a typical conference proceedings. As there were no formal presentations, there are no reprints of presented papers or verbatim records of the discussions provided. We appreciate that it is not possible to totally capture the spirit of what was, by necessity, an ephemeral event. Instead, this book attempts to document the products of the conference, while, as much as possible, preserving the process by which these products were created. Following this introduction, an overview of the conference synthesizes the conference deliberations, provides a summary of the learning outcomes and research strategies developed at the meeting, and presents suggestions for establishing a national museum learning research agenda. Next come revised versions of the seven background papers prepared by the social scientists, followed by three papers written by representatives of art, children's, and science museums that reflect both on the conference and on the directions in which the field should be heading. Final sections present author biographies, a list of conference participants, and resources.

We encourage readers to use this book as a resource, sampling sections and readings as appropriate to the need. We hope it will stimulate discussions and, for those who are willing, also serve as a framework for considering, in museums and other institutions, the creation of a plan of action for conducting research on long-term learning. We would be delighted if the Annapolis Conference and this book prove to be a point of departure. They are neither a beginning nor an end, however, but an important step in what is envisioned as an arduous, many-step, multi-institutional effort toward facilitating understanding of museum learning.

We also hope that this conference and book help catalyze efforts to build a national museum learning research infrastructure; without such an infrastructure, no significant progress will be attained. Although we certainly hope that some individuals and institutions take the information contained here and directly implement museum learning research, we do not assume that these ideas or approaches represent the only, or necessarily even the best, ideas and approaches. Our intention has always been to help move the field from merely talking about museum learning into actively investigating this subject. We not only welcome alternative research agendas and approaches, we encourage them. It is in this collaborative spirit that we share the readings and discussions of the 1994 "Public Institutions for Personal Learning" conference and encourage others to join us in establishing an active community of museum learning researchers.

John H. Falk and Lynn D. Dierking

References

American Association of Museums. 1984. *Museums for a new century: A report of the Comission on Museums for a New Century.* Washington, D.C.: AAM.

American Association of Museums. 1992. *Excellence and equity: Education and the public dimension of museums.* Washington, D.C.: AAM.

ASTC Newsletter. 1994. "Museum educators, others, tackle notion of informal learning." *ASTC Newsletter* 22 (March/April 1994), no. 2: 1-3.

Ausubel, D. P., J. Novak, and H. Hanesian. 1978. *Educational psychology: A cognitive view.* New York: Holt, Rinehart & Winston.

Bitgood, S., B. Serrell, and D. Thompson. 1994. The impact of informal education on visitors to museums. In *Informal Science Learning*, ed. V. Crane. Dedham, Mass.: Research Communciations, Ltd.

Dierking, L.D. and J. H. Falk. 1994. Family behavior and learning in informal science settings: A review of the research. *Science Education* 78, no. 1: 57-72.

Falk, J.H. 1988. Museum recollections. In *Visitor studies, 1988: Proceedings of the First Annual Visitor Studies Conference,* ed. S. Bitgood, et al., pp. 60-65. Jacksonville, Ala.: Center for Social Design.

Falk, J. H. and L. D. Dierking. 1992. *The museum experience.* Washington, D.C.: Whalesback Books.

Graburn, N. H. 1984. The museum and the visitor experience. In *Museum education anthology: 1973-1983,* ed. Nichols, et al., pp. 177-182. Washington, D.C.: Museum Education Roundtable.

Kimmel, P. S. and M. J. Maves. 1972. Public reaction to museum interiors. *Museum News* 51: 17-19.

Levins, R. 1968. *Evolution in changing environments.* Princeton, N.J.: Princeton University Press.

Russell, R. L. and R. M. West. 1994. Annapolis meeting explores research on learning in museums. *Informal Science Review* 8 (September/October): 1-2, 4-5.

Screven, C. and P. Shettel, eds. 1993. *Visitor studies bibliography and abstracts* Shorewood, Wis.: Exhibit Communications Research, Inc.

Yellis, K. 1985. Reverence, association, and education: Testing a typology of museum-goer needs. Unpublished MS.

Note

1. The word "museum" is used as a generic term to refer to a wide assortment of educational institutions including art, history and natural history museums; botanical gardens; nature centers; science centers and zoos.

Part 1

Defining Our Outcomes and Research Questions

What Do We Think People Learn in Museums?

John H. Falk, Lynn D. Dierking and Dana G. Holland

The Annapolis Conference was designed to accomplish two broad goals:

1. To develop a manageable list of learning outcomes that could result from a museum visit and be applicable across various types of museums; and

2. To take these outcomes, reframe them as research questions and develop research designs to investigate the learning that results from museum experiences.

The next two chapters describe the efforts of the 48 Annapolis Conference participants to accomplish these two goals. Rather than a detailed accounting of the conference, these two chapters seek to organize and synthesize the ideas and discussion generated at the meeting since there were no formal presentations or pre-organized panels, only large and small group discussion sessions. In developing these summary chapters we have treated the notes and comments of facilitators and participants as data, and then qualitatively analyzed these data to reveal patterns of differences and commonalties. The result is a synthesis of conference participants' thinking that we believe accurately reveals both the current opinions and perspectives of the museum community, as well as the complexity of the underlying structure of museum-based learning.

The first day of the conference was devoted to the effort of defining museum learning "outcomes" — stated plainly, what are the possible impacts on a person when he or she visits a museum. The implicit assumption of this exercise was that if we can delineate a set of learning "outcomes" that the museum community can agree are reasonable and valuable, then documenting the frequency and extent of their occurrence becomes a manageable way to "understand museum learning." The two activities that contributed to this task were a large group sharing of personally memorable and meaningful museum experiences and a small group effort to develop "short" lists of learning outcomes.

The sharing of personal "best" and/or "worst" museum experiences proved to be extremely impor-

tant. This seemingly simple task revealed the powerful emotional and intellectual experiences that museums can and do facilitate. It also framed museum "learning" as frequently a very personal, often unpredictable, experience quite different than the highly structured and prescribed "learning" typically associated with formal education. The themes that emerged in these personal recollections, such as the capacity of museums to provide a context for making intellectual connections; the importance of having a personal affinity for the ideas/objects being displayed; the important role that social interactions play in mediating learning; how feelings of cultural inclusion/exclusion influence a museum experience and the power of early museum experiences to shape future life decisions, were echoed in all of the later efforts to define museum learning outcomes. This exercise also set a tone for the necessity of broadly defining "learning" to encompass a wide array of experiences and perspectives.

For the task of generating museum learning outcomes, the conference attendees were organized into six small working discussion groups.[1] Each small group contained one of the domain specialists and one of the facilitators plus three to five other conferees. The charge for each group was to develop a short list of learning outcomes that were important, as well as generalizable, across diverse types of museums. Although groups were not to focus specifically on the domain of the social scientist present in their group, the group's discussions often were influenced and informed by their expertise and by the ideas fostered by pre-conference reading of their background papers. The other dynamic that was present in each group was the diverse mix of individuals representing divergent orientations from within the museum field — art, history and science; education, curatorial, administration, design, and funding; researchers and practitioners.

All groups needed to confront, directly or indirectly, the issue of "learning" as it applies to museums. At the start of his discussion group session, Jeff Hayward stated:

"'Informal learning' is an accepted phenomenon among people in the museum community, even though we may have different definitions of what it means. In general, we agree that a museum is an educational experience, and the public thinks so too ('educational' and 'informative' are two of the most common words that people use to describe museums). And we also agree that this educational experience [can be] worthwhile and satisfying — after all many people come to do this voluntarily and they do consider it an enjoyable use of their leisure time. So it seems reasonable and appropriate that 'informal learning' is becoming an important catch-phrase for the significance and value of a museum visit."

Hayward went on to question whether the field needs to engage in the relatively endless discussion of defining the characteristics of informal learning (characterized as "running in circles") or whether it was better to accept an approximate definition and get on with the more important task of documenting where and when it happens (characterized as "closing the circle"). Independently Hayward's group, and each of the other small groups, explicitly or implicitly, endorsed the "closing the circle" view.

Although discussions in at least three of the groups included issues related to the meaning and characteristics of "learning" in a museum context, it is important to note, that defining the meaning of learning was not an obstacle to expansive and productive discussion within any of the groups, a sign perhaps that the museum community appreciates the need to move forward in this arena. However, discussions about learning in both small groups sessions, and subsequently in large group sessions, often made the distinction between "learning" as it occurs in schools and "learning" as it occurs in museums. George Hein correctly pointed out that these distinctions are primarily "administrative." He further cautioned against using "school learning" as a "surrogate for outdated pedagogy" — equating schools with bad practice and museums with good practice — he reminded us that good and bad practice happen in both settings. Hein concluded that learning, whether in a museum or in a school, is by its very nature "complex, personal, social and experientially based".

In the end, conference participants easily embraced a broad, flexible and highly idiosyncratic notion of what constitutes "learning." All groups felt that a broad definition of learning with outcomes that might vary subtly from institution to institution was critical; they all further agreed that this type of learning can, and does, occur in museums. In other words, conference participants did not feel the need to debate if museum learning occurs, instead, they were willing to focus their attention on defining *what, where, when, why* and *for whom* museum learning occurs.

Nearly all of the small groups began their discussions very broadly, beginning with "lengthy, flowing conversation," and then, often with some difficulty, focused their discussion on developing a limited set of outcomes. Employing this general approach — from open and expansive, to more focused and narrow — was probably inevitable given the participants' diverse views and experiences, but perhaps more significantly the process reflected the nature of museums as places for holistic and multi-faceted experiences.

Categories of Learning Outcomes

Content
Process
Traits
Visit/Institution
Identity

Several groups devised strategies for systematically narrowing the range of the learning outcomes that they generated. Based upon their exhaustive learning outcome lists, two groups generated topical categories under which the outcomes were thematically subsumed. The categories determined by one group were:

1. *Content:* The subject matter of museums.
2. *Process:* Characteristics usually associated with the learning process.
3. *Traits:* Traits pertinent to personal experiences, i.e., courage, curiosity, caring.
4. *Visit/Institution:* The quality of the entire experience.
5. *Sense of Identity:* Personal, cultural, community.

Criteria for Learning Outcomes

Augment Understanding
Improve Service
Increase value
Measurable
Fundable
Achievable

Another group systematically and objectively evaluated the relative importance of the various learning outcomes they generated by devising a set of assessment criteria. Each criteria subsumed some practical and concrete aspect of real museum experiences and operations. The criteria effectively put each learning outcome to a pragmatic litmus test, designed to assess the usefulness, feasibility, and measurability of the outcome. The criteria were:

1. Will results help museums better understand visitors (tourists and residents)?

2. Will understanding this outcome better help us serve other important audiences to the museum (e.g., schools)?

3. Does the outcome have social value?

4. Is the outcome consonant with the museum's mission?

5. Is the outcome measurable?

6. Is the outcome fundable?

7. Can museums achieve the outcome and do it well?

Characteristics of the Museum Environment That Facilitate The Process of Learning

Process Outcomes
Direct experience
Personal and active
Socially mediated

The discussions of the six groups encompassed a myriad of factors important to visitor learning and to the institutional facilitation of that learning. The learning outcomes generated included the immediate as well as the long term, the social as well as the deeply personal, the concrete, as well as the abstract. Ultimately, discussions revolved around two issues; what characteristics of the museum environment facilitate learning — the processes of learning — and, the task at hand, *what* learning occurs as a consequence of museum experiences — the products or outcomes of learning.

It was difficult for many participants to separate the characteristics of museums and the **processes** of learning promoted there, from the potential products or outcomes of these learning experiences. Three important characteristics of museums and the processes that they can facilitate, emerged from the data.[2]

1. Museums provide "direct experience" with real objects in an appropriate context.

Having a direct experience with real objects, organisms, and phenomena (Provide encounters with examples of excellence such as artwork, unique objects, cultural pride)
Bring things to life. Make things real.

2. Museums facilitate a voluntary, highly personal and active style of learning.

How well does the museum engage the visitor in the PROCESS of learning? (I use the museum to actively engage in the dynamic process of learning and to investigate questions that are meaningful to me.)

Visitor Involvement
• Observed active participation in the opportunities for interaction presented by the exhibit
• Self-reported personal engagement in the experience
• Longer-term increased interest in the subject matter of the exhibit

3. Museums facilitate and encourage socially mediated learning.

Enhance social aspect of the visit.

Visitor Sharing of Learning and Inquiry
• Observed or reported cross-generational sharing of exhibit-related information
• Observed or reported sharing of information among initially independent social groups in the museums
• Recorded attempts by visitors to share exhibit-related information with museum staff

What role does social interaction play in the museum experience (particularly interaction with staff)?

Also imbedded in some of the groups' extensive learning outcome lists were notions about what museums can and should be for people.

In summary, there was support for the view that museums are, perhaps most uniquely, places for active, personal exploration. In addition, museums were seen as the agents responsible for the creation of environments within which this active exploration occurs. One group implicitly characterized museums as "facilitators." The responsibility for positive visitor learning outcomes was essentially placed on the museum (i.e., to "provide," "engender," "increase," "meet the needs," "change," etc.) Another group was in tune to visitors' experiential states while in the museum and after leaving, specifically visitors' feelings of capability, enthusiasm and sense of wonder (i.e., "inspire awe," "empower," "foster understanding," "bring things to life," etc.)

Learning Outcomes

As anticipated, the discussions about the characteristics of the museum environment that facilitate the process of learning strongly influenced the "product" outcomes that each group generated and reinforced the process/product nature of learning. Although each group's perspective, and their subsequent discussions, was often subtly different from one another's, there was considerable agreement when it came time to compile a manageable list of learning outcomes that can result from a museum visit and be applicable across various types of museums.[3]

Product Outcomes
Connections with and accessibility to learning
Comfort with different ideas
Promotion of identity
Interest and curiosity
Change in the way people think

The list that was generated includes what people learn as a consequence of museum experiences:

1.Museums make content and ideas accessible, facilitating intellectual "connections" and bringing together disparate facts, ideas and feelings.
How well does the museum allow/help visitors find a given discipline ACCESSIBLE? (From the visitors point of view: I realize that I can understand the world around me, and I can actively participate in investigating that world.)

Make diverse content accessible, allowing people to learn something new or see something in a different way.

How well does the museum help visitors find/make CONNECTIONS? (From the visitor's point of view: I can find relevance and make connections through seeing my own and other ways of understanding the world.)

Visitor Understanding
• Changes in subject matter knowledge
• Demonstration of the ability to connect ideas presented within an exhibit or set of exhibits
• Demonstration of the ability to put ideas in a new context, i.e. "seeing the big picture"

Experience epiphanies, inspire awe, provide memorable experiences.

Visitors are emotionally affected by the quality of the experience, whether: contemplative/aesthetic, social or through interaction with content.

Foster "ah-ha" experiences (epiphany/eureka/insight).

2. Museums affect values and attitudes, for example, facilitating comfort with cultural differences or developing environmental ethics.
How well does the museum assist visitors in becoming COMFORTABLE WITH DIFFERENCES? (From the visitor's point of view: In the museum, I find environments which accommodate and pro-mote a variety of perspectives and opportunities to learn and enhance my acceptance of and comfort with differences.)

Visitor Values
• Changes in attitude more closely reflecting the valuations presented in an exhibit
• Changes in behavior more closely reflecting those presented as desirable in an exhibit
• Increased self-examination relative to the topics presented in an exhibit

3.Museums promote cultural, community and familial identity.
Feel part of culture, values, traditions, part of family communication, part of shared experience. Expand communications.

Visitors realize a greater sense of identity with self, community and culture.

Help visitors identify with their community, identify professions.

Appreciating cultural heritage (qualifiers: one's own heritage or someone else's; the importance of access to cultural material; the museum does have a role in encouraging visitors to *appreciate* cultural heritage, which is more than just displaying it)

4. Museums foster visitor interest and curiosity, inspiring self-confidence and motivation to pursue future learning and life choices.
Empower people to learn, build self-esteem, validate the experience of the learner, build self-confidence, enable the visitor to learn.

Visitor traits of curiosity, caring, self-esteem, self-confidence and empowerment are enhanced.

Visitors learning experience is a gateway (not a gatekeeper) to further learning.

Stimulate ideas for later follow-through, such as "Hey, I could do this at home with my kids"

Do museums provide visitors with the confidence to enjoy and learn? Can they increase visitors' confidence to become competent learners, and engender interest in their visitors?

Influence visitor behavior (e.g., career choice). Make applications of knowledge gained.

Does the museum experience translate into/result in non-museum experiences?

Inspire people to want to do this again, here or somewhere else.

5. Museums affect *how* visitors think and approach their worlds, in contrast to what they think.

Learning how to learn, life long learning. Giving people the tools, confidence, open mindedness and belief that there is more to learn.

Visitor Methods of Inquiry
• Changes in the methods of inquiry and observation used to explore exhibit-related content areas
• Improved critical thinking skills
• Improved knowledge and appreciation of the methods of inquiry used by experts in a particular field

Foster an understanding of the process of creating, analysis, and scientific method.

Promote a greater depth of questions such that one might leave with more questions than one arrived with.

Institutional Learning Outcomes
Communicate learning opportunities
Offer multiple messages

A number of other issues also emerged during discussions that affected how conference participants approached this task. Since the discussion groups were essentially microcosms of the diverse museum community, these issues will likely emerge as important to the larger museum community as visitors' learning experiences are considered more seriously. In the process of discussing the relative importance of various outcomes, two groups hit upon the issue of "important for whom?" and "desired outcomes according to whom?" underscoring the relative, and perhaps, political nature of attributing significance to particular outcomes. In one discussion, tension between what "my institution sees" as opposed to the way "I see" was evident. The group facilitator, Mary Ellen Munley, elaborated on the issue:

"In reflecting on this element of our discussion ... I get the sense that the museum community is struggling with public (formal) and private (informal) definitions of its role and its potential for what it can contribute to education and life long learning. Individuals are comfortable, and even salutatory, of museums' capacity to assist them with powerful and personally beneficial learning experiences. Institutions, on the other hand, seem to need to remove the pro-

foundly personal from the acceptable (or achievable) list of goals. This tension between public and personal definitions of important learning may be at the heart of what we struggle with as we attempt to identify outcomes. Based on the nature of the memorable museum experiences reported by conference participants, and based on the distinctive features of museums as learning environments, I'm left believing that there is a need to move our public (institutional) definitions of success closer to our personal (individual) definitions of meaningful learning."

This issue also arose in other groups and, in fact, in response to this issue some groups generated institutional outcomes:

1. Museums effectively convey to visitors the nature and value of the opportunities they afford as part of the total educational infrastructure of a community.

Meet visitor expectations for a worthwhile experience (we assume that visitors' own definition of a worthwhile use of their time and money is a valid definition, it will be different for different people, and we should define this so that it's not just about marketing).

Are museums perceived as an "educational resource" by the community?

How well does the museum present itself as a LEARNING RESOURCE? (From the visitors' point of view: When I come to museums I discover new skills, awareness and understandings by using collections and other resources that invite me to continually learn.)

People want to return because of the quality of the experience. They perceive that the institution is a resource to which they can return.

An interesting variation on the issue of the institutional role of museums, related to where museums fit into the educational infrastructure of their communities. Several outcomes reflected this perspective:
What is the interplay between various "information" media — in particular, museums and schools, TV, film, radio and books?

What role does the public see the museum playing within the community — social, cultural, intellectual?

Visitors understand museums' role in society better. Create a portrait of the role of museums as learning facilitators in American society.

Identify the impact of individual characteristics of the museum's activities as facilitators of learning.

Another set of themes that ran through many discussions were issues related to how inclusive museums have been and for whom in current society these outcomes might resonate. It was perhaps best summarized by Mary Ellen Munley as follows:

To whom are the things currently selected for presentation in museum exhibits and programs valued and recognized as necessary to living a good life?

To whom are the topics and items selected for presentation meaningful?

For whom does the learning environment created by the museum staff evoke positive responses? And for what reasons do people feel comfortable in the museum?

Consequently, a few groups generated outcomes related to the issue of inclusion:

2. Museums communicate different messages to different people.

What do non-traditional audiences "get" out of the museum experience?

Who are the museum's constituencies and what is the relative success of museums in meeting the needs of these constituencies?

Despite the obvious diversity of opinion among participants about the many issues to be considered when documenting and analyzing the impact of museum experiences on visitors, there was tremendous consensus regarding the importance of doing so. The potential learning outcomes generated by the Annapolis Conference represent these individuals' efforts to transcend differences of discipline, institutional type and personal world view to generate broad learning outcomes that could be generalizable across a wide variety of different types of institutions. The hope, of course, was that such a list of outcomes would provide a concrete basis for investigating the *what, where, when, why* and *for whom* of museum learning. The next section summarizes conference participants' efforts to move from these broad generalizable outcomes to the development of specific research questions and possible research studies for investigating the learning that occurs in museums.

Notes

1. Originally, there were to be seven groups, but two small groups were combined.

2. Our synthesis is presented in bold; the direct quotes that follow each are drawn from group discussions. They are presented in no particular order and represent ideals. Since the examples are direct quotes, they differ considerably in style and presentation. They are included in this "raw" form to both illustrate the commonalties, as well as the subtle nuances, between the six groups.

3. As with the process items, bolding represents our attempt to synthesize the data generated in discussion; the examples that follow the bolded outcomes are direct quotes from the six small working groups. The outcome statements are presented in no particular order and represent the ideal.

How Should We Investigate Learning in Museums? Research Questions and Project Designs

John H. Falk, Lynn D. Dierking and Dana G. Holland

On the second day of the conference, participants again organized into six groups. The mission of each group was to generate potential research questions and devise research projects to investigate these questions. There were three major topics discussed by groups:

1. What would constitute an ideal research program investigating learning in museums?

2. How do we "operationally" define some interesting research questions? and

3. What specific research studies could be designed to investigate these questions?

Although the groups used the learning outcomes generated the day before as a springboard for this discussion, they did not have the benefit of the synthesis presented in the preceding chapter as they pondered these issues.[1]

The Ideal Research Program

Several groups discussed what would constitute an ideal research program and developed a series of criteria to systematically assess the relative merits of proposed research projects. Groups converged on some criteria and diverged on others.

I. Research Criteria

Generalizable
Multiple, cumulative experiences and sites
Relate to other educational experiences
Relate to larger contexts
Span a long period of time
Relevant and practical

Four separate groups concluded that research should:

•*Be generalizable across institutions*
In order for the study to be called research rather than evaluation, the investigation should attempt to provide information that is potentially useful in more than one context.

•Incorporate more than single or specific experience evaluations. [Our] suggestions for research studies includes recommendations for *multiple-site studies.*

Another area of general agreement was that research on informal learning in museums should relate peoples' museum experiences to other educational experiences, effectively placing museums and museum learning in a "larger societal context":

•*Place the museum experience in the context of other educational experiences.* In order for the real significance of museums to society to be understood, researchers must tackle the difficult problem of the role of museums relative to that of other educational experiences, both formal and informal.

•*Strive to understand the effects of museum visits in a larger context.* Questions were asked such as "How do conditions in the larger society affect people's decisions to use museums?" and "How does a person's cultural background and experiences affect whether they visit museums at all, what they do once they get there and what they take away from the experience?"

Although no one had answers to these questions, all concurred that they were extremely important issues in terms of the ability of museums to attract visitors and the ability of museum professionals to understand visitor outcomes.

Several groups concluded that the most significant research on learning should transcend immediate experiences and include longitudinal views and outcomes. Attendees felt that research should:

•*Look for effect over long time periods, in an order of magnitude of many years (10-20 years)*
•*Look at the effects of multiple visits, the* cumulative *effect of the museum experience*

•Focus on a global, expansive and longitudinal approach to museums and learning

In concurring, one group felt that the museum field has been, "missing out by conducting studies [that] focus on the immediate visit." As a remedy, "when appropriate, designs should allow visitors to compare their visit to other museum visits."

A final criteria for research was that project selection should be guided by practical considerations of [institutional] relevance and applicability:

•The basic question put to the group was:
What would you like to know more about so you could make informed decisions and improve practice?

Prerequisites to Long-term Research:

Defining:
Operational Terms
"What" is the content of museum learning
"Where and When" does learning take place
"Why" museum learning has value
Values of the museum culture
"Who" will be the focus of studies

---

1. Operationally Defining Research Questions
As groups began generating research questions, they quickly appreciated that in order to actually craft the questions and the studies, some precision in terms of the language used and the intent of that language was required. Terms such as "frequent visitor" or "awe-inspiring" might conjure up different images to different people unless there was an agreed-upon set of terms that would be used consistently by researchers, or researchers were very specific in describing their particular use of a term. When researchers focus on developing universal terms within a research study or program or clarify their particular use of a term they are said to be operationally defining the study. The discussions and the resulting research questions centered on defining only the "what," the "where and when," the "why" and the "for whom" of potential research projects.

2. What is the content of museum learning.
Not surprisingly, considerable attention was directed towards defining the "what" of museum learning. One group appreciated that it was very important to first operationally define what was meant by the content of museum learning. Specifically, they recognized that learning experiences can be characterized subjectively (by the visitors) or objectively (by museum staff). The criteria by which learning is assessed and measured was thought to have "enormous" implica-

tions for research:

> [Research should] be clearer about the characteristics of the (learning) process which we intend to observe and analyze. For example, will the process be grounded in whether visitors have perceived the main message and/or interpretive themes as *specified by the museum*, or will the process be based on whether visitors themselves think that the experience was educational, whether or not they learned the major points of content? There's not an easy answer to this question, and a reasonable answer might include some of each, but the implications for a research strategy are enormously different.

Another group discussed operationally defining terms generally, from nitty gritty concepts such as the frequency of visitation (e.g., "...how will you distinguish frequent visitation from infrequent visitation?...") to "tougher" concepts such as operationally defining learning.

3. Where and When does learning take place?
Although groups did not quibble about the meaning of "learning," several groups began their discussions by acknowledging that several intermediary steps are necessary between the conceptualization of a learning research study and the actual conduct of that research. Several groups discussed the need to "operationalize the concept" of informal learning so that "'we'll know it when we see it' and so that we'll have a reliable set of measures to indicate when it is happening." Jeff Hayward and his group recognized that the application of informal learning to "real situations and settings" raises questions such as: How well does this museum facilitate learning? Do we see this phenomenon throughout a museum visit, or only at some times and places? Hayward's group went on to define the nature and character of informal learning in museums:

> "We made an assumption that informal learning is a characterization of the entire experience that a visitor has at a museum/aquarium/zoo, etc. In other words, we don't view it as a "mode" that we step into and fall out of. If it were a "mode," then we should be measuring when it happens and where it doesn't happen in a museum. Does it only occur in exhibit galleries? Does it happen in the store? Are some people more pre-disposed to experience this? We decided we didn't want to study these types of questions. We think they illustrate the potential trap of quantifying this experience *so specifically* that we will forget that some informal learning happens before visitors even enter the museum building, and it can continue in thoughts and discussions after people have left. So instead of being a "mode" that we flip into or out of, we'd like to think of it as a characterization of a type of

experience—one that we could have by walking in the woods, or visiting a museum, or watching people work at a marina."

The same group also thought it was important that researchers consider the characteristics that define a place as museum-like in facilitating informal learning:

"[We need to] develop a way to specify the characteristics of the (different) settings in which informal learning takes place. Of course, our primary interest is museums, but we should recognize that informal learning takes place elsewhere too. If we agreed that it's characterized as places where people go voluntarily and which they consider to be at least somewhat educational, then we would rule out shopping malls and movie theaters, but not libraries or nature centers."

The relationship of the learning that occurs in museums to other venues and learning experiences was also an important theme in many of the research questions:

Does the visitor's behavior [broadly defined in ways relevant to informal learning] generalize to other situations and other learning experiences?

To what other experiences do visitors connect the museum experience?

Are there other experiences that might have a similar effect on a person as a museum visit has on a frequent visitor?

Do the learning approaches or skills acquired through museum experiences extend to other venues, over time?

Investigate post-visit behavior that might be attributable to museum visitation. Examples would be:
• books read or taken out of collections
• activities engaged in
• school course choices
• informal talk among visitors

Examples of research studies that appeared to be of this nature: Study of consequences of watching the "Square One" television program; Recent NIH and NSF programs for minority students that are tracking the participants school careers; Paulette McManus' studies on post-visit conversations.

Being even more specific, two groups felt that the most important research on informal learning should be exhibit-based:

•[Research should] be on exhibit-based experiences. In the minds of most museum professionals, decision makers and the public, exhibits are the raison d'etre for museums. Although an argument could be made for focusing on museum programs,

many tend to be based around specific exhibits.

Another group disagreed with the assumption of an exhibit-based orientation, articulating that research should:

•[Not] focus on the learning outcomes attributable to a visit to a single exhibit — or even, necessarily, to a single museum.

And still a third group developed a question that pertained to aspects of museum learning that are applicable to all (or at least many) museums:

Identify elements that cause visitors to continue informal learning experiences that transcend individual disciplines. Are there factors that are applicable to all museums that contribute to learning? We didn't know how to design this, but reference was made to some findings from market research that appear to apply to all types of museums.

4. Why does museum learning have meaning and value?

A large number of research questions were generated that related to the "why" of museum learning, questions that related to what people "value" about their museum experiences, what "meaning" they derive from them and what other experiences "connect" to them. A component of several of these questions was the role and impact of museums in society (as well as the impact of society on museums):

What about the museum experience do people value?

What meaning and value do visitors place on museum visits? (When possible, emphasizing the "s" on "visits" is the key; we should include members and frequent visitors in the sample, as well as people from out of town who are frequent visitors to other museums).

What do visitors expect? Are those expectations met? Is learning one of those expectations?

The group discussed the work of Marilyn Hood which shows that frequent museum visitors have similar values and perspectives to exhibit developers in how they select leisure-time activities and what they value. On the other hand, infrequent museum-goers utilize a different set of values in making those decisions. Hood's findings would suggest that museums will continue to have difficulties attracting new audiences since they don't share the same expectations. The group questioned whether learning was, indeed, an expectation of the average museum visitor and tended to disagree with the assumption that had been made in the large group discussion in the morning.

Do people self-select to go to museums because of a preferred way of learning, or do people learn a certain way because they are at a museum, or is it some combination of both?

Studies about the value of museums in people's lives. John Ogbu underscored the importance of not bypassing fundamental questions about museums, people, culture and learning. He was emphatic about the desirability of assuring that the frames of reference used to guide our research be informed by visitors' world views, not by the world view of museum boards, administrators, staff and frequent visitors. For this reason, the group felt that it is essential for museums to have answers to very basic questions such as:

• Why do people go to museums?

• Why don't people go to museums?

• Given their current structure, appearance and programs, what value do museums represent for people from different cultures?

Assuming that museums are educational institutions dedicated to serving a widely diverse society:

• What do we need to know about visitors' cultures and backgrounds in order to better understand them and to best support their learning

And finally,

• How do conditions in larger society affect people's decisions about the value they place in museums and the ways they use them?

5. Values of the Museum Culture

Research questions were also generated that related to understanding the world view of museum professionals; the feeling on the part of groups generating these questions was that investigations into the characteristics and implicit values of the "museum culture" would enable constructive self-reflection about the role and mode of operation of museums, both in the present and towards the future:

What does the museum staff think the visitor experience is? How does that compare to what the visitor thinks? A study designed to address this issue would include designers, content specialists and visitors reflecting on what is learned or to be learned from a museum exhibit. Contrasting these results would make an important contribution to understanding why exhibits often don't meet visitor expectations.

Have the courage to study ourselves. Perhaps it was inevitable that a group entwined in the perspective brought by an engaging and compelling anthropologist would turn introspective and think about themselves as members of the museum community, as part of a culture. This small group did just that. The participants placed great value in their discussions on bringing the perspective of the other (the visitor and non-

visitor) clearly into focus. One result was group members realizing that one potential - even desirable - outcome of research is to gain knowledge that will suggest and inform decisions about ways the museum must change. The group concluded that research about cultural differences is likely to suggest some fundamental changes in museum practice as it has been traditionally executed. If so, then we have at least one important question to ask ourselves about our "museum culture." The question got phrased this way:

How do we (board members, administrators, staff and supporters of museums) see the differences that exist between our "culture" and the cultures of many of our visitors and potential visitors? Using Ogbu's framework as a reference, are the differences seen as barriers or are they viewed as fundamental and unchangeable markers of identity? Given the answer to the preceding question, what does it say about the future of museums in this country?

In contrast, other questions focused more specifically on visitors' learning experiences as they related to a single exhibition or museum:

Is the message of an exhibit/museum perceived differently by different types of visitors?

How does the design [layout, size, arrangement, etc.] of the exhibit/museum affect what people learn? How does it affect the quality of the experience?

Does the experience that people have in the exhibit/museum increase the complexity of their cognitive schema?

Do visitors feel a greater sense of self-efficacy related to the domain of the exhibit?

The museum professionals wanted visitors to leave the exhibit with the sense that they had learned something new and were better able to understand, analyze, make decisions about and convey information related to the exhibit content.

Can museum visits change one's style of learning?

Can and do visitors raise their own questions? Do they demonstrate interest in the subject matter?

The museum professionals in the group thought that the most important outcome for museum visitors was increased interest in the subject matter to the point where visitors would ask and pursue their own questions.

6. Who is the focus?

Several groups believed that informal learning research should encompass diverse audiences and focus on voluntary museum visitors. These groups stated that research:

• Should focus on diverse audiences and account for the voluntary nature of learning that is a component of many museum experiences.

•*Focus on voluntary visitors.*

Although a great deal of work has been, and should continue to be done with visiting school groups, this group thought the initial research emphasis should be placed on voluntary visitors. Outcomes for voluntary visitors are less well understood. Voluntary visitors are presumably the ones who are most clearly responding to exhibit content. Many museums would also like to increase the number of voluntary visitors and therefore play a larger role in the community.

•*Attend closely to demographic diversity*

There are large differences in museum visitation rates among people of different cultural and educational backgrounds. Understanding these differences will be extremely important if museums hope to expand their influence.

One group specified that "small groups" are the most important unit of study (i.e., [Research should] utilize as the units small groups, including both "families" and school groups.)

A whole series of research questions relating to "for whom" were generated. Examples included:

What are the differences in learning approaches and outcomes between frequent visitors and museum novices (A participant mentioned the Denver Art Museum study which compared art museum experts to art museum novices)?

Look for long-term outcomes through interviews (self-reports) with specific populations. The idea is to find some audience segment and probe for the influence of museum visits on their current status. This is all within the context of the limiting criteria listed above. We are considering only long-term influence of multiple visits. Suggested segments included:

• random museum visitors
• successful people in a chosen subject field
• non-museum goers
• museum professionals

Examples of studies of a similar nature: Girl Scouts of America's study of successful women professionals who had been Girl Scouts; interviews with University biologists; Judy Diamond and Mark St. John's study of Exploratorium Explainers.

What children learn when they visit the museum? Do children talk differently about the domains after visiting the museum? Here the group examined whether the museum experience helps develop a language and reference point for children to talk about what they have learned.

Studies about the ways groups learn in museums.

Participants were interested in knowing more about the ways adults and children interact in the museum, and more particularly, the ways adults help or hinder children's learning. The research questions posed were:

• How do adults support/discourage learning by children in the museum?
• How do museum programs and exhibits help/hinder adults as they support/discourage children's learning?
• How do features in the museum environment and in exhibits support/hinder small group learning.

Develop a study that tied a school curriculum directly to a museum experience. This would help provide opportunities for learners to interact and reflect. Pre-visit preparation, etc. would also be important.

Finally, several groups felt it was important to explore the differences between people who visit museums and those who do not (or do so less frequently) utilizing open-ended methodologies:

What meaning and value do people who do not traditionally visit museums place on museum visits?

Are there differences between frequent visitors and those who do not utilize museums frequently?

Are people who visit museums different from those who do not (the Getty Foundation focus group study "Insights" was mentioned as an example of a study that investigated visitor and non-visitor expectations and reflections on their first visit to an Art museum)?

Do visitors feel a greater sense of connection to the subject matter?

Finally, the museum professionals wanted visitors to better understand the relevance of the subject presented in the exhibit to their lives. They wanted visitors to be able to place both themselves and the subject matter of the exhibit in a larger context.

Designing A Research Study
Visitor Perspective and Scope
Visitors' Prior Knowledge-Variables
Multiple Methodologies

Integrating the Visitor's Perspective

In conceptualizing research studies the groups appreciated that operationally defining terms related not only to a researcher's intent in using particular terms or to the choice of a particular research paradigm, but also to the best way to convey these terms to visitors during data collection. One group raised the concern that if researchers use the term "learning" to talk with visitors it might affect the outcome of the study, since "many of them might [associate] 'learning' with formal education and [therefore] have difficulty with the question."

Early in their discussions, most groups concluded

that research on informal learning in museums must be informed by visitors' own perspectives on learning, by authentic museum experiences and by the important outcomes generated the day before [outcomes described in the previous chapter]. One group felt that visitors should inform what constitutes a meaningful museum experience:

> [Useful research would] allow visitors to categorize and group their museum experiences in their own way.

Two groups proposed having visitors participate in the same activity undertaken by conference participants the previous day, that is, sharing their most positive and their most negative museum experience. This type of research would provide insight into visitors' perspectives of museum experiences:

> This discussion began with a theme that the first group had touched on the day before: What are the stories that the visitor makes out of their visit? What meaning do they give the visit? ...

> We were very excited after the morning's conversation and eager to begin discussing potential research questions and studies. One suggestion was that it would be fascinating to ask visitors the same questions we had all answered as a warm-up (best and worst experience as a visitor). Many of the positive stories shared centered on family involvement or being at the museum with certain social groups, as well as moments of revelation and inspiration. Many of the negatives included problems with the physical design, environmental crowding, noise and way-finding. The sharing had also emphasized the importance of the power of the object, demonstrated that many levels of learning are possible and that these learnings can be very deep and meaningful for some.

Two groups discussed the need for visitors' perspectives to inform the selection of museum learning outcomes:

> The session began with the facilitator posing the questions "What is the value of museums to visitors?" and "Why do people go to museums?" ... Although the participants could easily articulate a set of outcomes they thought were important for visitors, they asked how they could know what were meaningful outcomes from the visitor's perspective...

> Define "outcomes" of a museum visit from more than one perspective or constituency. Visitors need to participate in the discussion of what makes a museum visit worthwhile; it shouldn't only be defined by those of us in the museum profession.

Some of the discussion in Valerie Crane's group related to the likelihood that the views of various museum professionals — those responsible for conceptually and physically creating "stories" in the museums — probably diverge from the views of visitors. Exploration of these divergences were thought to be an interesting avenue of inquiry:

> These questions [relating to the visitors' perspective on the museum experience] led the group to discuss how there are different perspectives that get attention as exhibits or experiences are developed. First, there is the content expert and then the exhibit developer. Often the story they want to tell isn't the story that the visitor ends up creating out of their own experience. Understanding the stories that the visitors construct would be a useful approach to understanding the learning that occurs in museums.

Visitors' Prior Knowledge

In addition to integration of visitors' perspectives into the research process, several groups discussed the need to consider visitors' prior subject matter knowledge. One group discussed the probable role that prior knowledge plays in "how and why visitors make personal connections with the subject matter presented in an exhibit." Whereas some groups discussed prior knowledge as a contextual factor and/or intervening variable that must be addressed in research generally, one group proposed focused investigation into "the role existing interest and knowledge play in the museum experience."

Multiple Methodologies

Inevitably, discussions turned to methodology with several groups debating the relative strengths and weaknesses of various research approaches. Discussion often revolved around the relative appropriateness of qualitative versus quantitative approaches to conducting research:

> Barbara Rogoff, our domain expert, indicated that she might suggest utilizing qualitative, in-depth interviews in which the interviewer has a general agenda, but not specific questions. The interview is much more like a conversation, in-depth and open-ended. These interviews can get more "closed" at the end...

> Doug Herrmann mentioned the idea of doing exploratory factor analyses of outcomes (i.e. presenting subjects with lists of possible outcomes, asking them to rate the outcomes on some dimension, such as frequency with which the outcome has been personally experienced, or the extent to which the subject agrees that the outcome is important, and then examining a factor analysis of the responses for coherent clusters) in order to develop a taxonomy of the results of museum vis-

its. Others in the group thought that it might be a bit early to try to develop a taxonomy. Museum professionals are still trying to define reasonable, measurable, generalizable outcomes for which they could conduct a factor analytic study. The idea of using open-ended interviews and focus groups to begin to get some ideas for outcomes were discussed.

Several groups proposed very specific strategies for investigating museum learning; examples were:

Identify a group of frequent visitors and investigate their interactions with the same exhibit over time. If children return, for example, do they look at subject matter that is interesting to them, do they look at the same or different things over time?

Utilize visitor tracking, in combination with visitor conversation analysis. The goal would be to track the "process of inquiry," an effort to map how visitors encounter and utilize museums to develop understanding.

Determine the relationship between experience with "real objects" and further learning. Does exposure to objects lead to one or more of the elements of learning defined previously?

We believe that visitors' response to the "real thing" has a value beyond the pleasure of recognition, that it leads directly to "learning," (or is directly associated with some aspects of learning as we have defined it.) But what is that connection, and if it is actually present, can it be noted and documented?

Investigate some typical museum activity (such as camp-ins, school programs, or types of exhibit). Identify examples that are generally recognized as "good" models of that type of activity, and do naturalistic case studies documenting what they actually do. Then analyze this data to see if it is possible to identify components that are reasonably associated with learning.

This last approach was derived from an example provided by Jeremy Roschelle, one of the social scientists. He described a study that he had conducted with others to look at the consequences of student peer study groups in a college engineering course. Faculty agreed that these study groups were probably a good thing, but did not know why. The researchers videotaped the groups and then analyzed the tapes. Among other findings discovered was the fact that the groups generated many student questions, far more than usually came up in lecture formats. Assuming that asking questions is a positive indicator of "learning" then this finding can be considered a relevant charac-

teristic of the "good" discussion groups.

Sample Study Concepts

    A. Changes in Cognitive Schema
    B. Increasing Understanding of Our Audiences
Finally, after clarifying some general concepts and brainstorming important research questions, several groups chose one question and worked through some preliminary issues necessary to execute an actual research study. The following examples demonstrate the process undertaken by two groups to do this.

A. Measuring Cognitive Schema Complexity
One group elected to develop the following research question:
    Does the experience that people have in the exhibit/museum increase the complexity of their cognitive schema?
    The logic by which the group began to work through details of a potential research project included many of the general issues reported above. Discussion was as follows:
Clarifying the central concept
What qualifies as "increasing the complexity of a person's cognitive schema?" We were not implying that *factual information* is the primary outcome of a museum experience (an informal learning experience). We discussed the idea of a cognitive schema as different from an accumulation of facts. Similar to our feelings about informal learning, a cognitive schema is developed by individuals, based on their own perceptions and experiences. Also similar to our feeling about informal learning, we assume that this concept can work with different levels of complexity, and that it is affected by our own motivations and interests. So, the outcomes that would qualify as "increases the complexity of a person's cognitive schema" are:
• reinforcement of information and/or relationships in a schema
• new information or relationships added to a schema
• changes in the schema itself, e.g., its importance, or our perception of its structure

Issues to be considered in designing the study
    1. Accuracy/validity of information-based schema: Should we be concerned with whether the schema is based on accurate information, and would it still be a legitimate informal learning experience if a person added inadequate information to a schema?
    • We concluded that this was a supreme concern in using this question to define and measure informal learning, because not all information or relationships are dimensional (e.g., there isn't just one "correct" way to interpret history).

• However, sometimes this issue is critical because the point of a museum/exhibit is to reduce misconceptions and misunderstandings about certain things (someone gave an example of the public misperception that ozone depletion is due to global warming, but it isn't, so we wouldn't want to call it "informal learning" if people got this impression from an exhibit on global warming).

2. Prior knowledge: This issue is related to the first, but emphasizes the need to be able to measure prior knowledge if we want to investigate changes in a cognitive schema.
  • Exhibits are often designed so that no prior knowledge is needed, or assume that people have minimal knowledge about the subject; but would we design differently if we found out how much and what people know about already?
  • Sometimes prior knowledge and existing schema are a serious problem for exhibits which are designed to deliver a message and informational content (example: a creationist's worldview will prevent them from attaching new information to a schema about the history of human life).

3. Opportunity for interaction: In a research design on this question, we would like to see comparisons of settings with different opportunities for interaction - with people, objects, mechanics ("interactives"), and phenomena. The theory is that interacting, verbally or physically, is more likely to facilitate changes in the complexity of a schema, compared to only viewing something.

4. Interest/motivation: This should be another parameter of informal learning studies because they are voluntary experiences. If things are perceived as boring, people won't come; if they don't come, we lost the chance to increase the complexity of their cognitive schema. If they do come but "tune out" or get a case of "museum fatigue," we would assume that informal learning suffers.

5. Presentation: It would also be important to look at the influences of the presentation on informal learning experiences. We refer to the design of exhibit spaces and exhibit elements, to the presence of human facilitators (staff or volunteers) in an exhibit, as well as to the media and modes of experiencing a setting.

B. Increasing Understanding of Our Audiences
Another group developed the general parameters of a qualitative study to understand the "culture" of individuals and groups to whom the museum wishes to provide educational services:

An approach to research that will increase the likelihood that we will understand our audiences as they understand themselves. With the assistance of John Ogbu, the group sketched in broad strokes the kind of global study they felt would be of value to the museum profession.

The aim is to conduct investigations using observations and interviews with individuals and groups of people who represent cultures of interest to the museum because the museum wishes to provide educational services to the group. Interviews would be conducted in the museum among visitors and through the use of specially convened focus groups. Interviews and observations would also take place in situ — in homes, communities and other places where people live and spend their time.

The goals of the investigation would be: (1) to find patterns as they emerge from the people themselves; and (2) to identify patterns and variables that appear to make a difference in choosing to value and use a museum. The knowledge that could emerge from such investigations would be valuable to museums trying to expand their services to new audiences and to make decisions about ways the museum will need to change in order to best match itself to the cultural world views and needs of its constituents.

If such sociological studies were conducted over time, the museum community would begin to understand its audiences and potential audiences and would be able to have increased confidence in knowing the important questions to ask about why museums do and do not matter to people.

Conclusions
The small group discussions summarized above represent a tremendous wealth of ideas considering they were generated in only an hour or two of focused discussion. Although preliminary, the discussions raise important issues about the operational definition of terms and the possible scope of a museum learning research program. The preliminary efforts to define how to conduct such studies represent important initial steps in the creation of a national research agenda for investigating learning in museums. How to build on these initial ideas and truly activate a national effort to investigate learning in museums is the topic of the next section of this book.

Note
1. As in the preceding chapter, the notes and summaries of the discussion groups were analyzed and categorized; quotes appear as indented statements.

Establishing A Long-Term Learning Research Agenda For Museums

John H. Falk, Lynn D. Dierking and Dana G. Holland

The museum field has changed appreciably in the last ten to twenty years; perhaps in no way more than in the recognition that a diversity of informal learning institutions can, and should, all be considered "museums." It is a profound change that professionals at zoos and art museums, historic houses and science centers, nature centers and natural history museums now appreciate that they have more in common than not. As repositories of collections, art museums and zoos face very different concerns and problems; as free-choice learning institutions vying for the public's discretionary time and dollars, art museums and zoos face very similar concerns and problems.

Even as the differences fall away, though, the museum community is still faced with one overriding problem: **There does not currently exist a generally recognized and universally accepted public or professional understanding of the learning role of museums in present-day America.** This lack of knowledge about the learning potential of museums both resides with the general public, as well as among legislators, some sectors of the business community and federal, state and local government officials. Because these groups do not fully understand the important role that museums play within the information and education infrastructure of the society, because they do not fully appreciate the central role museums play in preserving and transmitting cultural heritage, because they do not fully understand how much museums help people learn, museums are facing the most significant fiscal and political constraints that they have ever faced. But who is primarily responsible for this dilemma?

As a field, museum professionals find it extremely difficult to state clearly and succinctly how museums meaningfully affect people's lives. This may be in part due to the complexity of a museum's role in society, but until we can develop a significantly better ability to articulate a museum's role in the educational infrastructure of a community we will continue to struggle with the existing perception of a museum's value in society. Until we better understand the nature of museum-based learning we will find it exceedingly difficult to improve our educational practices or market and promote our institutions more effectively to the public. As suggested in our introduction, what is needed is a concerted, conceptually consistent effort to conduct basic, long-term museum learning research. Moving that agenda forward was a major goal of the conference. Were we successful?

The Annapolis Conference

At many levels the effort was extremely successful. For two days in August, 1994, we were able to gather together a diverse group of the important stakeholders in the enterprise; museum researchers, museum professionals, representatives from national museum associations, funders and well-respected social scientists; to discuss the what's, where's and how's of launching a national research agenda focusing on the long-term impact of museum experiences. It was exciting as a high-level group of museum professionals; including administrators, educators, designers and curators actively engaged in discussions about basic research, with input from funders and museum association representatives.

It was helpful and reinforcing to have included well-respected social scientists in the endeavor. Not only did their papers serve as an excellent preparation for the meeting but their interest and commitment level, which noticeably piqued over the two day meeting as they became increasingly aware of the challenges and opportunities afforded by studying learning in museum settings, served to reinforce the importance and relevance of the task at hand. As "outsiders" they were able to reflect for us the capacity museums have to break new intellectual ground in understanding learning and in helping to redefine how and where learning research occurs. Fortunately, these interactions have not ended. We are aware of a number of conversations and continued collaborations that are occurring between these social scientists and participants at the conference. Since one intent of our efforts was to facilitate a dialogue between museum professionals and social science researchers in related fields, these results are heartening.

Our intent, of course, was to provide a forum in which this diverse group of people could arrive at some consensus about outcomes and research questions; and that this "research agenda" could be presented to the field and funding community as a first step in moving from rhetoric towards a plan of action for better assessing the impact of museums on people's lives. The conference generated a total of eight important learning outcomes — three learning process outcomes and five product outcomes.

Process Outcomes
Direct experience
Personal and active
Socially mediated

Product Outcomes
Connections with and accessibility to learning
Comfort with different ideas
Promotion of identity
Interest and curiosity
Change in the way people think

Though participants did not reach total consensus on all aspects of a museum learning research agenda, general consensus was reached on a number of important issues. Most fundamentally, all participants agreed that the museum field needs to begin actively supporting basic research into what, where, when, why and for whom long-term learning occurs in museums.

Conference Consensus for:
Commitment to basic research
Long-term studies
Studies in a larger societal context
Generalizable studies
Practical applications
Methodological diversity

Over the two days of the conference participants were able to clarify a variety of issues that are prerequisite to conducting long-term museum learning research; they also raised a variety of additional issues that future researchers will need to consider. Overall though, the questions posed at the beginning of the conference in terms of both the process of museum learning and the products of museum learning were validated by the conference discussions. Also reinforced by the conference was the importance of investigating museum learning from diverse intellectual perspectives — in terms of prior and subsequent experiences, in terms of social and cultural influences, in terms of micro and macro environments and in terms of motivation and attitudes. Despite the diverse perspectives represented at the conference, there was broad support for:

1. Conducting long-term research studies — studies that will probe the impact of visitor experiences over months and years, rather than minutes or hours or studies that will investigate the cumulative effect of multiple visits by groups or individuals.

2. Framing studies of museum learning within a larger social, cultural and educational context — studies that will determine how museums fit within the larger social, cultural and educational infrastructure of society.

3. Making investigations generalizable across a diversity of museum types; if possible, designing investigations that are conducted within a diversity of museum types.

4. Developing studies that yield practical applications to present and future museum practice, including marketing, education and outreach efforts.

5. Insuring methodological diversity — there were advocates for qualitative naturalistic studies as well as quantitative experimental studies, and a recognition that there is value in both.

The major message emerging from the conference was the strong belief that the museum community is justified in its assertion that museums are learning environments. What is needed, however, are answers to questions such as what, when and where, why and for whom are museums learning environments? The preceding two chapters represent important initial steps in this effort, but they are only initial steps. A much more comprehensive effort, launched over the next decade or two, must be undertaken to address these fundamental questions if museums are to flourish as an enterprise.

Towards A Museum Learning Research Agenda
At the most basic level, the challenge facing the museum community over the next decade will be to establish a credible definition of the central educational and cultural role that museums play in society. To do this, the museum community will need to build and sustain a sense of commitment for conducting basic learning research in museums. Clearly, there are those in the museum community who already appreciate the importance of conducting this type of research; certainly the American Association of Museums and Association of Science-Technology Centers appreciates and endorses the importance of

this undertaking. The National Science Foundation, by supporting this conference, obviously also appreciates the necessity of this type of research. Equally clear though, is the knowledge that this idea is not widely embraced by the field as a whole. The need to be resolute in this commitment will become ever more critical in the next several years as research results begin to trickle in from the myriad of small, scattered investigations currently being conducted. The temptation will be to latch onto these few preliminary findings and assume the job is done, rather than mount the comprehensive research program required in order to answer the complex and fundamental questions posed by learning in museums.

Even if there is no national research initiative, museum learning research will happen. This is true because there have been and continue to be a small cadre of individuals and organizations dedicated to conducting learning research in museums. These efforts tend to be small, poorly financed, often very local, conducted by a handful of investigators. All told, though, none of these efforts, no matter how successful, are likely to do more than scratch the surface. Such disparate efforts are *very* unlikely to lead to a major synthetic understanding of the problem — a scattered approach is likely to lead to a scattered understanding. For better or worse, as highlighted by the Annapolis Conference, understanding learning in museums is such a complex issue that its resolution will require *intensive, coordinated effort, over many years, by many researchers.* It is our opinion that *significant* understanding of the long-term learning that occurs in museums will require three things to succeed: 1) a well-conceived, over-arching set of research questions; 2) a major commitment of funding; and 3) a stable and expanded research infrastructure.

Towards a Research Agenda
   Define the research questions
   Commit funding
   Expand research infrastructure

Define Research Questions
The beginnings of a consensus forged over two days in Annapolis suggests that it should be possible to articulate a set of overarching questions and hypothesis for investigating museum learning. The Annapolis Conference reinforced the belief that not all research should follow a single approach nor even a single question. It also reinforced the feeling that in the absence of an over-arching conceptual framework for

research, efforts are likely to be scattered and haphazard. We propose that there be continued efforts to develop, refine and reach broad approval for a single research framework. The efforts of the Annapolis Conference participants represent a valuable starting point. A framework would provide the museum field with the most likely mechanism for insuring conceptually sound, practical results within a reasonable time frame. It would permit many investigators, from many institutions, using varied approaches, to develop mutually reinforcing studies with mutually reinforcing conclusions.

Funding
Basic research requires financial support. The type of fundamental research discussed in this book will require the commitment of substantial sums of money over a considerable period of time. However, increased funding resources alone will not be sufficient to solve this problem. Each museum must do its part by making itself available for research, perhaps even making staff time available for conducting research. Creative solutions that piggy-back support for research onto existing programs is a fundamental and appropriate strategy. While it may not be possible for all the research monies to be "new" monies, support for museum-based learning research may require a shift in current spending priorities and/or practices. Available funds may need to be reallocated so that a percentage of them are earmarked specifically for research. Funding agencies may need to form consortia, combining their resources to establish a single, substantial, museum-wide, non-disciplinary pool of monies available for museum learning research. Whatever the strategy, though, it is clear that unless sufficient resources are made available, over a substantial time period, significant progress is unlikely to be accomplished within a reasonable time frame — within the next ten to twenty years.

Inevitably and appropriately, to be successful in this research enterprise, the museum field will need to expand its efforts to involve quality social science researchers from outside the museum field. This does not suggest that the existing group of museum-based researchers are poorly suited to the task, but rather that they are both numerically ill-equipped to tackle the task and the complexity of the task could benefit from the multidisciplinary approach that social scientists from other disciplines would contribute. The field needs to have more investigators, including graduate students with appropriate guidance, willing to invest their time and talents in helping the museum community answer the fundamental questions facing the field. The most probable way enthusiasm for museum learning research can be fostered and a cadre of talented researchers from outside the museum field lured into the field is to find substantial financial support for such research. Fund it and they will come!

Research Infrastructure

Finally, an issue that has consistently emerged in all discussions about museum learning research, both at the Annapolis Conference and at other comparable gatherings, is the critical need for the development of a stable, extended museum learning research infrastructure. Such an infrastructure would support and nurture the research enterprise; once established it would be self-supporting and self-sustaining. It would include:

1. museums willing to serve as research museum centers where research would be conducted, data analyzed, compiled and shared with the field;

2. the development of a museum community of learners, a cadre of reflective practitioners who regularly engage in basic and

applied research as part of their everyday professional activities;

3. academic faculty and graduate students specifically focused on museum learning research;

4. one or more professional, peer-reviewed journals devoted to publishing museum learning research papers;

5. Internet or other electronic communication mechanisms for the sharing of ideas and distribution of research findings;

6. one or a consortium of professional organizations serving as a centralized clearinghouse and a forum for the sharing and discussion of research findings; and

7. potentially, the establishment of a museum learning institute or comparable "think tank" for academics and museum professionals where annual seminars or symposia would be conducted and where museum professionals could receive mid-career training in areas related to museum learning research.

Components of this infrastructure already exist, but even those that do, exist in only the most rudimentary way. Although there are academics and graduate students scattered around the country interested in museum-based learning, there is not a single U.S. university Ph.D. program dedicated specifically to museum learning and research (however, virtually every university in the country offers a Ph.D. for studying learning in either a laboratory or school setting). Even though journals such as *Curator, Journal of Research in Science Teaching, Science Education, Journal of Museum Education, Environment and Behavior,* and *Journal of Leisure Research* have all, at one time or another published museum-based research, none of these actively solicit or encourage such research. Currently, there is no regularly functioning journal dedicated *exclusively* to investigations into the learning that occurs in museums. The American Association of Museum's

Standing Committee on Audience Research and Evaluation (CARE) and the Independent Visitor Studies Association represent groups of individuals who share a common professional interest in issues related to long-term museum learning and each organization provides a forum open to the presentation of basic research results. At present, basic research presentations represent less than 5% of CARE's annual *Current Trends* poster presentations or Visitor Studies' annual meeting sessions.

In conclusion, there is much to be heartened by, but little to feel complacent about, regarding the status of museum learning research. There are significant efforts developing to begin the process, but little results, at present, to show for these efforts. A great deal was accomplished in Annapolis, but far more yet needs to be accomplished. We hope that the Conference, and this book, will move the process along and serve as a catalyst for a national effort to conduct basic, long-term research on learning in museums. With hard work, good fortune and the continued commitment of the entire museum field, such an effort can, and hopefully will, happen.

Part 2

Background Papers

Learning in Interactive Environments: Prior Knowledge and New Experience

Jeremy Roschelle
University of Massachusetts, Dartmouth

Educators often focus on the ideas they want their students to learn. But research has shown that a learner's prior knowledge often confounds an educator's best efforts to deliver ideas accurately. A large body of findings shows that learning proceeds primarily from prior knowledge and only secondarily from the presented materials. Prior knowledge can be at odds with the presented materials, and, consequently, learners will distort presented materials. The educator's neglect of prior knowledge can result in the learner's learning something opposed to the educator's intentions, no matter how well those intentions are executed in an exhibit, book, or lecture.

Consider a hypothetical book on wool production in Australia. Australian ranchers raise sheep in an extremely hot desert climate. The sheep are raised to have wool so thick that without yearly trimmings they would be unable to walk. To many children, these facts together are absurd. Children think wool is hot; if you put a thermometer inside a wool sweater, the mercury would go up (Lewis 1991). Wouldn't sheep grow more wool in cold places where they need to stay warm? Is wool hot because the sheep absorb the desert warmth?

Alternatively, consider a hypothetical exhibit on fish schooling. Fish follow each other in a close formation that looks highly organized. But no single fish is the leader, and none of the fish know how to command the others. Many people assume that any organized system is the result of a centralized planner who directs the others. They think "there must be an older fish, who is smarter than the rest, and who leads the school. If marine biologists believe otherwise, well I guess its true, but I'll never be a marine biologist!"

Then again, consider a hypothetical lecture on jazz. Upon a first listening, one might hear the music as ugly, chaotic, and meaningless —"it's just a lot of notes." Many years later, the same music provides a rich and rewarding experience, and with more listening, yet more difficult music becomes accessible. How can you learn jazz if all you understand is classical music or pop?

To the child who does not yet understand heat and temperature, no quick explanation can possibly resolve the contradiction between the hot desert and the warm wool; it takes weeks or years for this understanding to emerge (Lewis 1991). The adult who is unfamiliar with the possibilities of decentralized systems cannot be quickly convinced that schooling fish have no leader (Resnick 1992) and instead may be alienated. There is no way to give the first time jazz listener the epiphany available to more practiced ears. Prior knowledge determines what we learn from experience.

Prior knowledge also forces a theoretical shift to viewing learning as "conceptual change"(Strike and Posner 1985; West and Pines 1985). Previously learning was considered a process of accumulating information or experience, but prior knowledge is the bane of transmission-absorption models of learning. Mere absorption cannot account for the revolutionary changes in thought that must occur. The child simply cannot absorb knowledge about wool, because prior knowledge about heat renders incoming ideas nonsensical. The adult cannot assimilate fish schooling in a mindset that recognizes only centralized systems; distinct concepts for understanding decentralized systems must be developed. Jazz cannot be translated into rock; one must cultivate ears for its unique organization.

On the other hand, it is impossible to learn without prior knowledge. Eliminating prior undertanding of heat will not explain why that sweater is still so nice in the winter, or how thick-coated sheep can be raised in the desert. The idea of decentralized systems must be built from some anchor in prior experience. And it is easiest to appreciate unfamiliar music by starting with "crossover" artists who populate the periphery between jazz and rock or classical music.

The aspects of learning, prior knowledge and experience drawn out in these examples have a solid basis in research on learning. There is widespread agreement that prior knowledge influences learning and that learners *construct* concepts from prior knowledge

(Resnick 1983; Glaserfeld 1984). But there is much debate about how to use this fact to improve learning.

This paper presents a set of research findings, theories, and empirical methods that can help educators understand how prior knowledge affects learning, especially how designers of interactive experiences can work more effectively with the prior knowledge of their audience. It focuses on the central tension that dominates the debate about prior knowledge. This tension is between celebrating learners' constructive capabilities and bemoaning the inadequacy of their understanding. On one hand, educators rally to the slogan of constructivism: Create experiences that engage students in actively making sense of concepts *for themselves*. On the other hand, research tends to characterize prior knowledge as conflicting with the learning process, and thus educators try to suppress, eradicate, or overcome its influence.

The juxtaposition of these points of view creates a paradox: How can students' ideas be both fundamentally flawed and a means for constructing knowledge? The question cuts to the heart of constructivism—the idea that learners must construct knowledge for themselves— because new knowledge is constructed from old. But how can students construct knowledge from their existing concepts if their existing concepts are flawed? Prior knowledge appears to be simultaneously necessary and problematic. This version of the learning paradox (Bereiter 1985) is called the "paradox of continuity" (Roschelle 1991). Smith, diSessa, and Roschelle (1993) argue that educational reforms must include strategies that might avoid, resolve, or overcome the paradox. Throughout this paper, I endeavor to show how designers of interactive learning experiences can work with prior knowledge despite its apparent flaws and without succumbing to an irresolvable contradiction. This insight requires careful consideration of assumptions about knowledge, experience, and learning.

The paper is organized in three sections:

In the first section, I present findings both on how scientists learn and on how students learn science. Evidence on scientific conceptual change leads to a recommendation to view science learning as refinement of everyday ideas. This requires a long time and a rich social context. Consideration of how students learn science leads to additional recommendations: We should study successful learning, avoid interpreting prior knowledge in terms of dichotomies, see prior knowledge as providing flexible building blocks, and look for long-term transformations in the structure and coordination of knowledge.

The second section presents several major theoretical perspectives on the process of conceptual change. Jean Piaget emphasizes changes in the structure of prior knowledge. His theory and methods suggest that designers create tasks that engage learners and create tension between assimilation and accommodation. Engagement in physical aspects of a challenging task can lead to reformulation of intellectual aspects of the task. John Dewey emphasizes the conditions under which inquiry can resolve problematic experience. He suggests that designers discover that which is problematic for learners and establish conditions that support the process of inquiry: time, talk, and tools. L. S. Vygotsky emphasizes the role of social process in learning, suggesting that new concepts appear first socially and only gradually become psychological. He suggests that designers provide social models of appropriate activity, enable groups of learners to do activities more complex than they could handle individually, and use signs to enable people to negotiate the different meanings they find in social activity. Perspectives from information-processing and situated learning theories are also briefly discussed in this section.

The third discussion summarizes some useful empirical methods. Successful design of interactive learning experiences builds on an understanding of how learners think. This process requires using empirical methods to uncover prior knowledge. Traditional tests, written from the experts' perspective, label learners' differences as "errors." More modern and sophisticated methods allow educators to discover and work with the logic of learners' reasoning. These methods include clinical interviews, think-aloud problem solving, and video interaction analysis.

Empirical Findings in Science and Mathematics Learning

Because prior knowledge is usually specific to a subject matter, it is difficult to state general facts about prior knowledge across all areas of human interest. Therefore, this paper focuses on one area – science and mathematics learning – as a detailed example of prior knowledge at work. Prior knowledge has been studied more extensively in science and mathematics than in other areas. While the specific forms of prior knowledge in art or history may be different, we can expect that similar issues will arise.

Prior knowledge can be viewed from two perspectives, that of the accomplished scientist or that of the learner. Let's start with the scientist.

Science as Refinement of Prior Knowledge

In this section I discuss the role that prior knowledge plays in the thinking of accomplished scientists. I use the term "scientific knowledge" broadly here, referring both to concepts and to scientists' modes of perception, focus of attention, procedural skills, modes of reasoning, discourse practices, and beliefs about knowledge. It is conventional to think that scientific knowledge is different from everyday knowledge and that it must replace everyday knowledge. But when we look more closely, it becomes apparent that scientists reuse metaphors and ideas drawn from prior knowledge. Moreover, we see that the transformation from everyday knowledge to scientific knowledge occurs very gradually and depends on the social practices of the scientific community. Only over long periods of time and through extended conversations with their colleagues do scientist shape theories that are distinct from their commonsense roots.

The cartoonist presents the typical scientist as an Einstein scribbling mathematical formulae on a blackboard. Study of the scientific process reveals, however, that science does not always begin with mathematical abstractions or with empirical findings, but rather with ideas close to the surface of everyday knowledge. Albert Einstein, for example, rooted his own intellectual development not in mathematics but in everyday ideas of rigidity, simultaneity, and measurement (Einstein 1950; Wertheimer 1982; Miller 1986).

Einstein (1950) said that everyday knowledge provides a huge store of useful metaphors and ideas. From these, the scientist makes a free selection of a set of axioms and thereupon begins constructing a theory. Einstein thought the origin of his theory might relate to a childlike exploration of space, and he consulted with Piaget on the possible similarities between his personal intellectual development and that of children (Miller 1986). In analyzing the work of other scientists, philosophers (Black 1962; Kuhn 1970; Toulmin 1972) and historians (Miller 1986; Nercessian 1988) emphasize that science is a constructive activity. Its materials are drawn in part from the familiar images and metaphors of prior knowledge (Lightman 1989; Miller 1986).

If science draws upon everyday knowledge, why does scientific knowledge often appear so different from everyday knowledge in both form and content? In traditional accounts, philosophers searched for a "great divide" that separated scientific from everyday knowledge, much like the division between sacred and profane knowledge. If such a distinction could be made, scientific learning could be cut free of the biases of prior knowledge. These traditional accounts have not succeeded in establishing a firm divide between everyday and scientific knowledge.

An alternative to the "great divide" account comes from the work of sociologists, historians, and anthropologists who have studied scientific work (e.g., Latour 1987; Knorr 1981). From their inquiries, we learn that the properties of scientific knowledge arise from the social practices enacted by specific scientific communities. Discourse processes transform prior knowledge into refined concepts that can be applied consistently by members of the scientific community.

Scientific knowledge is not a *type* of knowledge but rather a refined product for which prior knowledge supplied the raw materials and social interaction supplied the tools.

The preceding discussion illustrates the contrast between replacement and reuse. New knowledge does not *replace* prior knowledge; rather new knowledge *reuses* prior knowledge. Reuse is made possible by a process in which prior knowledge is refined and placed in a more encompassing structure. The more encompassing structure comes in part from the social discourse norms that prevail within a community of practice.

The importance of time and social context becomes apparent when we consider how scientists learn. Kuhn (1970) argues that scientific knowledge does not always progress smoothly, but calls for "paradigm shifts" that involve large-scale conceptual change. To invent relativistic physics, Einstein had to depart from the very foundations of Newtonian science (Einstein 1961). In paradigm shifts, the paradox of continuity again arises: How can scientists formulate a better theory if all they have is a flawed prior theory?

Analyzing conceptual change, Toulmin (1972) argues that it is not the mere replacement of one theory by another. Conceptual change occurs slowly and involves a complex restructuring of prior knowledge to encompass new ideas, findings, and requirements. Thus Einstein did not merely replace Isaac Newton; he transformed Newtonian ideas and placed them inside a new, encompassing analysis of space and time. Toulmin emphasizes that conceptual change, like normal science, is continual and incremental. It is mediated by physical tools and regulated by social discourse. Only from the distant perspective of history does a paradigm shift appear as replacement. From a close-up perspective, conceptual change looks like variation and selection in a interrelated system of knowledge. Individual scientists vary the meaning of concepts and the use of methods. Given specific social rules and a long time over which to operate, selection can result in large-scale changes in concepts.

From this analysis of the scientific process comes a series of important lessons for those who study learning. Knowledge begins with the selection of ideas from everyday experience. The construction of scientific knowledge is a slow, continuous process of transformation taking place over a long period of time, involving successive approximation, and only gradually and incompletely becoming "different" from everyday knowledge.

In general, learning involves three different scales of changes. Most commonly, learners assimilate additional experience to their current theories and practices. Somewhat less frequently, an experience causes a small cognitive shock that leads the learner to put ideas together differently. Much more rarely, learners undertake major transformations of thought that affect everything from fundamental assumptions to their ways of seeing, conceiving, and talking about their experience. While rare, this third kind of change is most profound and highly valued.

These lessons have three implications for designers of interactive experiences. First, designers should seek to **refine prior knowledge**, not attempt to replace learners' understanding with their own. Second, designers must **anticipate a long-term learning process**, of which the short-term experience will form an incremental part. Third, designers must remember that **learning depends on social interaction**; conversations shape the form and content of the concepts that learners construct. Only part of specialized knowledge can exist explicitly as information; the rest must come from engagement in the practice of discourse of the community.

We next move to the viewpoint of learner, stressing similar points but drawing attention to specific difficulties that arise in trying to interpret learners' prior knowledge. First, I will review data that show the dominant the paradox of continuity in science education: Science learners need prior knowledge, but prior knowledge seems to mislead them. Then I present guidelines for resolving the paradox by reconsidering assumptions about learning. These guidelines may help educators interpret prior knowledge both in science and in other areas.

Studies of Science Learning: Deepening the Paradox

Studies of students' prior knowledge in science and mathematics began in the 1970s and have since produced a voluminous literature (see reviews in Confrey 1990; McDermott 1984; Eylon and Linn 1988). Interest in prior knowledge began with the careful documentation of common errors made by students in solving physics and mathematics problems. Analysis of interviews with these students revealed that the errors are not random slips but derived from underlying concepts.

For example, when students are asked to explain a toss of a ball straight up in the air, they describe the motion in terms of an "initial upwards force" which slowly "dies out" until it is "balanced" by gravity at the top of the trajectory. Physicists, in contrast, explain the ball toss in terms of a single constant force, gravity, which gradually changes the momentum of the ball: On its way upwards, the momentum is positive and decreasing; at the top, it is zero; and going down, the momentum is negative and increasing.

From analysis of students' thinking, researchers have determined that this "mistaken" explanation is not peculiar to this problem. Students commonly give explanations in terms of "imparting force," "dying out," and "balancing"(diSessa 1993). From these commonsense ideas, students can generate endless explanations for different situations. In many cases, these explanations disagree with conventional Newtonian theory.

The text below examines the complex findings that have emerged from investigations of students' concepts. Notice that research tends to deepen the paradox of continuity; as we learn more about students' prior knowledge, the construction of scientific knowledge not only seems slow but also increasingly improbable.

After they established the existence of prior concepts, researchers investigated the consequences of those concepts for subsequent learning. Most studies have looked at the role of prior knowledge in a conventional science course. The results depend on the nature of the task used to probe students' learning. If the task is procedural calculation, students can often learn to get the right answer independent of their prior knowledge. However, if the task requires students to make a prediction, give a qualitative explanation, or otherwise express their understanding, studies show that their prior knowledge "interferes. diSessa (1982), for instance, found students who were receiving an A grade in freshman physics at the Massachusetts Institute of Technology, but could not explain the simple ball toss problem correctly. Using their prior knowledge, students often construct idiosyncratic, nonconforming understandings of the scientific concepts.

The prevalence of this effect has been widely documented. Halhoun and Hestenes (1985a, 1985b) found that 30- to 40 percent of physics students who pass freshman physics at various universities misunderstood the concepts. The same misunderstanding has also been found at the elementary and secondary school levels, across both Western and non-Western cultures around the world. Indeed, some researchers suggest that 30- to 40 percent of physics teachers at the secondary school level misunderstand physics concepts because of their prior knowledge.

The processes by which misconceptions arise from a combination of prior knowledge and instructed subject matter are not unique to Newtonian mechanics. Children's concepts differ from those of scientists in biology (Carey 1985; Keil 1979), heat and temperature (Lewis 1991; Wiser and Carey 1983), electricity (Cohen, Eylon, and Ganiel 1983; Gentner and Gentner 1983), mathematics (Resnick and Ford 1981; VanLehn 1989), probability (Shaughnessy 1985), statistics (Tversky and Kahneman 1982) and computer programming (Spohrer, Soloway, and Pope 1989), and thus children encounter difficulties as they interpret the scientific theories of these subjects. Furthermore, children are not the only ones who produce mistaken interpretations by combining prior knowledge with instruction. Consider Tversky and Kahneman's (1982) findings about simple statistics. They have identified erroneous prior concepts about statistical phenomena that are widespread among professional psychologists – scientists who use statistics regularly. For example, both students and scientists suffer from "confirmation bias" that distorts experience to fit prior theory.

Prior knowledge exists not only at the level of concepts, but also at the levels of perception, focus of attention, procedural skills, modes of reasoning, discourse practices, and beliefs about knowledge. In Trowbridge and McDermott's (1980) studies of perception of motion, students perceived equal speed at the moment when two objects pass, whereas scientists observed a faster object passing a slower one. Anzai and Yokohama (1984), Larkin (1983), and Chi, Feltovich, and Glaser (1990) studied how students perceive physics problems and found they often notice superficial physical features, such as the presence of a rope, whereas scientists perceive theoretically relevant features, such as the presence of a pivot point. Larkin, et al. (1980) studied students' solutions to standard physics problems and found that they often reasoned backward from the goal toward the known facts, whereas scientists often proceed forward from the given facts to the desired unknown. Similarly, Kuhn, Amsel, and O'Loughlin (1988) studied children's reasoning at many ages and found that children only slowly develop the capability to coordinate evidence and theory in the way scientists do. Finally, studying students beliefs about the nature of scientific knowledge, Songer (1989) and Hammer (1991) found that these beliefs sometimes foster attitudes antagonist to science learning.

In summary, prior knowledge comes in diverse forms. It affects how students interpret instruction. While it may not prevent them from carrying out procedures correctly, it frequently leads to unconventional and unacceptable explanations. Prior knowledge is active at levels ranging from perception to conception to beliefs about learning itself. Moreover, its effects are widespread through the lay and professional population, from young children through to adults, and from low- to high-ability students.

Implications of Prior Knowledge: Learning as Conceptual Change

The overwhelming weight of the evidence has forced informed educators to make fundamental changes in the way science is taught. Learners are more likely to construct an interpretation that agrees with prior knowledge, and consequently disagrees with the viewpoint of the teacher. Thus the effects of prior knowledge require a change from the view that learning is absorption of transmitted knowledge to the view that learning is conceptual change (Resnick 1983; Champagne, Gunstone, and Klopfer 1985). Over time, learners need to accomplish the rarest form of change, a paradigm shift in their basic assumptions about the natural world and the accompanying ways they see, conceive, and talk about the world. Conceptual change is a process of transition from ordinary ways of perceiving, directing attention, conceptualizing, reasoning, and justifying. Slowly learners transform prior knowledge to accommodate new scientific ideas (Posner, et al. 1982).

Most of the data on science learning stress *differences* between prior knowledge and scientific knowledge rather than commonalities (Smith, diSessa, and Roschelle 1993). This emphasis has had an unfortunate consequence: rather than making education seem easier, it now appears impossible. Teachers get the impression that students *need* prior knowledge to learn new concepts, but prior knowledge *misleads* students to unconventional interpretations of concepts. Moreover, as the perception of a gap has increased, the metaphors used to describe the learning process have become more adversarial: prior knowledge must be confronted, challenged, overcome, replaced, eradicated, or destroyed in order for new knowledge to take its place. Educators celebrate students' constructive capabilities, then roll out the heavy artillery to destroy it. The weight of the evidence makes the paradox of continuity appear as a gaping void; there seems to be no bridge from prior knowledge to desired knowledge, with many apparent pitfalls along the way.

Undoing the Paradox of Continuity in Science Learning

Smith, diSessa, and Roschelle (1993) recently investigated the paradox of continuity that arises in science education research. They suggest a interpretive theoretical framework that accepts the flawed character of some prior knowledge but still gives it a positive role. The gist of their argument is that the paradox arises from implicit biases in theory and method. To undo the paradox, one must reconsider the implicit assumptions in science learning research.

First, one must recognize a bias in the data set. Almost all the data begin from identifying learning failure – examining a situation in which students make errors and then identifying the concept that causes the error. If we start, on the other hand, by identifying success and then investigating the concepts that enable success, we find an equally strong role for prior knowledge. Prior knowledge is properly understood not as a cause of errors or success but rather as the raw material that conditions all learning.

Second, biases in research methodology tend to produce "attributes" of prior knowledge that might be better understood as "attributes of the learning task." If prior knowledge is said to be resistant to change by conventional instruction, students might be resisting the learning experience and not the knowledge. For example, most conventional science courses focus on manipulating mathematical expressions that refer to idealized situations such as a frictionless plane. But we should not expect such an abstract experience to enable much change in familiar concepts of motion. When learning experiences are more concrete, related to familiar situations, and interactive, so-called "resistance" often disappears, and students construct new concepts quickly. Prior knowledge and conventional instructed knowledge may not be in conflict but more like ships passing in the night.

Likewise, research methods that compare expert and novice performance tend to characterize their findings in dichotomies. For example, Larkin (1983) suggests that scientific knowledge is abstract, whereas prior knowledge is concrete. Other popular dichotomies are general versus superficial, theoretical versus familiar, and structural versus superficial. A methodology based on dichotomies is well suited to sorting objects onto a bipolar spectrum but not to analysis of how emergent wholes integrate preexisting parts. For example, dichotomy-based methods mistakenly assert that science is abstract and cannot identify how scientific knowledge successfully coordinates both concrete and abstract elements. A bias to dichotomies obscures the continuing roles prior knowledge plays in a more encompassing knowledge structure.

Third, one must be careful about the status that is attributed to prior knowledge. Researchers have termed prior knowledge "preconceptions," "alternative conceptions," "naive conceptions," and "misconceptions" as well as "naive theories" and "alternative theories." Each term is loaded with theoretical connotations that may be quite misleading and inaccurate, even if unintentionally so.

Terms that ascribe the status of a theory to prior knowledge are particularly misleading. For example, some researchers have drawn analogies between students' ideas and historical theories, such as medieval impetus theory (McCloskey 1983). However, children are not "short scientists," nor are ordinary adults "medieval scientists." All people, including scientists, build knowledge from a pool of familiar metaphors like "balancing" and "dying out." This pool of metaphors is not structured like a theory; it is not necessarily consistent, complete, or deductively sound. Rather, it is a loose aggregate of useful ideas that can be flexibly applied. Although children and ordinary adults sometimes produce explanations that sound like medieval theory, they do necessarily hold their knowledge in the same regard that a scientist holds a theory.

Terms that focus on the mistaken or alternative status of prior knowledge are also misleading. Prior knowledge can produce mistakes, but it also can produce correct insights. Sometimes the same element of prior knowledge can provide both an incorrect alternative to one theory and be a component of a correct theory in another topic area. Consider the common idea of "force as a mover," for example, which holds that an applied force results in a proportional velocity (diSessa 1983). This idea is often misapplied to situation in which a constant force acts on a frictionless object. Conventional electromagnetism texts, however, assert that "an electron moves with a velocity proportional to the applied electromotive force." Thus "force as a mover" can be either a misconception or a sanctioned modeling concept, depending on the context. The consequence of such observations is that educators should treat prior knowledge as a store of generative metaphors, not a collection of wrong theories. Prior knowledge is like a set of building blocks, and not like an enemy fortress.

Fourth, one must beware of a reductionist bias in theorizing about prior knowledge. In general, research has focused on identifying a very small number of knowledge elements and attributing great power to each. Studies of science learning, to the contrary, remind us is that scientific thinking is comprised of many diverse components. Learning can occur by recontextualizing, reprioritizing, or refining the parts. For example, many "misconceptions" are correct elements of knowledge that have been overgeneralized. By specifying a narrower range of situations, the concepts become "correct." In mathematics, for instance, students often have the misconception that the x-intercept of a line is equal to the inverse of the b term in equations of the the form $y = mx + b$. This concept is correct, but only in the case where the slope of the line is 1 (Moschkovich 1992). One step in refining knowledge is adjusting the context in which the knowledge is applicable.

Similarly, as students learn science, knowledge elements change in priority (diSessa 1993). For example, we ordinarily think of surfaces as rigid. To understand the normal force, however, we must lower the priority of rigidity and raise the priority of springiness. In analyzing a book on a table, for instance, the scientist sees a heavy object compressing the surface of the table slightly, giving rise to a restoring force upwards. Thus the scientist, while understanding that books and tables are mostly rigid, gives a higher priority to springiness. Both springiness and rigidity are commonsense concepts; to accommodate Newtonian theory, only their relative priority shifts.

Likewise, Roschelle (1991) investigated how students develop a concept of vector addition suitable for understanding acceleration. Relevant prior knowledge for vector addition includes a commonsensical notion of addition as well as concepts of pulling, guiding, and hinging. Through concrete experience over time, students form a synthetic vector addition concept that draws upon these initial metaphors but is considerably more precise and specific. According to diSessa (1993), science learning involves many such shifts in generality, priority, and refinement. The net result is the transformation of a loose aggregate of knowledge into a crystalline structure of well-established priorities, tuned to the demands of conventional scientific theory.

In summary, we see that students quickly acquire many different kinds of knowledge but only slowly acquire the ability to coordinate and integrate these different sources of understanding. Students can learn to calculate from mathematical formulas and to give qualitative explanations, but it takes a long time to acquire to the ability to coordinate qualitative explanations with mathematical formulas that represent a theory.

The previous section on scientists' use of prior knowledge emphasized that knowledge changes slowly by restructuring, not replacement. This insight is equally true for science students. Moreover, to overcome the paradox of continuity for science learning, we should attend to several guidelines for interpreting prior knowledge:

• Study success, not just failure, and identify how prior knowledge enables success.

• Use methods that allow observations of students constructing integrated wholes, not just shifting valences on a bipolar scale.

• Be wary of viewing prior knowledge as an enemy fortresses that is wrong, alternative, or theoretical in character; instead, see prior knowledge as a disorganized collection of building blocks.

• Expect learning to occur through gradual refinement and restructuring of small component capabilities in a large, distributed system, with increasing coordination.

To this list, I would add that theories of prior knowledge tend to have an individualistic and psychological bias. This bias reflects, in part, in the selection of concepts as a focus of study. On every occasion of concept use, however, a learner is in a social and physical situation that powerfully affects the learning taking place (Roschelle and Clancey 1992).

Educational experiments that work with prior knowledge have realized considerable success in provoking and supporting conceptual change. Clement, Brown, and Zietsman (1989) have developed a science curriculum based on "anchoring analogies"— everyday concepts from which scientific concepts can grow. Similarly, Minstrell (1989) has developed classroom techniques for gradually restructuring students conceptions. White (1993) has developed a computer-based curriculum, called "ThinkerTools," that develops a scientific concept of motion gradually over several months. White's curriculum includes explicit attention to differences between scientific discourse and ordinary discourse (e.g. the meaning of "law") and organizes a social context that resembles the collegial environment of scientific work more closely than it resembles the authoritarian classroom. Roschelle (1991) studied students' learning from similar computer software and concluded that students learn the scientific concept of acceleration through a series of gradual transformations of their prior knowledge.

In reviewing teaching methods that work, Scott, Asoko, and Driver (1991) note two successful strategies, one based on explicitly working with conflicts, and the other based on building on correct prior knowledge. In any educational situation, there is likely to be some conflict, and some extensions to prior knowledge will take place. Learners can succeed in conceptual change as long as appropriate care is taken in acknowledging students' ideas, embedding them in an appropriate socially discourse, and providing ample support for the cognitive struggles that will occur.

In summarizing the broad sweep of research, perhaps the most important lessons are these. First, we must give up the notion of transmitting knowledge to absorbent minds; learning is a process of **conceptual change**. Second, conceptual change is a **slow, transformative** process. Rather than rejecting prior knowledge and accepting instructed knowledge, learners must gradually refine and restructure their prior knowledge. Third, to overcome the paradox of continuity, we should study success, avoid dichotomy-based empirical methods, see prior knowledge as providing building blocks, and look for learning as long-term transformation knowledge into larger, more systematically coordinated wholes.

Prior Knowledge in Theories of Learning

Research in science and mathematics learning has not yet produced a successful theory of learning, nor are theories available in other subjects. The current state of the art, as described above, merely suggests a set of framing assumptions that dissolve the paradox of continuity sufficiently to allow education to proceed.

But how does knowledge change and grow? To answer this question, we must turn to more general theories of learning. Philosophically, the issue of prior knowledge arises in epistemology, the study of justified true belief (Edwards 1967). Immanuel Kant (1724–1804) was concerned with identifying certain knowledge. He distinguished between *a priori* and *a posteriori* knowledge. *A priori* schemata consist of basic structures that enable us to detect regularities in the environment. Space and time were Kant's primary candidates for *a priori* status. Most other knowledge comes from synthetic combination of schemata with experience.

Most theories of conceptual change stick with this framework of *a priori* structures combining synthetically with new experience, though they vary the notions of schemata, experience, and the construction process in which schemata and experience come together. They also differ in emphasis: Piaget emphasizes psychological changes to schemata, Dewey emphasizes the transformative possibilities in experience, and Vygotsky emphasizes the role of social interaction in reconstructing the relationship of structures to experience. The few short pages available here present a quick tour of how these theories treat the issue of prior knowledge.

Piaget: Developmental Growth of Schemata

Jean Piaget's (1896-1980) theory (Inhelder and Piaget 1958; Ginsburg and Opper 1979; Gruber and Voneche, 1977) concerns the development of schemata in relation to new experience. Children, like adults, combine prior schemata with experience. However, children's notions of space and time differ qualitatively from adults' (Piaget 1970).

Piaget's theory of conceptual change focuses on the development of schemata from childhood to maturity, characterizing four stages, termed "sensimotor," "preoperational," "concrete operational," and "formal operational" (Murray 1994). At each successive stage, more encompassing structures become available to children to make sense of experience. For example, Piaget demonstrated that children cannot perform controlled experiments with variables, or reason with ratios, before the formal operational stage. Prior knowledge, in the form of structural schemata, thus play a determining role in how children make sense of interactive experience.

In Piaget's account of conceptual change, knowledge grows by reformulation. Piaget identified a set of invariant change functions, that are innate, universal, and age independent. These are assimilation, accommodation, and equilibration. Assimilation increases knowledge, while preserving structure, by integrating information into existing schemata. Accommodation increases knowledge by modifying structure to account for new experience. For Piaget, the critical episodes in learning occur when a tension arises between assimilation and accommodation, and neither mechanism can succeed on its own. Equilibration coordinates assimilation and accommodation, allowing the learner to craft a new, more coherent balance between schemata and sensory evidence. Reformulation does not replace prior knowledge but rather differentiates and integrates prior knowledge into a more coherent whole.

Piaget influenced educators not only by his theory but also by his method. He spent long hours coming to know children's modes of thinking (using the clinical interview, discussed later). After Piaget, we must assume that children will make sense of experience using their own schemata. Yet we also must carefully interview children, seeking an understanding of their form of coherence. Most followers of Piaget are constructivists who cultivate a deep appreciation of children's sense-making, and they design interactive experiences accordingly.

Piaget generated many innovative task settings in which children become involved in active manipulation of physical objects. Trying to achieve a goal in a physical task can promote conflict between assimilation and accommodation in the accompanying psychological task. Moreover, alternative physical actions can suggest different conceptual operations, and thus opportunities that arise in physical activity can inspire mental restructuring. Using these insights, Kuhn, Amsel and Papert (1988) show that children can learn to coordinate theory and evidence in a period of several weeks if provided with engaging, playful, thought-provoking tasks. Harel and Papert (1991) extend this point by suggesting that the best tasks for constructing ideas are those in which children have to build something that works. While construction and constructivism are not necessarily linked, they go well together. Dewey's theory, discussed in the next section, also identifies designing, making, and tinkering with real things as critical to conceptual change.

In summary, Piaget's work suggests that learners overcome the paradox of continuity with the help of slow maturational processes that operate when doing a task provokes conflict between accommodation and assimilation and support for equilibration between them. Thus designers of interactive experiences must invest the empirical effort needed to appreciate learner's perspective. From an understanding of this perspective, one can design tasks that are likely to attract learners, to provoke disequilibration, and to support the necessary but difficult work of knowledge reformulation. Tasks should be simple and direct, with individual concrete operations mapping closely to the conceptual operations at stake. Experience in which learners construct a working physical arrangement are often powerful for constructing knowledge. The best way to progress past prior understanding of a painting, for example, might be to try to paint one like it.

Dewey: The Conditions for Reflective Experience

Whereas Piaget developed a theory of the growth of structuring schemata, John Dewey (1859-1952) elaborate the experiential side of learning (Dewey 1938a). Piaget exposed Kant's *a priori* structures as genetic variants, not fixed truths. Dewey exposed the problematic nature of experience, which is not "given" to us either, but rather is created in our transactions with nature and with each other and thus depends on the prior knowledge that we bring to it.

In Dewey's account of learning (Dewey 1916; Dewey 1938b; McDermott 1981), problematic experience comes to the fore. For Dewey, primordial experience occurs in a physical and social situation. Moreover, learners are not "in" a situation like paint is "in" a bucket; rather experience is an active transaction that coordinates doing and undergoing (Dewey 1938a). Even in looking at a painting, we actively direct our gaze and undergo a transformation of our field of vision. Experiential transactions have simple qualities that we can directly apprehend; for example, they can be joyful, frightening, tasty, or harmonious.

In most of life, we proceed smoothly from one transaction to the next, using and enjoying the objects of our experience. But sometimes, experience has the quality of being problematic. By this Dewey means that we feel confused, uncertain, incoherent, unable to act. We are unable to coordinate prior knowledge and prior habit to cope with the exigencies of the moment. In the situation of problematic experience, we can engage a mode of life different from use and enjoying, which Dewey calls *"inquiry."*

Inquiry (Dewey 1938b), the reflective transformation of perception, thought, and action, reunifies experience into a more satisfactory whole. The process of inquiry involves reflection on experience; we apply tools like concepts, drawings, and gestures to point to features of experience that are troublesome. At the same time, we apply tools to project possible solutions. Through experiment and reflection, both schemata and perception are slowly transformed to bring coherence, coordination, and meaning to our transactions.

Inquiry involves psychological, physical, and social interaction. Schön (1979) gives a good example. A team of engineers was trying to design a synthetic paint brush, but the paint would not go on smoothly. One engineer decided to look very carefully at how a bristle brush works. As he slowly painted, the others watched. Gradually they saw that the real brush was not like a sponge. Metaphors of "pumping" and "channeling" came into discussion to describe how paint flowed smoothly down the bristles. Over time, the engineers transformed their notion of painting from absorbing paint to pumping and channeling paint. This transformation in their thinking enabled them to design a successful synthetic brush.

In this example, we see how a problematic experience involves prior knowledge. Prior knowledge was invoked both in creating the original problematic perception (seeing a brush as releasing paint) and the new understanding (seeing a brush as pumping and channeling paint). The process of inquiry involving

psychological, social, and physical interaction gradually enabled the engineers to transform their puzzlement into a new understanding.

Dewey is often viewed as a child-centered educator who emphasized growth of the child's interest and capabilities over the mandates of a curriculum. He took pains, however, to oppose any attempt to place a child's prior knowledge and a curriculum's desired knowledge in conflict or dichotomy (Dewey 1938). We should neither champion children's native desires over the hard-earned wisdom of disciplines nor impose static views into children's minds. Dewey urged a view of children's knowledge as fluid, flexible, generative, and unformed. By designing appropriate experiences, an educator should be able to move from children's interest and capabilities toward the more stable, definite, and structured content of organized subject matters. Thus an educator's responsibility is both to enable the child to engage in inquiry and to guide inquiry so it leads toward broader participation in the culture the child is to enter.

Dewey's lifework was concerned with understanding the conditions that enable inquiry to proceed, and herein lies the most salient inspiration for designers of interactive experiences. The key lesson is this: Attend to that which is problematic in an experiential transaction, from the point of view of the learner, and allow time and space for inquiry to occur as an activity in its own right. A secondary concern is to provide the tools that enable inquiry to be effective. Inquiry occurs not in the head, but in direct engagement with the world and with others. To succeed, learners need ways to sketch and explore ideas and phenomena and to test alternatives experimentally. Moreover, language (which Dewey calls the "tool of tools") can be an invaluable means for redescribing, reorienting, and restructuring experience. Attempts to coordinate one person's understanding with another gradually shifts idiosyncratic ideas toward a common ground. Thus educators interested in working with children's prior knowledge should look for situations in which that prior knowledge becomes problematic and should create three conditions that enable inquiry to proceed successful: time, tools, and talk.

Dewey's work overcomes the paradox of continuity by focusing on the nature of experience. Under the right conditions, a learner engaged with a problematic experience can effect a transformation of prior knowledge. This transformation restructures thought, perception, and action elements into a more integrated, coherent whole. Over a long time, with careful guidance, the net result of many local transformations can be an overall set of ideas and practices that approximates the central core of an organized subject matter.

Vygotsky: Social Reconstruction of Prior Knowledge

L. S. Vygotsky (1896–1934) developed his work partially in response to Piaget's neglect of social interaction. Whereas Piaget emphasized the maturation of schemata within the individual, Vygotsky([1934] 1986) argued that advanced concepts appear first in social interaction and only gradually become accessible to an individual. Thus Vygotsky emphasized the role of social interaction in transformation of prior knowledge.

In one of his studies, Vygotsky ([1934] 1986) specifically examined the role of prior knowledge in science learning. He argued that children have spontaneous concepts and scientific concepts and that these are not in conflict but rather are part of a unitary process. In this process, spontaneous concepts grow upward in generality, preparing the ground for more systematic reasoning. Simultaneously scientific concepts, which are introduced by instruction, grow downward to organize and utilize the spontaneous concepts. Upon achieving a through and systematic intertwining, the learner gains both the power of the abstract (maximum substitutability) and of the concrete (maximum applicability).

The restructuring process that intertwines spontaneous and specialized concepts occurs in social interaction and is mediated by sign systems, such as language and drawing. Whereas Piaget focused on disequilibration among schemata and Dewey focused on problematic experiences, Vygotsky turned attention to the zone of promixal development (ZPD) (Wertsch 1985; Newman, Griffith, and Cole 1989). The ZPD is formed by the difference between what a child can do without help and the capabilities of the child in interaction with others. In this construction zone, the child can participate in cultural practices slightly above his or her own individual capability. Successful participation can lead to internalization. In Vygotsky's account, the primary resources for restructuring prior knowledge come from culture. Moreover, the restructuring process itself occurs externally, in social discourse. Children share, negotiate, and try out meanings in social experience, and adults can shape those meanings by bringing them into the framework of cultural practice.

Recent translations of Vygotsky have inspired designers of interactive experience in several ways. First, the concept of the ZPD suggests that designers provide "scaffolding" to enable learners to participate in a more complex discourse than they could handle on their own (Brown and Ferrara 1985). This scaffolding can be in the form of social processes that manage some of the complexity of a task for learners, allowing them to participate while focusing on only one aspect. In addition, educators can engage in cognitive modeling whereby they act out and verbalize a reasoning process that usually occurs only in an expert's head (Palinscar and Brown 1984). Thus learners can acquire reasoning practices by imitation and apprenticeship (Collins, Brown, and Newman 1989; Rogoff 1990). Finally, Vygotsky inspires designers to create "mediational means" that enable learners to negotiate the meaning of a concept verbally (Hickman 1985). Mediational means can be a graphic notation system or a set of linguistic conventions that extend students' ability to talk about and act upon the relation between their understanding and another person's understanding.

Like the other theorists, Vygotsky's work overcomes the paradox of continuity by suggesting that learning coordinates spontaneous and specialized concepts in a gradual transformative process. Unlike Piaget's maturational account, Vygotsky saw structure coming from culture and gradually expanding into an individual's psychological repertoire through social interaction in the ZPD. By scaffolding, modeling, and negotiating, experienced adults are able to guide learning so as to bring the learner into a specialized cultural community.

Information Processing and Situated Learning

Piaget, Dewey, and Vygotsky developed their theories in the first half of the twentieth century. In the second half of the century, information-processing views have dominated, only recently to be challenged by a loosely coupled set of ideas called "situated cognition." I shall briefly survey the additional resources that these advances contribute to an understanding of prior knowledge.

Information-processing psychology builds on the metaphor of mind as a computer of symbolic data (Newell and Simon 1972; Posner 1989). Successful information-processing (IP) models utilize mechanisms similar to those described by Piaget: accommodation modifies a schema, or assimilation modifies data to fit an existing schema. However, IP modeling has worked best in areas where prior knowledge is weakest – in rule-dominated logic and gaming tasks. Modeling learning in areas where common sense is rich has proven to be an immense task. Moreover, the analogy between minds and computers quickly breaks down where prior knowledge is concerned: you can reprogram a computer, completely replacing its existing program with a different one, whereas human minds must make new knowledge from old. Likewise, computer models have impoverished capabilities for experience and social interaction.

To those interested in prior knowledge and learning, the major contribution of IP is the production of innovative representational systems and sound scientific methodology for analyzing learning processes. The relevant methodological contributions of IP are briefly summarized later in this paper. The representations can help in two ways. First, they can make it easier to describe prior knowledge precisely. For example, VanLehn (1989) showed how the concepts underlying mistakes in addition problems could be given a precise description. From this specific diagnosis, a teacher might decide to provide more focused instruction. Second, representations can be a tool that allows the learner to reflect. For example, children can use "semantic networks" to map the associations among ideas before, during and after learning. Likewise, tree diagrams can help students understand processes that are hierarchically composed rather than linearly composed, such as the generation of a geometric proof (Koedinger and Anderson 1990). Providing a tool for representing prior knowledge can enable learners to reflect more systematically on prior knowledge.

Situated learning (Brown, Collins, and Duguid 1989; Lave 1988) has emerged in the last decade as a critique of IP's focus on internal schemata and neglect of physical and social context. Situated learning, like Deweyan theory, holds that all learning occurs within experiential transactions – coordinations between personal agency and environmental structures. Like Vygotsky, situated learning also emphasizes the social construction of knowledge. Most striking in relation to the IP accounts is the overall conception of learning as *enculturation.* In place of relations between schemata and experience, situated learning accounts focus on relations among people, physical materials, and cultural communities (Lave and Wenger 1989). Knowledge is developed, shared, and passed on to the next generation by local communities that maintain a particular discourse or work practice, such as a craft guild or academic discipline. Growing ability *to participate* in a community-based culture has precedence over the ability *to know.* In fact, situated learning has relatively little to say about prior knowledge as such but focuses instead on how ordinary work and discourse practices can become specialized and how identities develop.

In its present (and quickly evolving) state, situated learning offers a constructive critique of Kantian-derived conceptions of learning. First, it reminds us that knowledge and social identity are tightly intertwined. A person's prior knowledge is part of his or her personal identity in society. Conceptual change almost always involves a transformation of identity – the specialization of concepts about motion, for example, not only enables a child to think more like a scientist but also to progress towards becoming a scientist. Becoming a participant in a community can be a stronger motivation than gaining knowledge. This insight is a useful corrective to educators who focus on the "right knowledge" and forget to ask who a learner is becoming.

Lave and Wenger (1989) offer the notion of legitimate peripheral participation (LPP) to make this more precise. LPP suggests that "becoming " requires participation in the activities of a community. However, learners often cannot participate in the core activities of a specialized group: an ordinary person, for example, cannot join a scientific laboratory. Thus learning often occurs on the periphery of the community, in specialized places that have been legitimized as entry points. Museums, schools, and clubs (such as 4-H clubs) can serve this purpose. LPP guides us to develop interactive experiences that form part of a legitimate trajectory toward full membership in a specialized cultural community. Because transformation of identity and conceptual change both operate gradually over a long period of time, it is important to specify an overall trajectory that could enable a learner to move from the periphery to the core of a community.

At the cutting edge of current work on prior knowledge, we find researchers concerned with the mutual interaction of social discourse practices with constructive, participatory experiences.

How to Investigate Prior Knowledge

Due to the pervasive influence of prior knowledge on learning, good designers of interactive experiences need to cultivate a sensitivity to the different points of view that learners will bring to an experience. This sensitivity is best gained by firsthand experience with others' points of view; no description in the literature can fully convey the character and constitution of a learner's prior knowledge. Fortunately, becoming sensitive to prior knowledge is not hard to do. One must simply look and listen closely as learners use your materials. When something strange and incomprehensible occurs, don't give in to the temptation to brush it aside; take the occurrence as opportunity to learn.

Understanding prior knowledge is 90 percent perspiration and 10 percent method. Standard tests are useless, because they are almost always written from the perspective of the expert. Instead, it is crucial to get learners to talk and then to pay careful attention to what they say and do. Three specific methods from research community can be helpful.

Piaget developed the clinical interview as a method for investigating children's sense-making. A clinical interview (Posner and Gertzog 1982; White 1985;) usually involves a task in which the learner manipulates some physical materials. Good tasks are simple and focus tightly on the concept at stake. Thus a strange set of actions in the task readily indicates a different sensibility. The interviewer then probes the learner's understanding by asking questions about things the learner has said or done, avoiding leading questions. As the interview progresses, it is often helpful to ask the learner to consider alternatives to see how stable a particular concept is. A transcript of the resulting interview provides a great deal of detail about prior knowledge.

Researchers in information-processing theory have developed the technique of the think-aloud protocol (Ericsson and Simon 1984; Simon and Kaplan 1989), which collects information about a learner's problem-solving process. The learner is trained to "think aloud" while performing a simple task, like addition. "Thinking aloud" means simply verbalizing the stream of consciousness, not explaining or justifying actions to the interviewer. The interviewer does not ask questions but merely prompts the learner to "say what you are thinking" whenever the learner stops talking. Then the learner is given the target problem-solving task and recorded on audiotape. The resulting "protocol" can then be analyzed for evidence of the prior knowledge and differences in thinking processes (Robertson 1990).

The situated learning community is developing techniques for using video recordings to study prior knowledge in full social and environmental context (Roschelle and Goldman 1991; Suchman and Trigg 1991; Jordan and Henterton 1995). Typically, a small group of learners is recorded on videotape as they work on and discuss a common task. The camera is set to a constant, wide-angle shot and left unattended so as to avoid intrusion. Care is taken to get good audio. When the video is finished, it may be put to several uses. Learners may review the video with an interviewer, creating an opportunity to interpret their own behavior. In addition, surprisingly diverse interpretations will often emerge when the video is reviewed by a multidisciplinary panel of colleagues. Finally, the strongest benefit of the video is that when a problematic event occurs, the investigator can review it repeatedly. With repeated viewing and conscious cultivation of multiple perspectives, an investigator will begin to sense each participant's prior knowledge and dispositions.

Conclusions: Prior Knowledge and Museum Assessment

Prior knowledge has diverse and pervasive effects on the learning. Museum experiences cannot eliminate or disable prior knowledge, but rather they must work with it. Thus museums, like all educational institutions, must come to grips with the paradox of continuity: Prior knowledge is both necessary and problematic. Conceptual change must somehow resolve, overcome, or avoid this paradox.

Prior knowledge is implicated in both failure and success; thus knowledge is best seen as raw material to be refined. Instead of assuming bipolar dichotomies where desired knowledge replaces prior knowledge,

designers should expect learning to occur through a transformative, restructuring process producing integrative wholes that coordinate preexisting parts. Refinement and restructuring occur incrementally and gradually; conceptual change is hard work and takes a long time.

Museums are potentially well positioned as sites for conceptual change. They provide the visitor with opportunities to experience authentic objects directly. Cognitive confrontations provoked by interaction with objects are at the heart of Piaget's theory as well as Dewey's. Museums allow visitors to learn socially in small, voluntary groups. Social discourse is the major means of conceptual change in Vygotsky's theory, as well as the contemporary views of situated learning. Museums can provide novel and challenging settings with opportunities for interaction, contemplation, and inquiry. Dewey's theory focuses attention on the problematic nature of learning experiences and the need for educators to anticipate the resources that learners will need to resolve the conceptual struggles that arise. Museums can provide intellectual, physical, and social resources to aid in the resolution of problematic experience.

But too often in my experience, museums do not rise to this challenge. Rather than acknowledging and working from the learner's point of view, museums present an aggressively professional point of view. Too often exhibits seem to assume that a good presentation will make underlying concepts obvious and therefore provide few or no resources when I find the exhibit problematic—alien, awkward, confusing, frustrating, inaccessible, incomprehensible, mysterious, offensive, opaque, strange, or just too exotic. Too often museums neglect the social nature of visits, and I find interaction difficult or uncomfortable.

Success, however, need not be hard to come by. Success begins with cultivation of the ability to look, listen, and understand the learner's viewpoint and to discover the seeds from which knowledge and identity can grow. Other institutions, especially schools, do a downright awful job of supporting conceptual change, as is well-documented throughout the literature. People are naturally active, lifelong learners. As Csikszentmihalyi points out in his paper in this volume, museums need not do much more than provide a high-quality experience that engages prior knowledge in an achievable intellectual challenge and help visitors assemble the physical, intellectual, and social resources they will need to succeed. Unlike schools, museums do not have to make visitors learn on a particular schedule; museums can focus on catalyzing a spontaneous reaction involving prior knowledge, authentic objects, social interaction, and resources for inquiry.

Assessing long-term success is a more difficult matter. As became clear during the Annapolis

Conference, museums have goals beyond subject matter content: encouraging curiosity, caring and exploration; providing a positive, memorable experience; supporting constructivist learning processes; and developing a sense of personal, cultural, and community identity. An excessive focus on *knowledge* can work to the detriment of these other goals and miss the importance of museum learning entirely. Throughout this paper, I have argued that dramatic conceptual change is a slow, unpredictable, and difficult process. It is thus inappropriate to expect deep conceptual change to occur predictably, in a single or short series of visits. Conversely, when deep conceptual change does occur, it will almost certainly involve resources beyond the museum's control such as books, videos, science kits, classes, clubs, and so forth. Assigning partial credit for long-term learning accomplishments is a dubious business at best. Finally, narrowing the museum's focus to changes in conceptual content may harm other, equally worthy goals. For example, curiosity and exploration may fall by the wayside in an attempt to focus on subject matter, and personal and cultural identity may become defined primarily in relation to the community that owns the subject matter rather than opening to diverse modes of participation.

Nonetheless, prior knowledge is implicated in all the museum's goals. Curiosity, caring, and exploration begin with what you know now. A memorable experience reaches unites prior knowledge, present experience, and future purposes in a coherent way. Constructivist learning requires attention to the continuity of knowledge. Knowledge and identity are bound together; we choose personal futures based on what we know and understand today. Thus in assessing museum learning, we can neither overemphasize nor ignore prior knowledge.

This insight suggests that long-term museum assessment should focus on how museums activate visitors' prior knowledge, opening new and effective roads for long-term learning. Do museums raise visitors awareness of alternative perspectives? Do visitors formulate personally relevant questions? Do visitors realize how they can tap their current knowledge to enter a new field of inquiry? Do museums provide models of constructive learning processes with which visitors can go on learning? Do visitors become aware of books, videos, and other resources that start from what they know already? Are museums a place where visitors can use prior knowledge to help their friends and family learn? Do museums provide a setting for integrating diverse views that comprise a rich understanding?

The many powerful and poignant stories related at the Annapolis Conference suggest that museums do activate prior knowledge in these and other remarkably significant ways. While assessment will not prove that museums *cause* long-term conceptual change, a variety of methods could bring to light the diverse ways in which museums can start with access points close to what a visitor knows already and can open the gate to those modes of inquiry, participation, and experience that our society values most highly.

References

Anzai, Y. and Yokohama, T. 1984. Internal models in physics problem solving. *Cognition and Instruction* 1:397-450.

Berieter, C. 1985. Towards a solution of the learning paradox. *Review of Educational Research* 13:233-341.

Black, M. 1962. Models and metaphors. Ithaca, N. Y.: Cornell University Press.

Boyd, R. 1986. Metaphor and theory change: What is "metaphor" a metaphor for? In *Metaphor and thought,* ed. A. Ortony, pp. 356-408. New York: Cambridge University Press.

Brown, A. L.. & Ferrara, R. A. 1985. Diagnosing zones of proximal development. In *Culture, communication, and cognition,* ed. J.V.Wertsch, pp. 273-305. New York: Cambridge University Press.

Brown, J. S., A. Collins, and P. Duguid. 1989. Situated cognition and the culture of learning. *Educational Researcher* 18:32-42.

Carey, S. 1985. *Conceptual change in childhood.* Cambridge, Mass.: MIT Press.

Champagne, A. B., R. F. Gunstone, and L. E. Klopfer. 1985. Consequnces of knowledge about physical phenomena. In *Cognitive structure and conceptual change,* ed. L. H. T. West and A.L. Pines, pp. 61-90. New York: Academic Press.

Chi, M. T. H., P. J. Feltovich, and R. Glaser. 1980. Categorization and representation of physics problems by novices and experts. *Cognitive Science* 5:121-52.

Clement, J., D. E. Brown, and A. Zietsman. 1989. Not all preconceptions are misconceptions: Finding "anchoring conceptions" for grounding instruction on students' intuitions. Paper presented at the annual meeting of the American Educational Research Association, San Francisco, Calif.

Cohen, R., B. Eylon, and U. Ganeil. 1983. Potential differences and current in simple electric circuits: A study of students' concepts. *American Journal of Physics* 51: 407-12.

Collins, A., J. S. Brown, and S. Newman. 1989. Cognitive apprenticeship: Teaching the craft of reading, writing, and mathematics. In *Knowing, learning, and instruction: Essays in honor of Robert Glaser,* ed. L. B. Resnick. Hillsdale, N. J.: Erlbaum.

Confrey, J. 1990. A review of the research on student conceptions in mathematics, science, and programming. *Review of Research in Education* 16: 3-56

Corsini, R. J. 1994. Encyclopedia of Psychology, 2nd Edition, New York: John Wiley, p 86-89.

Dewey, J. 1916. *Democracy and education.* New York: Macmillan.

———. 1938a. *Experience and education.* New York: Macmillan.

———. 1938b. *The logic of inquiry.* New York: Henry Holt.

diSessa, A.A. 1983. Phenomenology and the evolution of intuition. In *Mental models,* ed. D. Gentner and A. L. Stevens, pp. 15-33. Hillsdale, N.J.: Earlbaum.

————. 1993. Towards an epistemology of physics. *Cognition and Instruction* 10, nos. 2-3: 105-225.

————. 1982. Unlearning Aristotelean physics: A study of knowledge-based learning. *Cognitive Science* 6:37-75.

Edwards, P. 1967. *The encyclopedia of philosophy.* New York: Macmillan.

Einstein, A. 1950. *Out of my later years.* New York: Philosophical Library.

————. 1961. *Relativity: The special and general theory.* New York: Crown.

Ericsson, K. A. and H. A. Simon. 1984. *Protocol analysis.* Cambridge, Mass.: MIT Press.

Eylon, B. and M. C. Linn. 1988. Learning and instruction: An examination of four research perspectives in science education. *Review of Educational Research* 58:3, 251-301.

Gentner, D. and D. R. Gentner. 1983. Flowing waters or teeming crowds: Mental models of electricity. In *Mental models,* ed. D. Gentner and A. L. Stevens, pp. 99-129. Hillsdale, N. J.: Earlbaum.

Ginsburg, H. and S. Opper. 1979. *Piaget's theory of intellectual development.* Englewood Cliffs, N.J.: Prentice-Hall.

Glaserfeld, E. V. 1984. An introduction to radical constructivism. In *The invented reality,* ed. P. Watlawick. New York: W.W. Norton.

Gruber, H. E. and J. J. Voneche, eds. 1977. *The essential Piaget.* New York: Basic Books.

Halhoun, I. A. and D. Hestenes. 1985a. Common sense concepts about motion. *American Journal of Physics* 53:1056-65.

————. 1985b. The initial knowledge state of college physics students. *American Journal of Physics,* 53:1043-55.

Hammer, D. M. 1991. Defying common sense: Epistemological beliefs in an introductory physics course. Ph.D. diss., University of California, Berkeley.

Harel, I. and S. Papert, eds. 1991. *Constructionism.* Norwood, N.J.: Ablex.

Hickman, M. 1985. The implications of discourse skills in Vygotsky's developmental theory. In *Culture, communication, and cognition,* ed. J.V.Wertsch, pp. 236-257. New York: Cambridge University Press.

Inhelder, B. and J. Piaget. 1958. *The growth of logical thinking from childhood to adolescence: An essay on the construction of formal operational structures.* London: Routledge.

Jordan, B. and Henderson, A. Interaction analysis: Foundations and practice. Journal of the Learning Sciences 4, no. 1:39-103.

Keil, F. C. 1979. *Semantic and conceptual development. An ontological perspective.* Cambridge, Mass.: Harvard University Press.

Knorr, K. 1981. *The manufacture of knowledge: An essay on the constructivist and contextual nature of science.* Oxford: Pergammon Press.

Koedinger, K. R. and J. R. Anderson. 1990. Abstract planning and perceptual chunks: Elements of expertise in geometry. *Cognitive Science* 114, no. 4:511-50.

Kuhn, D., E. Amsel, and M. O'Loughlin. 1988. *The development of scientific thinking skills.* San Diego, Calif.: Academic Press.

Kuhn, T. 1970. *The structure of scientific revolutions.* Chicago: University of Chicago Press.

Latour, B. 1987. *Science in action.* Cambridge, Mass.: Harvard University Press.

Larkin, J. H. 1983. The role of problem representation in physics. In *Mental models,* ed. D. Gentner and A. L. Stevens, pp. 75-98. Hillsdale, N.J.: Earlbaum.

Larkin, J. H., J. McDermott, D. P. Simon, and H. Simon. 1980. Expert and novice performance in solving physics problems. *Science* 208:1335-42.

Lave, J. 1988. *Cognition in practice.* Cambridge, Eng.: Cambridge University Press.

Lave, J. and Wenger, E. 1989. *Situated learning: Legitimate peripheral participation.* Cambridge, Eng.: Cambridge University Press.

Lewis, E. L. 1991. The process of scientific knowledge acquisition of middle school students learning thermodynamics. Ph.D. diss. University of California, Berkeley..

Lightman, A. P. 1989. Magic on the mind: Physicists' use of metaphor. *American Scholar* 58, no. 1:97-101.

McCloskey, M. 1983. Naive theories of motion. In *Mental models,* ed. D. Gentner and A. L. Stevens, pp. 299-324. Hillsdale, N. J.: Earlbaum.

McDermott, J. J. 1981. *The philosophy of John Dewey.* Chicago: University of Chicago Press.

McDermott, L. C. 1984. Research on conceptual understanding in mechanics. *Physics Today* 37:24-32.

Miller, A. I. 1986. *Imagery and scientific thought.* Cambridge, Mass.: MIT Press.

Minstrell, J. 1989. Teaching science for understanding. In *Towards the thinking curriculum,* ed. L. B. Resnick and L. Klopfer, 133-49. Alexandria, Va.: Association of Supervision and Curriculum Development.

Moschkovich, J. N. 1992. Making sense of linear equations and graphs: An analysis of students' conceptions and language use. Ph.D. diss. University of California, Berkeley.

Newell, A. and Simon, H. A. 1972. *Human problem solving.* Englewood Cliffs, N. J.: Prentice-Hall.

Newman, D., P. Griffith, and M. Cole. 1989. *The construction zone: Working for cognitive change in school.* Cambridge, Eng.: Cambridge University Press.

Nercessian, N. J. 1988. Reasoning from imagery and analogy in scientific concept formation. *PSA* 1:41-7.

Palinscar, A. S. and A. L. Brown. 1984. Reciprocal teaching of comprehension-fostering and monitoring activities. *Cognition and Instruction* 1, no. 2: 117-75.

Piaget, J. 1970. *The child's conception of movement and speed.* New York: Basic Books.

Posner, G. J. and W. A. Gertzog. 1982. The clinical interview and the measurement of conceptual change. *Science Education* 66:195-209.

Posner, G. J., K. A. Strike, P. W. Hewson, and W. A. Gertzog. 1982. Accomodation of a scientific conception: Towards a theory of conceptual change. *Science Education* 66, no. 2:211-27.

Posner, M. I., ed. 1989. *Foundations of cognitive science.* Cambridge, Mass.: MIT Press.

Resnick, L. B. 1983. Mathematics and science learning: A new conception. *Science* 220:477-8.

Resnick, L. B. and W. W. Ford. 1981. *The psychology of Mathematics for Instruction.* Hillsdale, N. J.: Earlbaum.

Resnick, M. 1992. Beyond the centralized mindset:

Explorations in massively parallel microworlds. Ph.D. diss., Massachusetts Institute of Technology.

Robertson, W. C. 1990. Detection of cognitive structure with protocol data: Predicting performance on physics transfer problems. *Cognitive Science,* 14, 253-80.

Rogoff, B. 1990. *Apprenticeship in thinking: Cognitive development in social context.* Oxford: Oxford University Press.

Roschelle, J. 1991. Students' construction of qualitative physics knowledge: Learning about velocity and acceleration in a computer microworld. Ph.D. diss., University of California, Berkeley.

Roschelle, J. and W. J. Clancey. 1992. Learning as social and neural. *Educational Psychologist* 27:435-53.

Roschelle, J. and S. Goldman. 1991. VideoNoter: A productivity tool for video data analysis. *Behavior Research Methods, Instruments, and Computers* 23: 219-24.

Schön, D. 1979. Generative metaphor. A perspective on problem-setting in social policy. In *Metaphor and thought,* ed. A. Ortony, pp. 254-83. New York: Cambridge University Press.

Scott, P. H., H. M. Asoko, and R. H. Driver. 1991. Teaching for conceptual change: A review of strategies. In *Research in Physics Learning: Theoretical issues and empirical studies,* ed. R. Duit, F. Goldberg, and H. Niedderer, pp. 310-329. Kiel, Germany: IPN.

Shaughnessy, J. M. 1985. Problem solving derailers: The influence of misconceptions on problem solving performance. In *Teaching and Learning Mathematical Problem Solving,* ed. E. A. Silver, pp. 399-415. Hillsdale, N. J.: Erlbaum.

Simon, H. A. and C. A. Kaplan. 1989. Foundations of cognitive science. In *Foundations of Cognitive Science,* ed. M. I. Posner. Cambridge, Mass.: MIT Press.

Smith, J. P., A. A. diSessa and J. Roschelle. 1993. Misconceptions reconceived: A constructivist analysis of knowledge in transition. *Journal of the Learning Sciences* 3, no. 2:115-63.

Songer, N. B. 1989. Promoting integration of instructed and natural world knowledge in themodynamics. Ph.D. diss., University of California, Berkeley.

Spohrer, J. C., E. Soloway, and E. Pope. 1989. A goal/plan analysis of buggy Pascal programs. In *Studying the novice programmer,* ed. E. Soloway and J. C. Spohrer, pp. 355-99. Hillsdale, N. J.: Erlbaum.

Strike, K. A. and G. J. Posner. 1985. A conceptual change view of learning and understanding. In *Cognitive structure and conceptual change,* ed. L. H. T. West and and A. L. Pines, pp. 211-31. New York: Academic Press.

Suchman, L. and R. Trigg. 1991. Understanding practice: Video as a medium for reflection and design. In *Designing by doing: A tool box approach to collaborative system design ,* ed. J. Greenbaum and M. Kyng, pp. 65-90. Hillsdale, N. J.: Earlbaum.

Toulman, S. (1972). Human Understanding. Princeton, NJ: Princeton University Press

Trowbridge, D. E. and L. C. McDermott. 1980. Investigation of student understanding of acceleration in one dimension. *American Journal of Physics* 50:242-53.

Tversky, A. and D. Kahneman. 1982. Judgement under uncertainty: Heuristics and biases. In *Judgement under uncertainty: Heuristics and biases,* ed. D. Kahneman, P. Slovic, and A. Tversky, pp. 3-20. Cambridge, Eng.:

Cambridge University Press.

VanLehn, K. 1989. *Mind bugs: The origins of procedural misconceptions.* Cambridge, Mass.: MIT Press.

Vygotsky, L. [1934] 1986. *Thought and Language.* Translated by Alex Kozulin. Cambridge, Mass.: MIT Press.

Wertheimer, M. 1982. *Productive thinking.* Chicago: University of Chicago Press.

Wertsch, J. T. 1985. *Vygotsky and the social formation of mind.* Cambridge, Mass.: Harvard University Press.

West, L. H. T. and A. L. Pines, eds. 1985. *Cognitive structure and conceptual change.* New York: Academic Press.

White, B. Y. 1993. ThinkerTools: Causal models, conceptual change, and science education. *Cognition and Instruction* 10, no. 1:1-100.

White, R. T. 1985. Interview protocols and dimensions of cognitive structure. In *Cognitive Structure and Conceptual Change,* ed. L. H. T. West and A. L. Pines, pp. 51-9 New York: Academic Press.

Wiser, M. and S. Carey. 1983. When heat and temperature were one. In *Mental models,* ed. D. Gentner and A. L. Stevens, pp. 267-97. Hillsdale, N. J.: Earlbaum.

Museum Memory

Douglas Herrmann
Indiana State University
and

Dana Plude
Department of Psychology
University of Maryland

It has long been acknowledged that museums hold and protect collections valuable to society, but only in recent decades have museums been recognized as settings for learning (Falk and Dierking 1994; Melton, 1972). Consequently, researchers are just beginning to try to understand the basis of such learning.

Principles of modern psychology clearly indicate that the best explanation of the acquisition and retention of memories of museum visits lies in the uniqueness of the museum experience. Some principles of memory are generally applicable. For example, learning, retention, and remembering, which apply to information learned in school, events witnessed firsthand, advertisements, and athletic skills, also apply to museum memory.

When a specific kind of memory phenomenon occurs, however, these general principles are invariably coupled with specific principles that pertain to the particular situation. For example, the explanation of memory for information learned in school emphasizes processes of abstraction and concept learning, whereas the explanation of an eyewitness memory emphasizes perceptual learning and possibly the emotions associated with the witnessed event.

Some kinds of memory have more specific principles in common than other kinds. For example, the scientific explanation of memory for autobiography overlaps with the explanation of memory for biography. Both, however, have more in common with each other than with, say, memory for fiction. Furthermore, all three kinds of memory have much less in common with memory for meetings and almost nothing in common with the memory for a skilled motor movement such as flipping an omelette.

In this paper we review the fundamental principles of human memory as they apply to memories of museum visits, a kind of memory referred to here for convenience as museum memory. We begin by addressing what it is about the museum experience that is unique among human experiences. In doing so, we focus on what it is about this experience that results in a unique kind of memory. We examine the content of museum memories and identify what aspects set them apart from other kinds of memory phenomena. In identifying the uniqueness of museum memories we necessarily point out what this kind of memory shares with other kinds of memory, but ultimately it is the uniqueness of museum memories that makes it possible to understand the special properties of this kind of memory and to identify novel methods for investigating museum memory in the future.

Once we have established how the content of a museum memory is different (and similar) to other kinds of memory, we address how museum memories are acquired and used. Finally, we propose the kinds of investigations that might lead to better a understanding of museum memory and to the development of museum conditions that are better suited to promoting richer, more enduring, and more useful memories among museum visitors.

The Uniqueness of Museum Memories
Psychological Accounts of Memory in General
Until only two decades ago, the typical unit of psychological analysis of memories was the association. In its simplest form, an association is merely a connection between two items, such as words, held in memory. Hermann Ebbinghaus ([1885] 1964) was the first psychologist to document that associations could be formed simply on the basis of temporal contiguity; two nonsense syllables, for example, could be learned as a pair after sufficient study. Thus from the earliest studies of memory, most theories focused on the representation of associative links between concepts held in memory.

Although the focus on associations yielded a substantial literature within the verbal learning tradition (see, for example, Lachman, Lachman, and Butterfield 1979), it came to be criticized as too narrow and overly mechanistic (Searleman and Herrmann 1994). For example, one prominent difficulty with simple associationistic theories is that such

Table 1.
Kinds of Memory Representations

Autobiographical memory: for an event in one's life of personal significance

Conversation memory: for a previously experienced or observed conversation

Declarative memory: for statements

Discourse memory: for a previously heard passage

Event memory: for events of life, sometimes called episodic memory

Free recall memory: for a set of items without regard to order

Graphic memory: for drawings and patterns

Knowledge memory: for knowledge acquired in school or other settings

Paired associate memory: for pairs of items in which the second item in a pair was learned to be emitted in the presence of the first

Procedural memory: for a sequence of procedures, mental and/or physical

Prose memory: for a previously read or studied prose passage

Prospective memory: for actions that must be completed at a certain time

Retrospective memory: for one's past, includes both autobiographical and event memory

Semantic memory: for word meanings and for language generally, sometimes used to include knowledge memory

Sentence memory: for a sentence or list of sentences

Serial recall memory: for a set of items in order of presentation

Short-term memory: for briefly presented displays or information

theories are hard pressed to account for individual differences in learning as a function of emotional state. Despite continuing efforts on behalf of some theorists to cast learning and memory within associationistic principles (as evidenced in connectionist architectures for machine learning; see McClelland and Rummelhart 1985), there is current scientific consensus that memory in its broadest sense must incorporate more than simple associations to capture the richness and diversity of the construct (Searleman and Herrmann 1994). In addition to associations, research must focus on the content of experience.

Accordingly, many theories now define memories by the content of experience, including the requirements of a memory task. Table 1 lists many of the kinds of memory that researchers have used to account for the nature of memories formed in the laboratory and everyday life. Perusal of this list reveals that these kinds of mental content are involved in museum memories on one occasion or another. However, the list also reveals that no particular kind of memory captures the essence of the mental content of a museum memory.

The Museum Experience

The uniqueness of museum memories can be identified by considering the function of museums. No other institution in society serves this function. Museums are enjoined by society to provide experiences that are deemed important for people to have and that cannot be obtained elsewhere in society. This analysis of the museum's function deserves elaboration if we are to fully appreciate the unique content of museum memories.

In some cases the content of the museum experience overlaps with information taught in schools (such as knowledge about dinosaurs), or with information conveyed by the media (such as recent historic events), or with information picked up in the course of everyday life (such as the uniforms worn by members of different occupations). Thus, museums possess a scholarly legacy but since schools also have this legacy, the museum experience is not unique in this respect.

The essence of the uniqueness seems to us to be that the museum is expected to fill a very special educational role that schools do not and cannot fill. The museum offers knowledge and experience that has been deemed essential to a person's education in the broadest sense of that word. Implicit in the notion of the museum experience is that it should be incorporated into everyone's education, but that is not possible. Many museum exhibits are rare and cannot be distributed throughout society; many exhibits are too large to transport; many exhibits are too costly to be mass-produced.

Because the experience provided by museums is rare and must be sought out, rather than delivered, as public education is delivered, people in most societies regard their museums with both respect and reverence (Falk and Dierking 1992). Visitors expect a museum to provide an experience that will prove useful. They believe that these experiences are deemed important by society and to one's heritage. In principle, the ideal museum memory is therefore a heritage memory. Because visitors learn from exhibits about topics of value to society, the content of museum memories also bears on personal behavior and social responsibility. For example, museums may provide experiences with animals, artworks, or scientific principles that touch the lives of citizens in various ways: the protection of endangered species, an understanding of other cultures, or an appreciation for advances in technology (Falk, Koran, and Dierking 1986). Because the museum experience instills in the visitor a greater appreciation of societal values, the museum visit has an influence on personal philosophy. Thus museum memories may include philosophic content concerning one's relationship with the topics exhibited (see Ross, 1991), in addition to other content, such as factual information about the exhibits and episodic information about various events surrounding the visit.

We believe that the implied social contract that museums have with their visitors predisposes visitors to form memories that possess the special properties that we have just discussed: a reverential feeling and philosophic content about the value of the museum experience (in relation to, for example, science, nature, or the law). None of the various kinds of memory mentioned earlier or listed in table 1 are held to convey the special properties typically associated with museums. Although it is true that some kinds of memory – such as autobiographical memory – may on occasion include feelings of reverence and philosophic content, they do not necessarily do so (Falk and Dierking 1992). In contrast, our conceptualization of museum memories is that their content necessarily includes some sense of rarity or uniqueness with associated feelings of reverence and a philosophical content regarding the relationship between the visitor and the museum exhibits.

To the extent that a museum experience is redundant with experiences already available elsewhere, such as in school or in the media, the museum experience will be less likely to induce memories of reverence and philosophic content. Sometimes a museum exhibit will fall short and not produce memories with the ideal content. Sometimes an exhibit will have more modest ambitions and not seek to address issues pertinent to societal values. Sometimes visitors are not open to the full impact of an exhibit.

When a museum experience fails to register the unique properties associated with museum memory, the memory instilled by museum experience may be considered as equivalent with autobiographical memories (Conway 1990). In contrast, when maximally effective, the museum experience establishes a unique memory whose content differs from a typical autobiographical memory.

The Principles of Forming and Using Museum Memories

In that a museum memory is like autobiographical memory, it can be expected to include mental records of the physical environment (such as the settings of exhibits and their design), social interactions that occur during the visit and emotional responses elicited during the visit (Falk and Dierking 1992, 1994). In addition, a museum memory may include a record of the person's motivation during the visit and the physical conditions encountered in the museum building, including even the quality of the air, the temperature, and lighting of exhibit rooms. The memory may include as well the visitor's reflection on prior knowledge and on prior museum visits.

Museum researchers are well aware of the richness of museum memory, but they may not be aware of a recent theory that provides a framework for the acquisition, retention, and retrieval of museum memories. This theory provides a basis for explaining the registration of reverence and philosophical content expected of heritage memory. In the following section, we describe this new framework first in general and then with regard to the formation and use of museum memories.

The New Framework

The processes that influence the formation and use of memories in general are diverse. Research has shown that memories are affected not only by the memory system. Memories are affected by several other modes important to our psychology. These modes include, for example, physiological, chemical, affective, social, and psychomotor aspects of the learning situation (Herrmann, Rea, and Andrezejewski 1988; Herrmann and Searleman 1990; Herrmann, Weingartner, Searleman, and McEvoy 1992; Herrmann, Raybeck, and Gutman 1993; Herrmann and Parente 1994; Searleman & Herrmann, 1994; McEvoy, 1992).

Across several research areas, different variations of multimodal theory have been proposed for various

Table 2
Psychological Modes That Affect the Formation and Use of Memories

Active Modes
Mental manipulations: thought processes that foster encoding or the cueing of retrieval

Physical environment: the perception of aspects of the environment, or physical use of the environment to facilitate such perception, so as to foster encoding or the cueing of retrieval

Social Environment: the perception of aspects of the social environment, or the engaging in behaviors that facilitate such perception, so as to foster encoding or the cueing of retrieval

Passive Modes
Physiological states
    Physical condition: factors of daily living that fatigue a person
    Chemical state: chemicals consumed (stimulants, medicines)
    Health: minor and major diseases and disorders

Emotive states
    Attitudinal state: disposition to process certain information or to interact with certain people
    Emotional state: feelings of varied intensity, quality, and value (positive, neutral, or negative)
    Motivational state: awareness of rewards and punishments for performance of memory tasks

---

purposes. Multimodal accounts have been provided for the general functioning of memory (Searleman and Herrmann 1994; Newell 1990; Zacks and Hasher 1992), the improvement of memory in students and in nonstudent adults (Herrmann, Rea, and Andrzejewski 1988; Herrmann et al. 1992), the rehabilitation of memory problems in the neurologically impaired (Bracy 1986; Herrmann and Parente 1994), the changes in memory associated with aging (Cavanaugh et al. 1985; Poon 1980; Poon, Rubin, and Wilson 1992), and the difficulties associated with neurologically impaired memory (Bracy 1986). Next we provide a detailed description of the multimodal model. Then we discuss the implications of the multimodal model for research on museum memories. Finally, we consider the implications of the model for producing the ideal museum memory.

Specific Assumptions of the Multimodal Model
The current formulation of the multimodal model assumes that the psychological system consists of nine modes. Three of these modes are described as active in that they involve conscious thought processes, and six modes are called passive in that they tend to be controlled automatically. Both the active and passive modes affect memory because they influence encod-

ing and other memory processes (Herrmann and Parente 1994). Active and passive modes affect the availability, allocation, and informational bias of attentional processes, although the particular variables that affect these modes exert their effect on these three attentional processes in different ways (Herrmann, Mullin, and Searleman 1993). Table 2 summarizes the different psychological modes involved in encoding and remembering all memories, museum and otherwise.

Active Modes
The three active modes include mental manipulations of ideas and images to register or remember memories; using the physical environment to influence memory; and using the social environment to influence memory performance. All three active modes affect the content of the mental manipulation, either by directly altering the control of memory processes and strategies or by influencing what a person pays attention to and encodes into memory.

The active mode of mental manipulations involves mental processes that have always been the mainstay of memory training and rehabilitation (Bellezza 1981, 1982; Higbee 1988; West 1985; Ben Yishay and Diller 1981; Gianutsos 1991; Parente and AndersonParente

1991). Mental manipulations are thought processes that serve to transfer encoded information to long-term memory. These processes also affect the pattern of attributes that become longterm memories. The particular effect of mental manipulations can be expected to vary across individuals with different learning styles (Dierking 1991).

The nature of the memory formed as a result of a mental manipulation depends on several factors. Current memory theory holds that the sensory input and the cognitions it elicits will be registered in long-term memory in proportion to the kind and amount of processing given to this input and elicited cognitions. In addition, different kinds of information and experience are also registered (Tulving 1972).

A museum memory can be assumed to involve the information represented in displays, the percepts formed from observing the exhibit, and statements made by others during the museum visit. Falk and Dierking (1992, p. 123), state: "Museum visitors do not catalogue visual memories of objects and labels in academic, conceptual schemes, but assimilate events and observations in mental categories of personal significance and character, determined by events in their lives before and after the museum visit." However, because different parts of this content may be registered in different ways, subsequent access to different parts of the content can be expected to depend on the way the information was encoded (Tulving 1983). Thus, for example, if an observer consciously attends to an exhibit's salient labels, particularly if these labels possess the critical characteristics identified by Falk and Dierking (1992), e.g., reverence, then they will serve as an effective cue when the individual tries to remember his or her visit to that exhibit.

Research on the museum experience suggests that museum memories comprise both intentional and unintentional components. For example, Falk and Dierking (1992) have found that the size, position, and attractiveness of labels improve memory for the labels. Such factors also enhance memory because they capitalize on the mind's tendency to learn and remember better when stimuli are imageable and organized (Bransford 1979). However, if an observer only casually peruses the label on an exhibit without concentrating on the message, then the label (or the information it conveys) is unlikely to be an effective reminder at a later time. In this case, the memory for the exhibit may still be cued by a different source of information. For example, the visitor may be cued by whatever he or she was focusing on at the time of the visit—perhaps some aspect of the display itself or even some aspect of the crowd of onlookers.

The other two active modes support mental manipulations by processing cues in the physical and social environments. Social environmental cues may be used to elaborate on the memory record during initial learning or to facilitate remembering at a later date. During a museum visit, environmental cues may be used to elaborate upon the memory record by encoding salient features of the social setting and the physical environment. During remembering, recall of these social and environmental cues may facilitate remembering the appropriate information about the museum exhibit. In a museum, these cues include captions, descriptions, and other signs that convey information about exhibited materials (Evans 1994).

The use of the physical environment to affect memory performance can be quite deliberate. Objects may be intentionally positioned in a display to call attention to themselves and other high-priority information (Cohen 1989; Davies and Thompson 1988). When objects are arranged to enhance their memorability, the physical environment is employed as an external aid. Alternatively, when a visitor chooses to use an interactive display, the visitor may be consciously or unconsciously manipulating the physical environment to increase his or her memory for the exhibit. The visitor also creates permanent cues to take home if she or he extends the museum experience by purchasing souvenirs at the museum store that pertain to certain exhibits visited.

The use of the social environment to affect memory performance can be quite deliberate as well. When a museum arranges guided tours or questionandanswer sessions, the museum is manipulating the social environment to optimize the likelihood of memories' being encoded for the exhibits involved. Alternatively, if a visitor has the opportunity to ask questions and discuss exhibits with museum staff members or fellow visitors, the visitor is manipulating the social environment in ways that will increase her or his memory for the exhibit (Loftus, Levidow, and Duensing 1992). Indeed, any behavior in which the visitor engages in order to linger and extend the visit to learn more about what others are saying about an exhibit helps to keep attributes of the exhibit available in memory to be mentally manipulated.

Although a great deal of learning that occurs in museums is probably not the result of a deliberate intention to learn, prior orientation to a museum and its exhibits is known to make more of an impression than when plans about what exhibits to visit have not been made (Falk and Dierking 1992). The effects of prior orientation may be seen to involve the preparation of active processes for the content to be encountered in a museum visit. Memory research has sometimes found strikingly beneficial effects from planning. For example, a comparison of John Dean's testimony before the Watergate Committee and the tapes made in President Richard Nixon's Oval Office showed that Dean remembered his interactions with Nixon better if he had thought about them ahead of time (Neisser 1981).

Similarly, differences in exhibits can yield differential memorability. Interactive exhibits provide greater opportunity than noninteractive exhibits for many visitors to personalize cues. Moreover, general knowledge and expectations for a particular topic can also prepare visitors for exhibits concerned with the topic. Indeed, people have scripts for how to go about visiting different kinds of museums and the behaviors engaged in at different museums understandably vary. For example, people observe and move about more slowly and more quietly in an art museum than in a science museum. The differences in observational behavior dictated by the art museum script and the science museum script can be expected to affect what is learned in the two kinds of museums.

Passive Modes
Whereas the active modes directly affect the content of a museum memory, the passive modes do not directly affect what is learned or remembered. Instead, the passive modes affect a person's disposition to learn because the state affects either a person's current strength or motivation to attempt a memory task.

Three passive modes figure into a person's strength for memory and cognitive tasks. These modes pertain to a person's physiological states for mental work. These modes include a person's physical condition, chemical state, and health. For example, a person's physical strength rises and falls throughout the day. These socalled diurnal rhythms appear to be optimal for learning in mid-morning, suboptimal right after lunch (people are typically less alert after a meal, especially a large one; see Smith and Miles 1986), and optimal again in the middle of the afternoon. The effects of time of day on learning indicate that the amount that a museum visitor learns depends on when an exhibit is available and when visitors observe it (May, Hasher, and Stoltzfus 1993). Similarly, the chemical state and health of visitors also affect what they learn from a display. Visitors are likely to learn less from their museum experience in the winter because they often have colds and flus that, along with medications taken for these illnesses, interfere with memory.

Another three passive modes pertain to a person's emotive states that influence ones readiness to learn (Csikszentimihalyi and Hermanson, in this volume; Roschelle, in this volume). These modes include a person's attitudinal, emotional, and motivational states (Hertel 1992). They determine what kinds of experiences and information the person is expecting or open to. Negative attitudes about a topic limit what a person will learn about it. Topics that engender an emotional response will elicit more interest and learning than boring topics, but topics that produce a strong negative response will dispose people to turn away and learn less (Freud 1901; Matlin and Stang 1978). Situations that elicit anxiety (Dixon, Hertzog, and Hultsch 1986; Meichenbaum 1972), induced stress (Fisher and Reason 1988; Reason 1988), or produce depression (Zarit, Gallagher and Kramer 1981) impair memory performance.

The passive modes continually change, from hour to hour or day to day, and in some cases from minute to minute. The reason that these modes are called passive is because, relative to the active processes, they typically require little deliberate action to regulate them.

The indirect effect of the passive modes on memory processing originates from the two ways they influence effectiveness. All six modes affect a person's strength for engaging in active processing of the exhibits being viewed or, in somes cases, with which the person interacts. In addition, the person's attitudes, emotions, and motivation determine which particular stimuli or information will be the focus of attention and, therefore, likely to be learned.

The effect of a museum experience on the passive modes can critically influence what an individual learns from visit in a museum. If a visitor is fatigued before arriving at a museum, it is unlikely that he or she will learn a great deal during the visit. If a museum visit is fatiguing, the visitor will learn less than if the visit is not fatiguing. And if the visitor has experienced personal stress before arriving at a museum, the best exhibits and staff practices in the world are unlikely to enable him or her to pay attention and learn. Alternatively, to the extent that a museum provides an opportunity for visitors to initially rest and unwind, richer museum memories will be formed.

The Relationship of the Modes to Memory Performance
The active and passive processes together determine what is ultimately learned, retained, and remembered from a museum visit. The relationship of the various modes to each other is summarized in figure 1, which has been adapted from Herrmann and Searleman 1992 and Herrmann and Parente 1994, in part to address the formation of memories during a museum visit.

The solid lines in the figure connect the active processes with the sensory, response, and cognitive systems. These lines represent the assumption that active processes operate directly on the sensory mechanisms that generate sensations and perceptions that become part of a memory, the memory system, and the expression of responses that show others what one knows. The dotted lines in the figure represent the assumption that passive processes operate indirectly on the sensory, memory, and response systems. It is also assumed that the passive processes influence the active processes, although this is not illustrated in

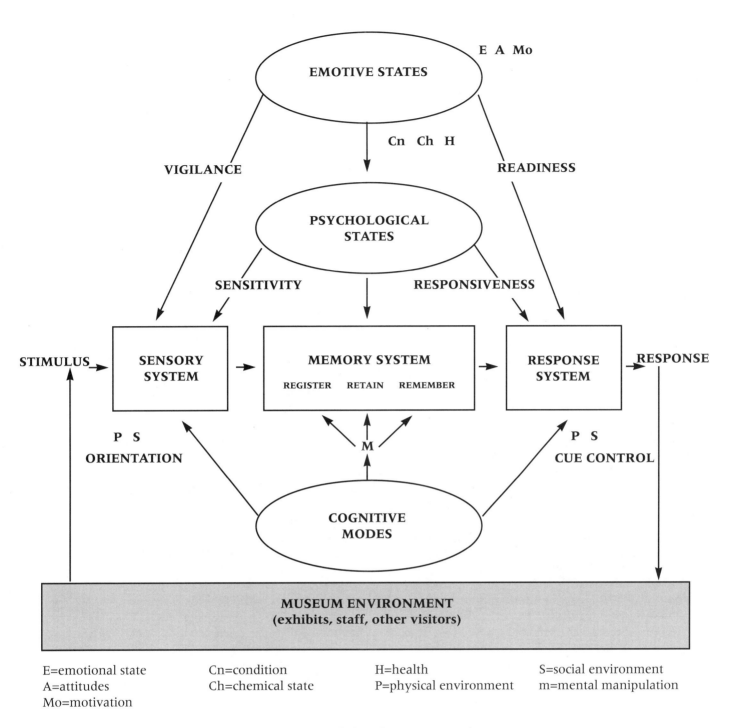

E=emotional state   Cn=condition   H=health   S=social environment
A=attitudes   Ch=chemical state   P=physical environment   m=mental manipulation
Mo=motivation

Figure 1. The multimodal model of memory as applied to the museum environment.

the diagram. The model accounts for a variety of memory tasks, such as trying to learn the name of a new acquaintance or remembering a recently observed exhibit.

Finally, a solid line is shown in the lower part the figure that links the response system to the museum environment which is also presented to the sensory system. This solid line represents a feedback loop by which a museum visitor may influence subsequent memory processes. Thus by altering the world (such

as by talking with a museum staff member, taking notes on an exhibit), the museum visitor can deliberately change the stimulation that otherwise would be provided by the museum. Interactive displays are specifically designed to give the visitor a chance to alter what an exhibit presents and thereby facilitate learning.

Ultimately, the effects of the different modes on memory hinge critically on attentional processes. Recent theorizing about the role of the different modes holds that they affect memory performance by influencing a person's attentional processes (Herrmann, Mullin, and Searleman 1993). The passive modes have a general effect on attention—that is, they affect how much a person pays attention because they determine how much capacity a person has at any given moment to pay attention. The active modes affect what is to be the object of attention—that is, how well one pays attention to an object when there are other objects calling for attention as well.

It should be pointed out that the multimodal model is similar to the human factors approach proposed by Hedge in this volume for optimizing museum learning in that both approaches emphasize trying to improve cognition by considering a variety of psychological modes. The primary difference in these approaches is that the human factors approach may emphasize the importance of the physical environment more than the multimodal approach and, conversely, the multimodal approach emphasizes the coordination of the different modes more than the human factors approach. Otherwise these approaches to museum learning are mutually supportive.

Implications of the Multimodal Model for the Investigation of Museum Memory

In this section, we illustrate how the multimodal model helps to formulate research questions about museum memories and identify new practices that museums might employ to enhance museum memories. In essence, the model suggests hypotheses about how museums may alter the museum experience so as to enrich the memories visitors take away. Obviously, any step that a museum can take to get museum visitors to pay more attention to exhibits will increase the amount of detail registered in museum memories. Because the model shows that attention is affected by all nine psychological modes, research should investigate the formation of museum memories as a function of all nine modes. Below we illustrate some of the hypotheses about how each mode may influence the formation of museum memories.

Active/Cognitive Modes

Mental Manipulations

It seems likely that museum exhibits can increase the memorability of labels and exhibits by designing them to be mnemonically friendly. Verbal displays might provide the visitor with specific mnemonic devices for remembering the name of a certain species. For example, the label for an exhibit of a Tyrannosaurus rex might have a phonetic spelling alongside this term (such as "tie ran a sore us," see Gruneberg 1992). The use of such mnemonic devices to learn technical terms may be regarded by some as silly, but research shows that people are more likely to remember what

the terms stand for than if no mnemonic device is provided (Patten 1990).

Physical Environment

From one perspective, exhibits are the most important way for a museum to induce memories (Falk, Koran, and Dierking 1986; Koran and Koran 1986). Nevertheless, the advent of the modern memory aid promises to add to a new dimension to the memorability of exhibits. Recent research in the memory field has focused on how external objects and devices can aid individuals in both learning and remembering (IntonsPeterson and Newsome 1992; Herrmann and Petro 1990).

One way an aid can improve learning is to provide the visitor with a summary of an exhibit's goals. An audio component might include a onesentence summary of information activated by the push of a button. This information could be repeated as many times as needed by the visitor to consolidate the message in memory and facilitate later retrieval.

Another way to enhance the durability and richness of museum memories might be to equip visitors with a memory aid summarizing the content of their visit that they can take home with them. Research has also shown that reminiscence is central to a healthy attitude on life. Thus external aids that capture the gist of what the visitor experiences will enable him or her to continue learning after the visit because the aid encourages reflection whenever the aid is examined. Each reflection on such an aid strengthens the memory for the content of the visit. For example, visitors might be given not only a pamphlet that describes the entire museum but also pamphlets that describe particular exhibits. These pamphlets may be prepared ahead of time or generated on the spot by interactive displays. For example, the visitor might indicate via a computerized checklist the exhibits she or he has seen; the computer could then generate a pamphlet that summarizes the content of the exhibits mentioned. We realize that this procedure has been used before; our point is that this procedure should be investigated for its effects on museum memories with the view that such pamphlets might be made a standard feature of museum visits.

Microprocessors have come into increased use in museums. These devices allow the visitor to participate in her or his learning from an exhibit (Matusov and Rogoff, in this volume; Roschelle, in this volume). Compact disk players with video capability are becoming increasingly popular and affordable and are likely to prove valuable as aids to museum learning. For example, there already exists a compact disk that potential visitors to the Smithsonian Museum can use to prepare for an upcoming visit (American Interactive Media 1991). This interactive disk allows the potential visitor to explore different parts of the museum and to see high-quality pictures of some of the exhibits in each portion of the museum. Since preparation for a museum visit has been shown to benefit a visitor's memory for a museum experience, it seems likely that disks will become common for major museums.

Compact disk technology is still very new, but research indicates that people may learn more easily with this technology than with other automated forms of learning, including video courses and personal computers (Plude and Schwartz 1994). It therefore seems likely that this technology will be used increasingly by museums in the future to prepare visitors for a museum visit. Additionally, this technology will probably be used a great deal in exhibits, opening the door to even richer museum memories.

Social Environment

Museum visits are often used as a vehicle for people to socialize (Dierking 1989). Social interaction facilitates the information a person picks up from exhibits. Research might begin by examining the effects of staff interactions with visitors and the nature of interactions giving rise to the richest and most durable memories. For example, it may be that a courteous hello on the part of a museum staff member may foster better registration of memory for an exhibit.

Beyond a simple greeting, a staff member may probe visitors about their impressions of exhibits. Probes have the advantage of stimulating the visitor to become a participant in his or her learning (Matusov and Rogoff, in this volume). For example, a staff member may ask visitors what they think of the exhibit (a general query) or whether they understood a certain point of the exhibit (a specific query). It is an open question which probe, general or specific, would enhance memory the most or even whether these probes enhance memory above that provided by a greeting. Additionally, a staff member may provide supplementary information about an exhibit, such as a fact or a set of facts. Again, it is up to research to determine whether staffsupplied supplementary information enhances memory or how many facts produce the optimum effect. It might be argued that such staffing is too costly for most museums, but this view might change if it were demonstrated that the costs were offset by increased effectiveness and visitations. Also, costs could be curtailed by having museum volunteers greet, probe, or provide supplementary information at exhibits.

Passive Modes

Physical Condition

A person's memory performance is affected by aspects of his or her physical state, such as one's health, chemical state and physical condition. As mentioned earlier, relatively inconspicuous variables, such as the time of day (May, Hasher, and Stoltzfus 1993) that a museum is visited, will affect museum learning because a person's strength rises and falls during the day.

Thus research is needed that examines the effects of the timing of museum visits and that attempts to determine the optimum time to direct visitors to certain kinds of exhibits. For example, people can be expected to register a more detailed museum memory by visiting a museum an hour or so after eating (Smith and Miles 1986). Tours immediately after lunch should be avoided. Visitors who have just eaten probably should be encouraged to see simpler exhibits. Nevertheless, research should investigate the kinds of exhibits that are best visited when people are drowsy, sleepy, or tired and the kinds of exhibits that are best visited when people are alert, awake, and energetic.

Research is also needed to determine the appropriate pace for museum visits so that a visitor's energy and interest are sustained and mental fatigue is avoided (Evans, in this volume). People can improve their memory for a museum visit by mixing exercise and rest appropriately. Museum space is at a premium, but, nevertheless, museums should investigate whether the availability of rest areas near exhibits might enhance memory, presumably by ensuring that visitors have time to reflect on (and hence rehearse) what has been learned from the exhibit. If people can sit on a bench and look at an exhibit or at least sit and ponder the exhibit after looking at it, they will remember far more than when the only place to rest is in the cafeteria or snack bar.

Attitudinal State

Attitudes influence a person's disposition to perform memory tasks. Once engaged in a task, attitudes influence the efficiency and nature of responding. We acquire information that protects our ego (Greenwald 1981; Neisser 1988; Sehulster 1988), and we tend to learn more readily if we believe that we are superior at a certain learning task (Sullivan 1927; Rapaport 1942). A good deal of evidence has shown that memory performance is improved by appropriate changes in a person's attitudes. Increased positive attitudes in a person's memory abilities and increased self-confidence result in better memory performance in both normal children and retarded children (Borokowski, Carr, and Rettinger 1987), as well in older adults (Lachman, Steinberg, and Trotter 1987). Experience that corrects negative stereotypes facilitates memory performance (Best 1992).

Thus, museum visitors may be more likely to retain what they have learned from a museum visit if they are presented with information pro and con about the importance of an exhibit. Quotations from famous people such as well respected entertainers, sports figures, and members of government can make the visitor more receptive to an exhibit.

Emotional State

As mentioned earlier, various aspects of emotional states may affect memory (Hertel 1992). Memory registration and retrieval are often impaired by negative emotions (Matlin and Stang 1978) or very intense emotions (Freud 1901), anxiety (Dixon, Hertzog, and Hultsch 1986; Meichenbaum 1972), stress (Fisher and Reason 1988; Reason 1988), and depression. Worse yet, events that threaten ones core values may even be repressed (Erdelyi and Goldberg 1979).

Because a museum experience can be expected to elicit a variety of emotional responses to exhibits and people at the museum (Hayward and Jensen 1981), it would also be expected that museum memories will include these emotional responses. Museum research should investigate the effects of attempts to influence mood and emotion on museum memory. It is generally held that memory is enhanced by congruency between a person's mood and information to be acquired (Ellis, Thomas, and Rodriguez 1984; Johnson and Magaro 1987; Singer and Salovey 1988). Thus a visitor's motivation to encode unpleasant information can be heightened by mood induction techniques, such as directing the visitor to adopt the appropriate mood.

Quotations, background music, photographs, and drawings can be selected not only to support the theme of an exhibit but also to create an emotional backdrop consistent with the exhibit. Sometimes museums attempt to create an appropriate mood but often exhibits appear to be designed without consideration of the effects of the exhibit on the visitor's mood and how mood affects memory.

Research might also address the effects of the arrangement of exhibits on mood and memory. For example, museums that deal with upsetting material, such as is the case with the United States Holocaust Memorial Museum, sometimes arrange exhibits so that people cannot avoid spending some time thinking about the material. It is an empirical issue about how much time is optimal for visitors to observe an exhibit in order to derive the appropriate mood.

Stress reduction seems to be an especially fruitful topic for investigation of memory in the context of museums. When learners are anxious, elaxation is a wellestablished technique for facilitating learning (Yesavage, Sheih, and Lapp 1992). Because many visitors take time to visit a museum specifically to avoid stress, some museum practices could be fashioned to cater to those seeking an escape from stress. It seems likely that these visitors will learn more if given a chance to relax on arriving at the museum or in the process of their visit. As stated earlier, it may be worthwhile for research to investigate the effects of convenient rest areas on museum memory, particularly for the harried visitor.

Implications of the Multimodal Model for Museum Practices

When all modes are at their optimum, the memory formed will likely be a heritage memory, one that is full of reverence for the museum experience (Falk and Dierking 1992) and of philosophic content that enlarges the relationship between the visitor and the topic of an exhibit. However, certain modes appear to be especially important to forming such memories. In particular, it seems likely that reverence and philosophic content are likely to be incorporated into a museum memory when the museum context fosters a proper attitude and mood and a heightened awareness of the social implications of an exhibit.

The Attitude Mode

Research should examine the effects of attempts to impart positive attitudes about the importance of an exhibit. For example, labels that suggest that the exhibit presages the future might make it more likely that the visitor will develop reverence for the information conveyed. The mode of attitude presentation might be one of the first goals of such research. One example might involve comparing the effects of taped messages with tapes of messages against a music background that is consistent with the message.

The Emotional Mode

Earlier it was suggested that music and labels might increase the detail included in a museum memory if the mood elicited by the music and labels is consistent with the topic of an exhibit. Research might specifically seek to identify music that tends to induce a sense of awe or reverence (such as Tchaikovsky's 1812 Overture, the theme from Star Wars, or patriotic songs such as "America the Beautiful") and then determine if such pieces induce a heritage memory more often than more pedestrian music. Similarly, certain quotations may have the power of inducing heritage memories more so than others. Obviously not every exhibit in a museum can have inspiring music played behind it or sit under majestic quotations. Nevertheless, music and language could probably be used to better effect than they are now, and research could help establish the nature of that effect.

The Social Mode

Finally, the social mode seems to be especially important to conveying reverence and instilling the philosophic importance of an exhibit within the visitor. There are several ways that an exhibit might call attention to the social implications of an exhibit; it would remain to research to determine which, if any, of these ways might actually be effective. A perception of reverence might be enhanced by pointing out the importance of the knowledge conveyed by an exhibit to all people. The reasons why different peoples or different religions value the knowledge may similarly elicit the feeling of reverence (Ogbu, in this volume). Most museums can point to many exhibits that cannot be seen anywhere else in the world or at least to exhibits that would not be presented in the same way at another museum. Recognition of the uniqueness of an exhibit adds a special feeling to the museum experience, as if the visitor has just joined a secret society with knowledge known only to the initiates of the society.

An appreciation of the issues that are pertinent to one's personal philosophy may be enhanced by calling attention to certain social issues pertinent to an exhibit. First, the language attending an exhibit may enhance a person's sense of social responsibility. To the extent that the visitor takes pride in being a responsible person, information about social responsibility can elicit motivation above and beyond inherent interest value and improve the registration of the facts addressed by an exhibit (Csikszentimihalyi and Hermanson, in this volume). For example, most animals are interesting to learn about; knowing that a particular animal is an endangered species increases the interest value further and identifies a person who is aware of that status to others as a caring individual and as a responsible citizen.

Second, if museums point out that visitors are smarter and more valued members of society because of what they have learned in their visit, the visitor is likely to retain more from the museum experience (Klatsky 1984). Thus visitors will know not only how to respond more responsibly to a certain topic but also recognize that their possession of this knowledge makes them valuable citizens. For example, an exhibit of lunar landers is interesting to most people. An exhibit on this topic could point out that knowing details about the space program identifies the visitor as a supporter of the program and puts him or her in the company of people whom many consider to be patriots.

Similarly, because the information obtained from many museum exhibits has considerable social currency, a visitor becomes more valuable after a visit because she or he now has information that is of interest to others as well. A museum may, therefore, point out that a museum visit may enhance the visitor's subsequent social interactions (Best 1992; Searleman and Herrmann 1994; Wyer and Srull 1990).

Third, museums may point out how the visitor may reconceptualize his or her place in the world or universe, with respect to the topic of the exhibit and related information (Roschelle, in this volume).

Pondering the similarities between humans and other life forms makes many people feel closer to nature. Considering the vastness of space makes many people consider the finiteness of life.

Research is needed to determine in which of these ways the museum experience might elicit reverence and philosophic content so that they become part of museum memories for that experience. It was suggested earlier that museum memories differ from other autobiographical memories. For example, a museum memory (such as for a display about an endangered species) should involve reverence and philosophically personal truths far more than autobiographical memory for mundane details of daily living (such as for what groceries are to be picked up on the way home from work). If this analysis of the difference of museum memories and other autobiographical memory is correct (Falk and Dierking 1992; see also Wyer and Srull 1990), then research should be able to detect differences between these two kinds of memory for social and emotional variables that reflect the awakening (or strengthening) of philosophically personal truths.

Discussion

Until now, psychology has paid little attention to the memory associated with a museum experience. We suspect that psychological research in the memory field was not devoted to museum memories previously because such memories appear to be autobiographical in nature and thus explainable within the context of existing theories of memory (Bransford 1979). However, our analysis of the content of museum memories indicates that these memories are not ordinary autobiographical memories. Rather, museum memories appear often to include a sense of reverence for a museums topic and a judgement of the personal philosophic relevance of the exhibit (Falk and Dierking 1992, 1994). Ideally, museum memories address some aspect important to the visitor's cultural heritage.

Museums have the power to instill an extraordinary autobiographical memory because museums show objects and provide experiences rarely or never shown elsewhere. It is because museums hold special things that museum visitors sometimes revere what they have seen, heard, smelled, or touched and engage in thought about the significance of these objects for their understanding of their own place in the environment, the country, the world, or the universe.

As has been pointed out here, the unique properties of museum memories have important implications for museum research. It should also be pointed out that the identification of museum memories has important implication for the science of human memory. Memory research has evidenced almost no interest in the attribute of reverence or of philosophic content. It seems likely that investigations of museum memory may be pertinent to memories acquired in religious contexts because of the attribute of reverence and possibly to memories acquired in therapy because of the attribute of philosophic and personal content.

In addition to showing that museum memories of ideal museum experiences have special content, we have endeavored to show that museum memories are best addressed by a multimodal theory. Many examples were offered here to demonstrate that museum memory is multimodal and lends itself to interpretation within a multimodal framework, as extrapolated from multimodal models of memory that have been developed for memory improvement, memory rehabilitation, and memory theory generally.

Acknowledgements

We thank John Falk and Lynn Dierking for providing us the opportunity to study the role of memory in the museum experience.

Further Reading

Cohen, G. 1989. *Memory in the real world.* Hillsdale, N.J.: Erlbaum. *This book reviews findings pertaining to memory as manifested in a wide variety of situations in everyday life.*

Conway, M. 1990. *Autobiographical memory.* Milton Keynes: Open University Press. *This book provides the most comprehensive review of research on autobiographical memory to date.*

Searleman, A., and D. Herrmann. 1994. *Memory from a broader perspective.* New York: McGraw-Hill. *This book reviews the classic, and the latest, scientific findings in memory according to the multimodal interpretation of memory phenomena.*

References

American Interactive Media. 1991. *Interactive treasures of the Smithsonian: A compact disk program.* Los Angeles, Calif.: Phillips Corporation.

Ben Yishay, U., and L. Diller. 1981. Cognitive deficits. In *Rehabilitation of the Head Injured Adult*, ed. M. Rosenthal, pp. 122–149. Philadelphia: F. A. Davis.

Best, D. 1992. The role of social interaction in memory improvement. In *Memory improvement: Implications for memory theory*, ed. D. Herrmann, H. Weingartner, A. Searleman, and C. McEvoy, pp. 122-149. New York: Springer Verlag.

Bellezza, F. S. 1981. Mnemonic devices: Classification, characteristics, and criteria. *Review of Educational Research* 51:247275.

Bellezza, F. S. 1982. *Improve your memory skills.* Englewood Cliffs, N.J.: PrenticeHall.

Borkowski, J. G., M. Carr, and E. Rellinger. 1987. Selfregulated cognition: Interdependence of metacognition, attributions, and selfesteem. In *Dimensions of therapy*, ed. B. Jones, pp. 53-92. Hillsdale, N. J.: Erlbaum.

Bracy, O. L. 1986. Cognitive rehabilitation: A process approach. *Cognitive Rehabilitation* 4:1017.

Bransford, J. D. 1979. *Human cognition: Learning, understanding, and remembering.* Belmont, Calif.: Wadsworth.

Cavanaugh, J. C., D. A. Kramer, J. D. Sinnott, C. J. Camp, and R. P. Markley. 1985. On missing links and such: Interfaces between cognitive research and everyday problem solving. *Human Development* 28:146168.

Cohen, G. 1989. *Memory in the real world.* Hillsdale, N.J.: Erlbaum.

Conway, M. 1990. *Autobiographical memory.* Milton Keynes: Open University Press.

Davies, G. M. and D. M. Thomson. 1988. *Memory in context: Context in memory.* Chichester, England: Wiley.

Dierking, L. D. 1991. Learning theory and learning styles: An overview. *Journal of Museum Education* 16:46.

Dierking, L. D. 1989. The family museum experience: Implications from research. *Journal of Museum Education* 14:911.

Dixon, R. A., C. Hertzog, and D. F. Hultsch. 1986. The multiple relationships among metamemory in adulthood (MIA) scales and cognitive abilities in adulthood. *Human Learning* 5:165178.

Ebbinghaus, H. [1885] 1964. *Memory.* Translated by A. Ruger and C. E. Bussenius. New York: Dover.

Ellis, H. C., R. L. Thomas, and I. A. Rodriguez. 1984. Emotional mood states and memory: Elaborative encoding, semantic processing, and cognitive effort. *Journal of Experimental Psychology: Learning, Memory, and Cognition* 10:470482.

Erdelyi, M. H. and B. Goldberg. 1979. Let's not sweep repression under the rug: Toward a cognitive psychology of repression. In *Functional Disorders of Memory*, ed. J. F. Kihlstrom and F. J. Evans, pp. 355–402. Hillsdale, N. J.: Erlbaum.

Falk, J. H. and L. D. Dierking. 1992. *The museum experience.* Washington, D.C.: Whalesback Books.

Falk, J. H. and L. D. Dierking. 1994b. Recollections of elementary school field trips. Unpublished. Annapolis: Science Learning, Inc.

Falk, J. H., J. J. Koran, and L. D. Dierking. 1986. The things of science. *Science Education* 70:5038.

Fisher, S. and J. T. Reason. 1988. *Handbook of life stress, cognition and health.* New York: Wiley.

Freud, S. 1901. *The Psychopathology of Everyday Life.* Harmondsworth: Penguin.

Gianutsos, R. 1991. Cognitive rehabilitation: A neuropsychological specialty comes of age. *Brain Injury* 5: 35368.

Greenwald, A. G. 1981. Self and memory. In *The psychology of learning and motivation*, ed. G. H. Bower, vol. 15. New York: Academic Press.

Gruneberg, M. M. 1992. The practical application of memory aids: Knowing how, knowing when, and knowing when not. In *Aspects of memory*, ed. M. M. Gruneberg and P. Morris 2:16895. London: Routledge.

Hayward, D. G. and A. D. Jenson. 1981. Enhancing a sense of the past: Perceptions of visitors and interpreters.

Museum Science 12:411.

Herrmann, D. J., and S. Petro. 1990. Commercial memory aids. *Applied Cognitive Psychology* 4:43950.

Herrmann, D. and A. Searleman. 1990. The new multi-modal approach to memory improvement. In *Advances in Learning and Motivation,* ed. G. H. Bower, 26:175205. New York: Academic Press.

Herrmann, D. J., P. Mullin, and A. Searleman. 1993. An explanation of the effects of extrinsic variables on memory performance. Paper presented at the meeting of the Psychonomic Society, November, Washington, D.C.

Herrmann, D. and R. Parente. 1994. A multi-modal approach to cognitive rehabilitation. *NeuroRehabilitation* 4:133-42.

Herrmann, D. J., D. Raybeck, and D. Gutman. 1992. *Improving student memory.* Toronto: Hogrefe & Huber.

Herrmann, D. J., A. Rea, and S. Andrzejewski. 1988. The need for a new approach to memory training. In *Practical Aspects of Memory,* ed. M. M. Gruneberg, P. E. Morris, and R. N. Sykes, 2:41520. Chichester, England: Wiley.

Herrmann, D., H. Weingartner, A. Searleman, and C. McEvoy, eds. 1992. *Memory improvement: Implications for theory.* New York: Springer Verlag.

Hertel, P. 1992. Improving memory and mood through automatic and controlled procedures of mind. In *Memory improvement: implications for theory,* ed. D. Herrmann, H. Weingartner, A. Searleman, and C. McEvoy, pp. 43-60. New York: Springer Verlag.

IntonsPeterson, M. J., and G. L. Newsome III. 1992. External memory aids: Effects and effectiveness. In *Memory Improvement: Implications for Memory Theory,* ed. D. Herrmann, H. Weingartner, A. Searleman, and C. McEvoy, pp. 101-21. New York: Springer Verlag.

Johnson, M. H. and P. A. Magaro. 1987. Effects of mood and severity on memory processes in depression and mania. *Psychological Bulletin* 101:28-40.

Klatzky, R. L. 1984. *Memory and awareness.* New York: W. H. Freeman.

Koran, J. J. Jr., and M. L. Koran. 1986. A proposed framework for exploring museum education research. *Roundtable Reports* (now *Journal of Museum Education*) 11:1216.

Lachman, R., J. Lachman, and E. C. Butterfield. 1979. *Cognitive Psychology and Information Processing: An Introduction.* Hillsdale, N.J.: Erlbaum.

Lachman, M. E., E. S. Steinberg, and S. D. Trotter. 1987. Effects of control beliefs and attributions on memory selfassessments and performance. *Psychology and Aging* 2: 26671.

Loftus, E. F., B. Levidow, and S. Duensing. 1992. Who remembers best? Individual differences for events that occurred in a science museum. *Applied Cognitive Psychology* 6:93108.

Matlin, M., and D. Stang. 1978. *The Pollyanna principle.* Cambridge, Mass.: Schenkman.

May, C. P., L. Hasher, and E. R. Stoltzfus. 1993. Optimal time of day and the magnitude of age differences in memory. *Psychological Science* 4:32630.

McClelland, J. L. and D. E. Rumelhart. 1985. Distributed memory and the representation of general and specific information. *Journal of Experimental Psychology: General* 114:15988.

McEvoy, C. L. 1992. Memory improvement in context: Implications for the development of memory improvement theory. In *Memory improvement: Implications for memory theory,* ed. D. Herrmann, H. Weingartner, A. Searleman, and C. McEvoy, pp. 21030. New York: Springer Verlag.

Meichenbaum, D. 1972. Cognitive modification of test anxious college students. *Journal of Consulting and Clinical Psychology* 39:37080.

Melton, A. W. 1972. Visitor behavior in museums: Some early research in environmental design. *Human Factors* 14:393403.

Neisser, U. 1981. John Dean's memory: A case study. *Cognition* 9:122.

Neisser, U. 1988. Time present and time past. In *Practical aspects of memory,* ed. Gruneberg, P. E. Morris, and R. N. Sykes, pp. 545-60. Chichester, England: Wiley.

Newell, A. 1990. *Unified Theories of Cognition.* Cambridge, Mass.: Harvard University.

Parente, R., and Anderson Parente, J. 1991. *Retraining memory: Techniques and applications.* Houston, Tex.: CSY Publishing.

Patten, B. M. 1990. The history of memory arts. *Neurology* 40: 34652.

Plude, D. and L. Schwartz. In press. The Promise of Compact Disc-interactive Technology. In *Basic and Applied Memory: Theory in Context,* ed. D. Herrmann, C. McEnvoy, C. Herzog, P. Hertel, and M. Johnson. Mawah, N.J.: Erlbaum.

Poon, L. W. (1980). A systems approach for the assessment and treatment of memory problems. In *The comprehensive handbook of behavior medicine,* ed. J. M. Ferguson and C. B. Taylor 1: pp. 191212. New York: Spectrum.

Poon, L., D. Rubin, and B. Wilson. 1992. *Everyday cognition in adult and late life.* New York: Cambridge.

Rapaport, D. 1942. *Emotions and memory.* Baltimore: Williams & Wilkins.

Reason, J. T. 1988. Stress and cognitive failure. In *Handbook of Life Stress, Cognition and Health,* ed. S. Fisher and J. T. Reason, pp. 405-19. New York: Wiley.

Ross, B. M. 1991. *Remembering the personal past: Descriptions of autobiographical memory.* New York: Oxford University Press.

Searleman, A. and D. J. Herrmann. 1994. *Memory from a Broader Perspective.* New York: McGraw-Hill.

Sehulster, J. R. (1988). Broader perspectives on everyday memory. In *Practical Aspects of Memory: Current Research and Issues,* ed. M. M. Gruneberg P. E. Morris, and R. N. Sykes, pp. 323-8. New York: Wiley.

Singer, J. A. and P. Salovey. 1988. Mood and memory: Evaluating the network theory of affect. *Clinical Psychology Review* 8: 21151.

Smith, A. P. and C. Miles. 1986. The effects of lunch on cognitive vigilance tasks. *Ergonomics* 29:125161.

Sullivan, E. B. 1927. Attitude in relation to learning. *Psychological Monographs* 36:1149, 104:16391.

Tulving, E. 1972. Episodic and semantic memory. In *Organization of Memory,* ed. E. Tulving and W. Donaldson. New York: Academic Press.

Tulving, E. 1983. *Elements of Episodic Memory.* Oxford: Oxford Unversity Press.

West, R. 1985. *Memory fitness over forty.* Gainesville,

Fla.: Triad Publishing Company.

Wyer, R. S. and T. K. Srull. 1989. *Memory and cognition, In its social context.* Hillsdale, N.J.: Erlbaum.

Yesavage, J. A., J. I. Sheikh, and D. Lapp. 1992. Mnemonics as modified for use by the elderly. In *Everyday cognition in adulthood and late life,* ed. L. Poon, D. Rubin, and B. Wilson, pp. 598-614. New York: Cambridge.

Zachs, R. T., and L. Hasher. 1992. Memory in life, lab, and clinic: Implications for memory theory. In *Memory improvement: Implications for memory theory,* ed. D. Herrmann, H. Weingartner, A. Searleman, and C. McEvoy, pp. 23248. New York: Springer Verlag.

Zarit, S. H., D. Gallagher, and N. Kramer. 1981. Memory training in the community aged: Effects on depression, memory complaint, and memory performance. *Educational Gerontology* 6:1127.

Intrinsic Motivation in Museums: Why Does One Want to Learn?

Mihaly Csikszentmihalyi
and
Kim Hermanson
The University of Chicago

One often meets successful adults, professionals, or scientists who recall that their lifelong vocational interest was first sparked by a visit to a museum. In these accounts the encounter with a real, concrete object from a different world — an exotic animal, a strange dress, a beautiful artifact — is the kernel from which an entire career of learning grew. For others with an already developed curiosity about some field such as zoology, anthropology, or art, the museum provided an essential link in the cultivation of knowledge — a place where information lost its abstractness and became concrete. In either case, many people ascribe powerful motivation to a museum visit, claiming that their desire to learn more about some aspect of the world was directly caused by it.

Granted that these accounts of "crystallizing experiences" (Walters and Gardner 1986) attributed to museums might often be embellished and exaggerated in retrospect, it would be rash to dismiss them entirely, for the fascination of museums seems to be a very real psychological phenomenon. The question rather becomes, How do museums motivate viewers to learn? Is there a unique, *sui generis* "museum experience" that helps viewers start on the long journey of learning? How do museums present information in a meaningful way, a way that deepens a person's experience and promotes further learning? To begin answering these questions, it will be useful to review what we know about human motivation in relation to learning.

Children are born with a desire for knowledge, and some of the most stupendous feats of learning — to walk, talk, get along with others, to take care of oneself — are accomplished without seeming effort in the first few years of life. It would be difficult to see how a species as dependent on learning as we are could have

survived if we did not find the process of making sense of our environment pleasurably rewarding. But this spontaneous propensity is often extinguished as children's desire to learn is rechanneled in new directions by societal goals and expectations. The abstract, externally imposed tasks children confront in school undermine the motivation to learn for many, often for the rest of life. Research indicates that the natural motivation to learn can be rekindled by supportive environments (Deci et al. 1981; Deci 1992; McCombs 1991); by meaningful activities (Maehr 1984; McCombs 1991); by being freed of anxiety, fear, and other negative mental states (Diener and Dweck 1980; McCombs 1991); and when the challenges of the task meet the person's skills (Csikszentmihalyi 1990a, 1990b).

The view of learning taken in this paper is broader than mere knowledge acquisition, although that is certainly an important part of it. In our view, learning involves an open process of interaction with the environment. This experiential process develops and expands the self, allowing one to discover aspects of oneself that were previously unknown. Thus the learning experience involves the whole person, not only the intellectual but the sensory and emotional faculties as well. And when complex information is presented in a way that is enjoyable — intrinsically rewarding — the person will be motivated to pursue further learning.

Extrinsic and Intrinsic Motivation

Human action is motivated by a combination of two kinds of rewards: extrinsic and intrinsic. Action is *extrinsically* motivated when the anticipated rewards come from outside the activity. In this case, performance is simply a means to some other end — to obtain praise or to avoid punishment, to get a degree, or to live up to societal expectations. A person acts for the sake of intrinsic rewards when the performance itself is worth doing for its own sake, even in the absence of external rewards. For example, most

The authors wish to acknowledge the helpful suggestions of the participants at the Annapolis conference, and especially Margie Marino and Mark Harvey for their assistance with the literature on museum visitors research.

sports, games, and artistic activities are intrinsically motivated, because except for a few professionals, one gets no rewards from performing them beyond the experience itself. Usually we are motivated by both extrinsic and intrinsic rewards at the same time. I might go to work every day primarily because, if I don't, I will get fired, and I need the job to pay my bills. But if in addition I also enjoy my job, the quality of my life will improve, and I am likely to get better at what I am doing.

This general principle holds for learning as well. Most learning in schools is extrinsically motivated (Csikszentmihalyi and Larson 1984). The acquisition of knowledge is rarely enjoyed for its own sake, and relatively few young people would continue to learn in schools in the absence of parental and societal pressures. Because of the stress on external incentives in formal education, intrinsic motivation in schools has been rarely studied. Classic examples are studies that seek to find ways to make the task of learning subject matter and participating in classroom activities more intrinsically motivating (see, e.g., Benware & Deci 1984; Lepper and Cordova 1992).

Learning is intrinsically motivated when it is spontaneous. The most clear examples of intrinsic motivation may be found watching children at play. When playing, children pay attention because they want to, because they find the information interesting and important in its own right. People are intrinsically motivated when they are freely expressing themselves by doing what interests them (deCharms 1968; Deci and Ryan 1985; White 1959). Dweck (1986) and others (Nicholls, Patashnick, and Nolen 1985; Heyman and Dweck 1992) describe students who are intrinsically motivated as having "learning goals," while students who are extrinsically motivated have "performance goals."

Students who are intrinsically motivated tend to have higher achievement scores (Hidi 1990; Lepper and Cordova 1992; Gottfried 1985), and they develop their aptitudes further over time (Csikszentmihalyi, Rathunde, and Whalen 1993). Intrinsic enjoyment of learning appears to be associated with higher creativity as well (Amabile 1983, 1985). Under certain conditions, external rewards appear to undermine intrinsic motivation and to decrease performance (see, e.g., Deci 1971, 1972; Lepper and Greene 1978; McGraw 1978). When one's mind becomes focused on meeting an external goal or requirement, attention or "psychic energy" is split and no longer fully focused on the task at hand.

Schools can afford to ignore intrinsic rewards to a certain extent, because they have strong external incentives—grades, truant officers—to enforce learning. Of course, such extrinsically motivated learning is very wasteful and inefficient. But museums, without external means to compel a visitor's attention, must rely almost exclusively on intrinsic rewards. How, then, can intrinsic rewards be made a part of the museum experience?

The Origins of Intrinsic Motivation

Psychologists began to write about intrinsic motivation in the late 1950s, when some researchers concluded that the basic physiological needs for food and security did not seem to explain why rats explored new territory, were willing to work just to see novel sights, and experimented with challenging tasks (Csikszentmihalyi and Nakamura 1989). These findings suggested that the basic list of "drives" had to be expanded by adding novelty, curiosity, and competence drives (Butler 1957; Harlow 1953; Montgomery 1954; White 1959). More recently, Deci (1992) stated that the inherent psychological needs are competence, self-determination, and relatedness (see also White 1959). In any case, the desire to learn for its own sake appears to be a natural motive built into the central nervous system. A species could not survive long if it did not find pleasure in processing information (Butler 1957; Hebb 1955; Miller 1983, p.111; Montgomery 1954; Tiger 1992; Csikszentmihalyi 1993). As Miller wrote, "The mind survives by ingesting information."

Clearly, however, not all information is equally attractive. Because a person cannot process more than a limited amount of information at a time (Kahneman 1973; Hasher and Zacks 1979; Csikszentmihalyi 1978, 1993), environmental stimuli compete for attention with each other. Attention is a scarce resource — perhaps the most precious scarce resource there is (Simon 1969, 1978). Even though we are surrounded by exponentially increasing waves of information, the amount of it that any person actually notices and then retains in memory may be less than it was in the days of our cave-dwelling ancestors, and it certainly cannot be much more. Therefore what information we select to attend to, and how intently, is still the most important question about learning.

Curiosity and Interest

In the first instance, we choose what information to attend to in terms of curiosity and interest. Curiosity refers to individual differences in the likelihood of investing psychic energy in novel stimuli. For instance, if we say that Mary is curious we mean that compared to other persons she will devote more effort to find out things she does not know (or is not supposed to know). Of course we are all curious to a certain degree, in that our attention is attracted by novel or unexplained stimuli — a loud noise, a sudden bustling activity, a strange animal, or a mysterious object. It is by appealing to this universal propensity that museums can attract the psychic energy of a visitor long enough so that a more extensive interaction, perhaps leading to learning, can later take place.

Interest refers to a differential likelihood of investing psychic energy in one set of stimuli rather than another. To say that Mary is interested in horses means that she is likely to talk about horses, to seek out information about them, to think about them, and to wish that she could feed, groom, and ride horses more than she does these things in relation to, say, dogs, cats, elephants, or gerbils. If we had no interests, the sensory world would be completely confusing, because we would literally not know where to turn. As William James ([1890] 1950, p. 402) remarked over a hundred years ago:

> The moment one thinks of the matter, one sees how false a notion of experience that is which would make it tantamount to the mere presence to the senses of an outward order. Millions of items in the outward order are present to my senses which never properly enter into my experience. Why? Because they have no *interest* for me. *My experience is what I agree to attend to.* Only those items which I *notice* shape my mind—without selective interest, experience is an utter chaos. (James 1890, 402).

Interests are partly universal, partly the result of individual experiences and one's idiosyncratic personal history. Most people are interested in food when hungry, in the opposite sex, in whatever gives them power or acclaim, in babies and pets. But beyond these few common targets, interest soon becomes unpredictable. Some people are attracted to car engines, others to ancient Mesopotamian toothpicks, some to maps, and others to baseball cards.

Most researchers regard interest as a phenomenon that emerges from an individual's interaction with the environment, and they distinguish between situational interest and individual interest (Krapp, Hidi, and Renninger 1992). Situational interest occurs when one encounters tasks or environments with a degree of uncertainty, challenge, or novelty. These environments nourish our built-in propensities for curiosity and exploration. According to Berlyne (1960, 1974), certain structural stimulus characteristics, such as novelty, surprisingness, complexity, and ambiguity, lead to motivational states that result in curiosity and exploratory behavior.

Contextual characteristics that evoke situational interest—or curiosity—tend to be similar between individuals. These contextual stimuli provide the "hook" for museums to capture visitor attention. Without such situational interest, viewers may not attend to an exhibit at all. Hence unobtrusive observation of how visitors allocate attention is one of the most videly used techniques for assessing the effectiveness of museums (Loomis 1987; Serrell and Ralphling 1993).

But because situational interest "tends to be evoked suddenly by something in the environment, it often has only a short-term effect and marginal influence on the subject's knowledge and reference system" (Krapp, Hidi and Renninger 1992, p. 6). Thus situational interest may not affect one's motivation to learn more. In contrast, individual interest is defined as a relatively enduring preference for certain topics, subject areas, or activities (Hidi 1990). The pursuit of individual interests are usually associated with increased knowledge, positive emotions, and the intrinsic desire to learn more (Krapp, Hidi & Renninger 1992).

In *Interest and Effort in Education* (1913) John Dewey described the importance of individual interest. Students who are not genuinely interested in learning a particular subject do not identify with the material and only put out temporary, marginal effort. Dewey described this type of learning as forced and coercive. He believed it resulted in mechanical knowledge and did not effect a qualitative change in the individual (see also Schiefele 1991, p. 300). On the other hand, individual interests are intrinsically motivating, propelling an individual to pursue further learning opportunities. While interests tend to be individually unique, they are broadly characterized as having high personal meaning (Dewey 1913; Maehr 1984; Schiefele 1991). But an activity need not be already meaningful to a person in order for it to provide intrinsic rewards. For instance, John may reluctantly agree to join his friends in a game of bridge, expecting it to be a waste of time. Yet after a few hands the stimulation provided by the game turns out to be so enjoyable that John can hardly leave the table.

Museum visitors may at first attend to an exhibit because of curiosity and interest. But unless the interaction with the exhibit becomes intrinsically rewarding, visitors' attention will not focus on it long enough for positive intellectual or emotional changes to occur. Therefore it is important to consider what makes an experience rewarding in and of itself, so as to understand what may motivate a person to look and think about an exhibit for "no good reason"—that is, in the absence of external rewards.

The Flow Experience

Studies conducted in a great variety of settings by different investigators have shown that a common experiential state characterizes situations in which people are willing to invest psychic energy in tasks for which extrinsic rewards are absent. Chess players, rock climbers, dancers, painters, and musicians describe the attraction of the activities they do in very similar terms, stressing the fact that what keeps them involved in these demanding activities is the quality of the experience that ensues. Many activities that are also well rewarded with money and prestige, such as surgery or computer programming, also seem to offer intrinsic rewards in addition to the extrinsic ones; and these are similar to the ones that artists and athletes mention. We have called this common experiential state the flow experience, because it is generally described as a state of mind that is spontaneous, almost automatic, like the flow of a strong current (Csikszentmihalyi 1975, 1990a). If a museum visit can produce this experience, it is likely that the initial curiosity and interest will grow into a more extensive learning interaction.

A general characteristic of activities that produce flow is that they have clear goals and appropriate rules. In a game of tennis, or of chess, one knows every second what one would like to accomplish. Playing a musical instrument, one knows what sounds one wishes to produce. A surgeon has clear intentions during an operation, and it is this clarity of purpose that allows people to become so thoroughly involved with what they are doing. Conflicting goals or unclear expectations divert our attention from the task at hand. In addition to clear goals, flow activities usually provide immediate and unambiguous feedback. One always knows whether one is doing well or not. Musicians find out immediately if they hit a wrong note, tennis players if they hit the ball badly, and a surgeon knows right away if he has made a mistake. This constant accountability for one's actions is another reason one gets so completely immersed in a flow activity.

Another universally mentioned characteristic of flow experiences is that they tend to occur when the opportunities for action in a situation are in balance with the person's abilities. In other words, the challenges of the activity must match the skills of the individual. If challenges are greater than skills, anxiety results; if skills are greater than challenges, the result is boredom. This equation holds for the broadest possible range of skills: for instance, it includes physical, mental, artistic, and musical talents. I will be frustrated reading a book that was "above my head" and bored when reading a book that is too easy and predictable. As skills increase, the challenges of the activity must also increase to continue the state of flow. The skills involved are those perceived by the individual, however, and not necessarily the actual ones. If one thinks of himself as an incompetent football player, this perceived incompetence will affect performance regardless of its validity. Even if one is involved in an activity that typically induces flow, flow cannot be attained if he or she is worried about performance or if other negative mental states prevail.

Research has substantiated the importance of a positive state of mind for learning. McCombs (1991, p. 119–20) writes that "in the absence of insecurity (e.g., feeling afraid, being self-conscious, feeling incompetent), individuals are natural learners and enjoy learning. . . . Insecurities and other forms of negative cognitive conditioning interfere with or block the emergence of individuals' natural motivation to continually learn, grow, and develop in positive and self-determining ways." Negative mental states such as self-consciousness, depression, anxiety, loneliness, or anger also disrupt the flow experience (Csikszentmihalyi 1985). Dweck and her colleagues' (Dweck 1975; Diener and Dweck 1980) research on "learned helplessness" highlights the serious effects of low self-esteem and anxiety on learning achievement. The intrinsically motivated learning state is characterized by unselfconsciousness, joy, serenity, involvement, and happiness (Csikszentmihalyi 1985).

When goals are clear, feedback is unambiguous, challenges and skills are well matched, then all of one's mind and body become completely involved in the activity. Attention is focused and concentration is so intense that there is no attention left over to think about anything irrelevant or to worry about problems. In the flow state, a person is unaware of fatigue and the passing of time; hours pass by in what seems like minutes. This depth of involvement is enjoyable and intrinsically rewarding. In many cases, individuals describe the experience as becoming "one" with the environment — the painting, the music, the team. People often mention a sense of self-transcendence, as when chess players feel their moves becoming part of a universal field of forces or when dancers feel the rhythm that moves them as part of the "harmony of the spheres."

Flow activities lead to personal growth because, in order to sustain the flow state, skills must increase along with the increased challenges. Flow involves the person's entire being and full capacity. Since flow is inherently enjoyable, one is constantly seeking to return to that state, and this need inevitably involves seeking greater challenges. In the process, flow activities provide a sense of discovery; we discover things about ourselves as well as about the environment. Flow activities, whether they involve competition, chance, or any other dimension of experience, provide a sense of discovery, a creative feeling of being transported into a new reality. They push us to higher levels of performance and lead to previously unexperienced states of consciousness. In short, they transform the self by making it more complex. In this growth of the self lies the key to flow activities. One cannot enjoy doing the same thing at the same level for long. We grow either bored or frustrated; and then the desire to enjoy ourselves again pushes us to stretch our skills or to discover new opportunities for using them.

If these conditions are present, it is possible for individuals to be in flow in any activity, be it conversation, solving differential equations, or driving a car.

A participant in one of our studies was in flow while watching the Chicago Bulls play basketball on television. He knew in detail each of the players' strengths, weaknesses, and definitive plays. "I can totally shut away everything else. . . . I played basketball when I was in high school. I think it's the most talent-demanding of professional sports. . . . You get to know what people do, and you get sucked into their techniques because you can practically predict [their next move]." However, when the New York Knicks game came on, he became distracted and bored, as he was not as familiar with the play patterns of this team. A person who becomes interested in hockey will feel that it is the "most talent-demanding of professional sports," and the same holds for soccer or baseball; in other words, what we invest a great deal of attention in is bound to become ever more interesting and salient.

It is often assumed that for learning cognitive processes are more important than affective processes. But as Schiefele (1991) points out, it is likely that affective processes are at least as important for evoking broader conceptual understanding rather than simple fact retention. Because emotional factors may influence learning only indirectly by stimulating cognitive processes, their importance is easily underestimated (Schiefele 1991, p. 316; Isen, Daubman, and Gorgoglione 1987; Pekrun 1990).

From Flow to Enduring Meaning
When a person is in flow, or fully enjoying an intrinsically motivated activity, he or she usually describes two dialectically related characteristics. On the one hand, when involved in the activity, the individual fully expresses the self. In the process, he or she discovers previously unknown and unrealized potentials and skills. Following Aristotle's views on the purpose of life, Dante wrote: "In every action . . . the main intention of the agent is to express his own image. . . . In action the doer unfolds his being" (quoted in Csikszentmihalyi and Rochberg-Halton 1981, p. 48). The statement: "It is like designing, discovering something new," is the one most strongly endorsed by people as being similar to the phenomenology of the flow experience (Csikszentmihalyi 1975). One recent study participant told us that she finds "learning often comes as a surprise." This process of discovery and learning about who we are could be thought of as *differentiation* — the process of developing a unique self.

On the other hand, people in flow tend to feel connected with other entities, such as nature, a team, the family, or the broader community. Or in the case of many solitary pursuits, the activity connects one with a system of thoughts or beliefs. A rock climber may declare that climbing is for him a form of "self-communication" (Csikszentmihalyi and Csikszentmihalyi 1988). Cameron (1992, p. 53) says

that "attention is an act of connection." When we fully attend to something, we connect with life and thus fulfill the basic human need for relatedness. "The flow experience . . . is symbolic because it brings together the psychic processes of the person and unites them with a set of objective stimuli in the environment. This is opposite from the state of alienation, in which one feels separated from oneself and from the elements of one's life" (Csikszentmihalyi and Rochberg-Halton 1981, p. 247). This process of connection could be referred to as *integration*. Moore (1992, p. 261) says that "when we allow the great possibilities of life to enter into us, and when we embrace them, then we are most individual." When this integration occurs, an activity becomes meaningful, and we become both more connected and more differentiated.

Meaningful experiences are those that are both differentiated and integrated. This dialectical process of integration and differentiation is necessary for psychological development and personal growth (Damon 1983; Fowler 1981; Kohlberg 1984; Loevinger 1976; Maslow 1968). For example, the psychiatrist H. F. Searles (1960, p.30) states this dialectic as follows:

The human being is engaged, throughout his life span, in an unceasing struggle to differentiate himself increasingly fully, not only from his human, but also from his nonhuman environment, while developing, in proportion as he succeeds in these differentiations, an increasingly meaningful relatedness with the latter environment as well as with his fellow human beings.

This dialectic between integration and differentiation is the process by which we learn and grow. On the one hand, we must discover the limits of our being by expressing the purposes and potentials inherent in our biological organism. Only through self-control, through shaping events to our intentions, can we learn who we are and what we are capable of. On the other hand, we must find ways to expand our limited selves by forging ties with other human and nonhuman systems. Motivational research has highlighted the importance of both individual autonomy and connection for facilitating intrinsic learning.

Implications of Intrinsic Motivation for Museums
How do these general principles apply to the kind of learning that can take place in museums? A schematic representation of the process of intrinsic motivation at work in museums is presented in figure 1. Following the steps of this process, it will be easier to see the concrete implications of motivational theory. Of course, such a schematic approach cannot deal with all the practical problems museums face. One of the major obstacles to an easy movement from theory to

Figure 1. The development of learning through intrinsic motivation in museum settings

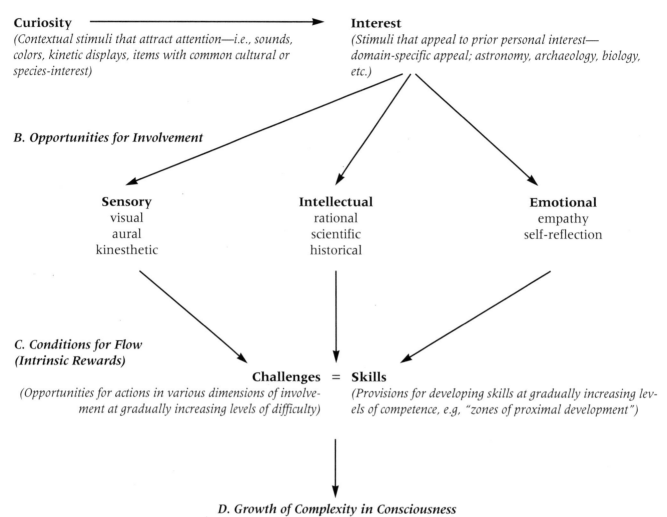

A. The "hook"

Curiosity ⟶ **Interest**
(Contextual stimuli that attract attention—i.e., sounds,   *(Stimuli that appeal to prior personal interest—*
colors, kinetic displays, items with common cultural or   *domain-specific appeal; astronomy, archaeology, biology,*
species-interest)   *etc.)*

B. Opportunities for Involvement

Sensory　　　　　　　**Intellectual**　　　　　　**Emotional**
visual　　　　　　　　　rational　　　　　　　　empathy
aural　　　　　　　　　scientific　　　　　　self-reflection
kinesthetic　　　　　　historical

C. Conditions for Flow
(Intrinsic Rewards)

Challenges　=　Skills
(Opportunities for actions in various dimensions of involve-　　*(Provisions for developing skills at gradually increasing lev-*
ment at gradually increasing levels of difficulty)　　*els of competence, e.g, "zones of proximal development")*

D. Growth of Complexity in Consciousness
(If involvement is intrinsically rewarding, visitors wish to maintain the flow experience. This requires increasing challenges to
avoid boredom, and increasing skills to avoid frustration. The consequence of this dynamic involvement is a growth of sensory,
intellectual and emotional complexity.)

---

practice is the fact that visitors come with such a broad range of interests and backgrounds that no single recipe for motivating them could possibly apply across the board. Nevertheless, these broad outlines can be quite helpful if one takes the trouble of adapting them to particular specific conditions.

The "Hook"

The first step in the process of intrinsically motivated learning suggests that the museum exhibit must capture the visitors' curiosity. Michael Spock, as experienced a professional as they come, says that dinosaurs and mummies are the surest exibits to attract attention. Probably the reason for this attraction is overde-

termined: both dinosaurs and mummies are ancient and therefore mysterious; both invoke awe and a thrill of fear without actual danger. These seem to be universal reasons for people to want to pay attention. Others are pleasing displays with bright colors, interactive exhibits, large size, and other stimuli that provide the situational interest necessary to attract attention.

Museum researchers have already demonstrated that visitors remember better displays to which they have paid more attention (Falk 1991; Koran, Foster, and Koran 1989). However, we still are far from knowing what the fundamental dimensions of situational interest are. Until we collect systematic knowledge on this topic, we shall have to proceed by trial and error, finding out which components of an exhibit are most attractive, for whom, under what conditions. In other words, museum work will continue to be an art rather than a science. Although this is not necessarily bad, a larger contribution of scientific knowledge would surely help.

After the individual's curiosity is aroused, the exhibit must engage sustained interest in order for learning to take place. While individuals vary in what they are interested in — astronomy, sports, mechanics, archeology, biology and so on — some general guidelines could be proposed. Most important, the link between the museum and the visitor's life needs to be made clear. To inspire intrinsic motivation, the objects one finds and the experiences one enjoys, while possibly inspiring awe and a sense of discovery, should not feel disconnected from one's own life. Moore (1992, p. 285) asserts that "when art is removed as the province of professional artists, a dangerous gulf develops between the fine arts and the everyday arts. The fine arts are elevated and set apart from life, becoming too precious and therefore irrelevant. Having banished art to the museum, we fail to give it a place in ordinary life." What Moore says about art could be said of museums in general. It is to be hoped that the museum experience will inspire visitors to see the relationship between the exhibits and their own concerns and perhaps be stimulated to create art, pursue science, and so on, after leaving the museum.

For example, an exhibit on rock formations may be informative and pleasantly arranged. In addition, the exhibit may have features that are challenging and allow one to explore and develop skills. But the features of the exhibit that will induce the motivation to learn more are the deeper sense of meaning it provides. How does this exhibit pertain to me? How does knowing about these rock formations link me to other people and times, the larger cosmos? Education should "speak to the soul as well as the mind" (Moore 1992, p. 36). How does knowledge of rock formations provide a "soulful" connection? Unless we make progress in answering such questions, the information provided in the display is likely to disappear from the visitor's consciousness without leaving any trace in memory.

Opportunites for Involvement

Learning involves the use of sensory and emotional faculties, as well as intellectual ones, and this connection leads us to the third step in the process. To engage intellectual faculties, the exhibit should encourage what Langer (1993; see also 1989) has termed "mindfulness." Mindfulness is the "state of mind that results from drawing novel distinctions, examining information from new perspectives, and being sensitive to context. It is an open, creative, probabilistic state of mind in which the individual might be led to finding differences among things thought similar and similarities among things thought different" (Langer 1993, p. 44). Exhibits that facilitate mindfulness display information in context and present various viewpoints. For example, Langer (1993, p.47) contrasts the statement "The three main reasons for the Civil War were . . ." with the statement "From the perspective of the white male living in the twentieth century, the main reasons for the Civil War were . . . " (p. 47). The latter approach calls for thoughtful comparisons. For example, How did women feel during the Civil War? the old? the old from the North? the black male today? and so on.

Information that is presented as true without alternative perspectives discourages the motivation to explore and learn more. Langer (1993, p. 45) terms this situation a "premature cognitive commitment," denoted by rigid beliefs mindlessly accepted as true (see also Langer and Imber 1979). In sum, intrinsically motivated learning is an open process involving uncertainty and the discovery of new possibilities. A fixed presentation of the material thwarts such further exploration. It is only through the conscious choice of various possibilities that one can learn who one is, what one's interests and beliefs are, and where one's unique talents lie (Csikszentmihalyi and Rochberg-Halton 1981; Csikszentmihalyi and Robinson, 1990).

But when we are intrinsically motivated to learn, emotions and feelings are involved as well as thoughts. For example, our wish to know about peoples in faraway places includes not only the desire for intellectual understanding but the desire to feel emotionally connected to them as well. We are often drawn to exhibits containing diaries and personal letters because they connect us with another's feelings. As Moore (1992, p. 208) states:

> We have spiritual longing for community and relatedness and for a cosmic vision, but we go after them with literal hardware instead of with sensitivity of heart. . . . Our many studies of world cultures are soulless, replacing the common bonding of humanity and its shared wisdom with bites of information that have no way of getting into us deeply, of nourishing and transforming our sense of ourselves. Soul, of course, has been extracted from the beginning because we conceive of education to be about skills and information, not about depth of feeling and imagination.

Museum researchers have become increasingly aware that it is not enough to attract the fleeting attention and interest of visitors; to be effective, museums must provide opportunities for the kind of deep absorption that leads to learning (Harvey,

Birjulin, and Loomis, forthcoming; Thompson 1993). This is what Bitgood (1990, p. 1) calls "simulated immersion," or "the degree to which an exhibit effectively involves, absorbs, engrosses, or creates for visitors the experience of a particular time and place."

Conditions for Flow

When the visitor is interested in an exhibit and engaged through sensory, intellectual, and emotional faculties, he or she should be ready to experience an intrinsically rewarding, optimal experience. But for this experience to occur, the conditions for flow must be present. In the previous section, we have seen that one of the main requirements for flow is to have clear goals. Unfortunately, one of the complaints visitors most often voice is that they do not know what to do when they enter a museum. Helping visitors set manageable goals, both for the entire visit and for each stop at an exhibit, is one way to make the experience more enjoyable. Without feedback, however, involvement is unlikely to be sustained. Successful displays tend to be those that ask visitors to commit themselves to make guesses, to evaluate, to respond — and then provide information by which the visitors can compare their responses to some other standard (Bitgood 1990).

Another feature of successful exhibits is that they offer opportunities for involvement that can be matched with a broad range of visitor skills. This notion was made familiar to the museum community through the "social design movement," one of whose principal aims is to increase the fit between people and their environment (Sommer 1972) or between visitors and informal learning environments (Screven 1976).

In this regard, Vygotsky's (1978) zone of proximal development provides a framework for understanding how to moderate challenges so that they are at the right level. The zone of proximal development is "the distance between the actual developmental level as determined by independent problem solving and the level of potential development as determined through problem solving under adult guidance or in collaboration with more capable peers" (Vygotsky 1978, p. 86). When individuals are assisted in particular tasks, they can learn at different levels. With assistance, one third-grade student may learn at a fifth-grade pace, while another learns at a fourth-grade pace. In developing exhibits, it is useful to ask: How much assistance is available for visitors with different levels of knowledge and ability? Do exhibits present gradually increasing levels of difficulty? And are there provisions for developing skills at gradually increasing levels of competence?

In addition to a balance of challenge and skill, the visitor must be able to concentrate and devote full attention to the given exhibit or activity. Well-known physical distractions include crowds, noise, intimidating guards, hunger, bladder pressure, and fatigue. In addition, preconceived notions may provide internal distractions. Concentration can be hindered by rigid expectations — either one's own or someone else's. For example, as Falk and Dierking (1992, p. 54) point out, museum visitors often have the expectation that they "should see the entire museum." Such prior expectations decrease the openness necessary for a meaningful learning experience by causing fixation on an external goal and anxiety over the ability to meet that goal. Another example frequently occurs in art museums when patrons feel they "should" be getting something out of the experience (Csikszentmihalyi and Robinson 1990, p. 144). When visitors feel intimidated or fearful, or when they try to sustain some rigid self-concept or achieve some predefined result, they also lose the openness necessary for an enjoyable learning experience. The physical sources of distraction can be remedied by physical means — reducing crowds, providing better facilities — while the psychological causes must be addressed through information and education.

In addition to negative expectations a person may bring to the museum, negative mental states can be caused by the social context (Deci et al. 1981; McCombs 1991). Thus, the museum environment can either facilitate or hinder flow. Anxiety, embarrassment, or self-consciousness usually vary depending on where we are and whom we are with. Social environments that facilitate intrinsically motivated learning support personal autonomy and responsibility rather than trying to control behavior. These supportive environments provide people with choices (Zuckerman et al. 1978) and acknowledge their perspectives or feelings (Koestner et al. 1984). We express who we are through our conscious choice of actions. Thus it is important to allow individuals to choose whenever possible. People are more open to learning when they feel supported, when they are in a place where they can express themselves and explore their interests without fear of embarrassment or criticism, and when there are no predefined expectations constraining their behavior. Support, security, and trust are critical for allowing openness to discovery and intrinsically motivated learning. For personal growth and development, one must become less dependent on, or constrained by outside guidance, so that spontaneous motivation will have a chance to awaken.

Growth of Complexity in Consciousness

If a museum exhibit induces the flow state, the experience will be intrinsically rewarding. The visitor will be motivated to explore, and as he or she learns more, skills will increase. The consequence of this dynamic involvement is a growth of sensory, intellectual, and emotional complexity. This growth is especially important to realize now that we live in an information society, when multimedia technology and computers are rapidly changing how we learn and how we are entertained. By pressing a button, in the comfort of our own home, we can learn about the entire history of art, complete with detailed images on the screen; we do not need to enter a museum. But museums offer the opportunity to interact with a real environment, one in which the objects are still imbued with the blood, the tears, the sweat of their makers. Does this contact with the facticity of the historical object actually matter? Or will virtual reality experienced in the communications room of one's home give an even more vivid learning experience than museums now provide?

The jury is still out on these questions. In one respect, however, museums seem to have a distinct advantage over solitary media-induced experiences. They provide information in a public space, where there is a potential to develop the integrative dimension of personal growth. We learn about connectedness through rituals — such as ceremonies or rock concerts — and whenever we are exposed to an event that is shared with others that feeling of connectedness is reaffirmed and strengthened. In modern society, however, there are fewer and fewer venues to experience such shared events. Perhaps one of the major underdeveloped functions of museums is to provide opportunities for individually meaningful experiences that also connect with the experiences of others.

It is essential to realize, however, that current knowledge is insufficient to provide a basis for a thoroughly informed museum practice. While we are getting to understand general principles of motivation tolerably well, the necessary details are still largely lacking. For instance, we have no table where we could look up the elements that will attract the curiosity of different types of visitors; we cannot anticipate the interests of the audience; we have only a rudimentary understanding as to how to balance the challenges of the exhibit with the visitors' skills; we are not sure how to nurture the growth of complexity in the visitors' consciousness after the first sparks are struck. Many of these issues will take decades of basic research to resolve.

In the meantime, however, it seems that each museum could generate knowledge about these pressing questions by taking a more experimental approach, by becoming a more active learning institution. If even 10 percent of museum space and staff efforts were devoted to collecting systematic information about how visitors are affected by the visit, we would soon have a much better idea of what learning takes place within the walls. Only by experimenting with one alternative after the other, in an iterative

process, can we learn what works and what does not (Screven 1976). Trying out different displays, different signage, different ways of involving visitors—while making sure that only a single variable is changed at a time—and then measuring the results will yield useful results. It is important to remain flexible in one's policies, so that mistakes can be corrected swiftly and successes can be built on. These are the main features of the experimental method on which all of science is based. But then, as the philosopher Karl Popper said, science is but common sense writ large. There is no reason museums could not use more common sense and develop the habit of writing it large. We would all benefit from it, and museums could go on performing their educational function with a clearer purpose and a renewed sense of self-confidence.

Acknowledgments
The authors wish to acknowledge the helpful suggestions of the participants at the Annapolis Conference, and especially Margie Marino and Mark Harvey for their assistance with the literature on museum visitors research.

References
Amabile, R. M. 1983. *The social psychology of creativity.* New York: Springer-Verlag.

———. 1985. Motivation and creativity: Effects of motivational orientation on creative writers. *Journal of Personality and Social Psychology* 48: 393-97.

Benware, C., and Deci, E. L. 1984. The quality of learning with an active versus passive motivational set. *American Educational Research Journal* 21: 755-65.

Berlyne, D. E. 1960. *Conflict, arousal and curiosity.* New York: Grove.

———.1974. Novelty, complexity, and interestingness. In *Studies in new experimental aesthetics,* ed. D.E. Berlyne, pp. 175-80. New York: Wiley.

Bitgood, S. 1990. The role of simulated immersion in exhibition. Report 90-20. Jacksonville, Ala.: Center for Social Design.

Butler, R. A. 1957. The effect of deprivation of visual incentives on visual exploration motivation. *Journal of Comparative and Physiological Psychology* 50: 177-79.

Cameron, J. 1992. *The artist's way: A spiritual path to higher creativity.* New York: Putnam.

Csikszentmihalyi, M. 1975. *Beyond Boredom and Anxiety.* San Francisco: Jossey-Bass.

———. 1978. Attention and the wholistic approach to behavior. In *The stream of consciousness,* ed. K. S. Pope & J. L. Singer. New York: Plenum, pp. 335-58.

———. 1985. Emergent motivation and the evolution of the self. *Advances in Motivation and Achievement* 4: 93-119.

———.1990a. *Flow: The psychology of optimal experience.* New York: Harper Collins.

————.1990b. Literacy and intrinsic motivation. *Daedalus,* 119: 2, 115-40.

————. 1993. *The Evolving Self.* New York: Harper Collins.

Csikszentmihalyi, M., and R. Larson. 1984. *Being Adolescent.* New York: Basic Books.

Csikszentmihalyi, M., and J. Nakamura. 1989. The dynamics of intrinsic motivation: A study of adolescents. *Research on motivation in education* Vol. 3, Goals and cognitions. New York: Academic Press.

Csikszentmihalyi, M., and K. Rathunde. 1993. The measurement of flow in everyday life. *Nebraska Symposium on Motivation* 40: 58-97.

Csikszentmihalyi, M., K. Rathunde and S. Whalen. 1993. *Talented Teenagers: The roots of success and failure.* New York: Cambridge University Press.

Csikszentmihalyi, M., and R. Robinson. 1990. *The art of seeing.* Malibu, CA: J.P. Getty Press.

Csikszentmihalyi, M., and E. Rochberg-Halton. 1981. *The meaning of things: Domestic symbols and the self.* New York: Cambridge University Press.

Csikszentmihalyi, M., and I. Csikszentmihalyi, I., eds. 1988. *Optimal experience.* New York: Cambridge University Press.

Damon, W. 1983. *Social and personality development.* New York: Norton.

deCharms, R. 1968. *Personal causation: The internal affective determinants of behavior.* New York: Academic Press.

Deci, E. L. 1971. Effects of externally mediated rewards on intrinsic motivation. *Journal of Personality and Social Psychology* 18: 105-15.

————. 1972. Intrinsic motivation, extrinsic reinforcement, and inequity. *Journal of Personality and Social Psychology* 22: 113-20.

————.1 992. The relation of interest to the motivation of behavior: A self-determination theory perspective. In *The role of interest in learning and development,* ed. K.A. Renninger, S. Hidi, and A. Krapp. Hillsdale, N.J.: Erlbaum.

Deci, E. L. and Ryan, R. M. 1985. *Intrinsic motivation and self-determination in human behavior.* New York: Plenum.

————.1991. A motivational approach to self: Integration in personality. In R. Dienstbier (ed.), *Nebraska symposium on motivation: Vol. 38. Perspectives on motivation.* Lincoln: University of Nebraska Press.

Deci, E. L., A. J. Schwartz, L. Sheinman, and R. M. Ryan. 1981. An instrument to assess adults' orientations toward control versus autonomy with children: Reflections on intrinsic motivation and perceived competence. *Journal of Educational Psychology* 73: 642-50.

Dewey, J. 1913. *Interest and effort in education.* Boston: Riverside Press.

Diener, C. I. and C. S. Dweck. 1980. An analysis of learned helplessness: The process of success. *Journal of Personality and Social Psychology* 39: 940-52.

Dweck, C. S. 1975. The role of expectations and attributions in the alleviation of learned helplessness. *Journal of Personality and Social Psychology* 31: 674-85.

Dweck, C. S. 1986. Motivational processes affecting learning. *American Psychologist* 41: 1040-48.

Falk, J. H. 1991. Analysis of the behavior of family visitors in natural history museums. *Curator* 34: 44-51.

Falk, J. H. and L. D. Dierking. 1992. *The museum experience.* Washington, D. C.: Whalesback.

Fowler, J. W. 1981. *Stages of faith.* New York: Harper & Row.

Gottfried, A. 1985. Academic intrinsic motivation in elementary and junior high school students. *Journal of Educational Psychology* 77: 631-45.

Harlow, H. F. 1953. Motivation as a factor in the acquisition of new responses. In *Current theory and research on motivation,* pp. 24-29. Lincoln: University of Nebraska Press.

Harvey, M. L., A. A. Birjulin, and R. J. Loomis (in press). A virtual reality and human factors analysis of a renovated diorama hall. In *Visitor Studies: Theory, Research, and Practice,* ed. D.R.Thompson, A. Benefield, and S. Bitgood. Vol. 6: Jacksonville: Center for Social Design.

Hasher, L. and R. T. Zacks. 1979. Automatic and effortful processing in memory. *Journal of experimental psychology* 108: 356-88.

Hebb, D. O. 1955. Drives and the C.N.S. (Conceptual Nervous System). *Psychological Review* 62, no. 4: 243-54.

Heyman, G. D. and C. S. Dweck. 1992. Achievement goals and intrinsic motivation: Their relation and their role in adaptive motivation. *Motivation and Emotion* 16, no. 3: 231-47.

Hidi, S. 1990. Interest and its contribution as a mental resource for learning. *Review of Educational Research* 60: 549-71.

Isen, A. M., K. A. Daubman and J. M. Gorgoglione. 1987. The influence of positive affect on cognitive organization: Implications for education. In *Aptitude, learning, and instruction,* Vol. 3, *Conative and affective process analyses,* ed. R. E. Snow and M. J. Farr. pp. 143-64. Hillsdale, N. J.: Erlbaum.

James, W. [1890] 1950. *The principles of psychology.* 2 vol. New York: Dover.

Kahneman, D. 1973. *Attention and effort.* Englewood Cliffs, N.J.: Prentice-Hall.

Koran, J. J. Jr., J. S. Foster, and M. L. Koran. 1989. The relationship among interest, attention and learning in a natural history museum. In *Proceedings of the Annual Visitors Studies Conference,* ed. S. Bitgood, A. Benefield, and D.Patterson, pp. 239-44. Jacksonville, AL: Center for Social Design.

Koestner, R., R. M. Ryan, F. Bernieri, and K. Holt. 1984. Setting limits in children's behavior: The differential effects of controlling versus informational styles on intrinsic motivation and creativity. *Journal of Personality* 52: 233-48.

Kohlberg, L. 1984. *Essays on moral development.* Vol. 2, *The psychology of moral development.* San Francisco: Harper & Row.

Krapp, A., S. Hidi and K. A. Renninger. 1992. Interest, learning and development. In *The role of interest in learning and development,* ed. K. A. Renninger, S. Hidi, and A. Krapp. Hillsdale, N. J.: Erlbaum.

Langer, E. J. 1989. *Mindfulness.* Reading, Mass.: Addison-Wesley.

————.1993. A mindful education. *Educational Psychologist* 28, no. 1: 43-50.

Langer, E. J. and L. Imber. 1979. When practice makes imperfect: The debilitating effects of overlearning. *Journal of Personality and Social Psychology* 37: 2014-25.

Lepper, M. R. and D. I. Cordova. 1992. A desire to be taught: Instructional consequences of intrinsic motivation. *Motivation and Emotion* 16, no. 3: 187-208.

Lepper, M. R. and D. Greene. 1978. *The hidden costs of reward: New perspectives on the psychology of human motivation.* Hillsdale, N. J.: Erlbaum.

Loevinger, J. 1976. *Ego development.* San Francisco: Jossey-Bass.

Loomis, R. J. 1987. *Musuem visitor evaluation: New tool for management.* Nashville, Tenn.: American Association for State and Local History.

McCombs, B. L. 1991. Motivation and lifelong learning. *Educational Psychologist* 26, no. 2: 117-127.

McGraw, K. O. 1978. The detrimental effects of reward on performance: A literature review and a prediction model. In *The hidden costs of reward,* ed. M. R. Lepper & D. Greene, pp. 33-60. Hillsdale, N. J.: Erlbaum.

Maehr, M. L. 1984. Meaning and motivation: Toward a theory of personal investment. In *Reseach on motivation in education,* Vol. 1, Student motivation. New York: Academic Press.

Maslow, A. H. 1968. *Toward a psychology of being.* New York: Van Nostrand.

Miller, G. A. 1983. Infomavors. In *The Study of Information,* ed. F. Machlup and U. Mansfield. New York: Wiley.

Mills, R. C. 1991. A new understanding of self: The role of affect, state of mind, self-understanding, and intrinsic motivation. *Journal of Experimental Education* 60, vol. 1: 67-81.

Montgomery, K. C. 1954. The role of exploratory drive in learning. *Journal of Comparative and Physiological Psychology,* 47: 60-64.

Moore, T. 1992. *Care of the soul.* New York: Harper Collins.

Nicholls, J. G., M. Patashnick, and S. B. Nolen. 1985. Adolescents' theories of education. *Journal of Educational Psychology* 77: 683-92.

Pekrun, R. 1990. Emotion and motivation in educational psychology: General and European perspectives. In *European perspectives in psychology,* ed. P. J. Drenth, J. A. Sergeant, and R.J. Takens, 1: 265-95. Cambridge, Eng.: Cambridge University Press.

Schiefele, U. 1991. Interest, learning, and motivation. *Educational Psychologist* 26, nos. 3-4: 299-323.

Screven, C. G. 1976. Exhibit evaluation: A goal-referenced approach. *Curator* 19:271-91.

Searles, H. F. 1960. *The nonhuman environment.* New York: International Universities Press.

Serrell, B. and B. Ralphling. 1993. The momentary shrine: A new way of thinking about visitors, exhibits, and time. Typescript.

Simon, H. A. 1969. *Sciences of the artificial.* Boston: MIT Press.
———. 1978. Rationality as process and as product of thought. *American Economic Review* 68:1-16.

Sommer, R. 1972. *Design awareness.* San Francisco: Rinehart Press.

Thompson, D. R. 1993. Considering the museum visitor: An interactional approach to environmental design. Ph.D. diss., University of Wisconsin, Milwaukee.

Tiger, L. 1992. *The pursuit of pleasure.* Boston: Little, Brown.

Vygotsky, L. S. 1978. *Mind in society: The development of higher psychological processes.* Cambridge, Mass.: Harvard University Press.

Walters, J., and H. Gardner. 1986. The crystalizing experience: discovering an intellectual gift. In *Conceptions of Giftedness,* ed. R. J.Sternberg and J. E. Davidson, pp. 306-31. New York: Cambridge University Press.

White, R. W. 1959. Motivation reconsidered: The concept of competence. *Psychological Review* 66: 297-333.

Zuckerman, M., J. Porac, D. Lathin, R. Smith, and E. L. Deci. 1978. On the importance of self-determination for intrinsically motivated behavior. *Personality and Social Psychology Bulletin* 4:443-446.

The Influence of Culture on Learning and Behavior

John U. Ogbu
Department of Anthropology
University of California

Introduction

This paper is about how culture influences behavior and learning. It is organized in three sections. The first section focuses on the meaning of culture; the second section reviews cultural influences on behavior; and the third section examines the influence of culture on learning.

Culture

Culture is a fundamental concept in anthropology. Unfortunately, at the present time the concept is problematic both within anthropology and outside the field. Freilich (1989, p. 1) notes that culture was the integrating construct that gave anthropology "a distinctive personality among the social sciences." Eventually many other disciplines found culture to be a useful concept and incorporated it as a part of their frameworks. Note, however, that while other disciplines have adopted the concept, my interdisciplinary experience is that nonanthropology colleagues often do not treat culture in the sense that anthropologists do. The difference is especially apparent in the context of learning and human development. Here culture is often equated with "family environment" or family characteristics due to socioeconomic status of parents. Occasionally, researchers include "population environment and social norms," but they rarely show how the latter enter into development or learning (Ogbu 1987, p. 156). A more serious threat to the concept of culture is its popularization, which has almost taken away its anthropological meaning. This threat is evident in current popular political and academic discourses on cultural diversity (Carroll and Schensul 1990; Ogbu 1990, 1992).

Within cultural anthropology, there is no agreement as to what culture means. Different schools hold very divergent views of culture. These schools include interpretive anthropology, cognitive anthropology, symbolic anthropology, and ecological anthropology, to name a few. Furthermore, within each school anthropologists differ in their definitions of culture. Indeed, in a review more than four decades ago Kroeber and Kluckhohn (1952) found more than 150 definitions of culture. These definitions, according to Freilich (1989:6) focused differentially on "history, normativeness, on values, adjustment and human psychology, learning, sharedness, sublimation, structures, ideas, symbols, and human association." That differential definitions continue can be seen from a sampling of works by educational anthropologists assigned in my course on education and culture (Cohen 1971; Gearing 1976; Kneller 1965; LaBelle 1976; Musgrove 1953; Wilson 1972).

How one defines culture affects how he or she perceives the influence of culture on behavior and learning. For example, a cognitive anthropologist who equates culture with information will conceptualize learning as a transaction. That is, learning takes place when the learner's cognitive map changes as a result of receiving information from a teacher's cognitive map (Gearing 1976). For an ecological anthropologist who defines culture as an adaptation, learning is the process by which culture "shapes the mind" of children to create the kind of persons who, as adults, will "be able to meet the imperatives of the culture" (Cohen 1971, p. 19).

My own view lies within the ecological school. Culture is a people's adaptive way of life. Following LeVine (1973), I suggest that analytically culture has five components:

1. customary ways of behaving (e.g., of making a living, eating, expressing affection, getting married, raising children, responding to illness and to death, getting ahead in society, dealing with the supernatural, going for a job interview, holding conferences, etc.)
2. codes or assumptions, expectations and emotions underlying those customary behaviors
3. artifacts—things that members of the population

Prepared for Museum Learning Conference, Annapolis, MD, August 1994. Revised 12/20/94

make or have made—that have meanings for them (e.g., airports, cars, family homes, freeways, museums, restaurants, schools, supermarkets, television, wristwatches)

4. institutions—economic, political, religious and social, what Cohen (1971) calls the imperatives of culture – which form a recognizable pattern requiring knowledge, beliefs, competencies or skills and customary behaviors in a fairly predictable manner

5. patterns of social relations.

The five components constitute a kind of "cultural world" in a given population. People create, change and pass on their culture to their children, who in turn may change it. But their culture also influences them. For example, U.S. children are born into a free-enterprise competitive economic system and are brought up to function as competent adults in this "free enterprise," competitive economic system (Ogbu 1981a; see also Cohen 1971; Edgerton and Langness 1968; LeVine 1973; Spradley 1979).

When children are born, they do not yet possess the ideas, values, emotion, perceptions, skills and behavior patterns that are shared by members of their society, all of which they will need to achieve social competence as adults. These are "cultural products" that have been constructed out of the people's past experience (Hansen 1979). They are different for different populations. Children are, of course, born with the human capacities and predispositions to learn such things. As they "develop" or reach different phases of maturation, children learn appropriate phases and types of their society's customary behaviors, thoughts, and emotions that accompany and support such behaviors. They gain knowledge and understand the meanings of cultural artifacts or symbols and of societal institutions, and they learn the practical skills that make those institutions work. They recognize patterns of social relations and behaviors, with their supporting assumptions.

Children are able to acquire culturally valued attributes because of biological capacities, not merely because of parental and other social teachings. However, children learn what they have to learn about their culture through formulas developed within their culture for this purpose (e.g., child-rearing practices, games and play, folktales or storybooks, proverbs, formal education, museum exhibitions, etc.). The attributes and behaviors rewarded by the culture in specific cultural tasks usually permeate other areas of life. Thus, cultural learning, or enculturation, helps children to become competent – that is, to become contributing members of their society.

Culture and Behavior

Culture influences behavior because people learn, as they grow up, to behave, think, and feel in the "cultural world" of their population. Each human population lives in a somewhat different cultural world and consequently members of different populations think, feel, and behave differently. Culture is the framework or "window" through which members of the population see the world around them, interpret events in that world, behave according to acceptable standard, and react to perceived reality. To understand members of different populations, it is necessary to understand their cultures (Edgerton and Langness 1968; Spradley 1979).

An example of a cultural or customary behavior in the United States is the ritual of caring for the mouth (Miner 1956, pp. 503-7). The assumptions underlying this customary or cultural behavior are the American people's belief that the body houses two dangerous elements—namely, debility and disease—that must be prevented from breaking out. Consequently every home in the United States contains a shrine for a daily mouth ritual (brushing of teeth) and occasionally Americans consult a "holy-mouth-man" or dentist, who is a specialist in the magical care of their mouths.

Another customary behavior limited to one segment of U.S. society is the "stylin' out" of the black preacher through a special "code talk." The preacher's code talk is specialized to facilitate in-group or population feeling and to conceal the aspirations and feelings of black Americans from the dominant white Americans. Whites have difficulty understanding the language and style of the black preacher; thus, a white American may attend a storefront church service and not comprehend the preacher's message to his congregation about white Americans (Holt 1972).

Other examples of customary behaviors in the United States are baby showers, buying a home, celebrating the Fourth of July, dining out, employment interviews, grocery shopping, letters of recommendation, retirement, Thanksgiving dinners, and waiting in line. Underlying assumptions make these customary behaviors meaningful to Americans, but not necessarily to people from other cultures.

Cultural Differences and Behavior
Different populations—even populations within one society – may differ in culture (i.e., they differ in their adaptations) for several reasons. One is that human populations may live in different physical or social environments requiring different adaptations. Furthermore, populations may have had different historical experiences that shaped how they perceive, interpret, and respond to things, situations and events within their environments, and their relationship with one another and with outsiders. Thus members of different populations may behave differently with different assumptions toward the same phenomenon. The essential point is that populations differ in culture because of their different environments and historical

experiences, which produced different solutions to common human life problems.

The influence of culture on behavior can be readily observed by comparing the solutions of different populations to common human problems – the way their members make a living (economy and technology); govern themselves (polity); organize their domestic life for reproduction (family and raising children); manage their relationship with the supernatural (religion) and communicate with one another (folk "theory of speaking"). Each solution both requires and promotes its own repertoire of customary behaviors (practical skills), knowledge, assumptions and emotions that support the behaviors.

When people from different cultures meet, they bring with them those attributes and behaviors they learned in their cultures for living in their cultures. And when children from different cultures come together in a learning situation, they bring with them attributes and behaviors they acquired and are expected of them in their respective cultures.

Cross-Cultural Examples

The influence of culture on behavior is most readily observed when comparing behaviors of members of different cultures, as the following examples will show.

Consider the raising of one's eyebrows. For most people in the United States, raising the eyebrows means a surprise; for people of Marshall Islands in the Pacific, it signals an affirmative answer. But for the Greeks it is a sign of disagreement (Taylor 1988). Thus these three cultures more or less compel their members to interpret raising eyebrows differently.

A second example is the customary behavior for getting ahead, or social mobility, in a society. Different cultures prescribe and inculcate different strategies and attributes for getting ahead. Mainstream middle-class American culture emphasizes individual competition. Members of this culture believe that social mobility, upward or downward, depends on the individual's ability or fate. In the culture of the Lowland Christian Filipinos in the Philippines, the individual achieves and is expected to achieve social mobility through group cooperation. Members of this culture believe that social mobility depends on one's ability to cooperate with others and work with them in competing with other groups. The culture of the Kanuri of northern Nigeria exhibits the third variant; here the aspirant is expected to achieve social mobility through a patron-client relationship. Thus an aspirant usually attaches himself to and serves a patron, who rewards him with desired position or wealth after the aspirant has served the patron in culturally approved manner and has demonstrated his "trust" by showing loyalty, obedience, servility, and compliance to the patron.

The attributes and behaviors that enhance getting ahead in each society are valued and taught to children by parents and other educational agents. Compare how mainstream middle-class Americans and the Kanuri of northern Nigeria respectively raise their children to get ahead in life. In mainstream American culture the attributes that promote social mobility valued by parents who teach them to their children include independence, self-reliance, initiative, foresight, industriousness, and "daring" (LeVine 1967). In contrast, the rewarding attributes that Kanuri parents value and foster in their children are obedience, servility, respect, and flattery. The Kanuri, according to Cohen (1965), describe the relationship between inferiors and superiors metaphorically as the proper father-child relationship, known as *barzum*. Cohen points out that the *barzum* relations are a person's most important "asset" for achieving higher economic, political, and social status. Kanuri parents perceive the behavioral dimensions of the barzum relations —namely, obedience and servility—as virtues to inculcate in their children. As Cohen (1965, p. 363) puts it, this

> mode of interaction is taught to the child as the proper relationship between a father and his son. Later the *barzum* relationship is shown to the young child, but most especially to boys, to be the thing that must be used between himself and all his superiors. He is told that his koranic teacher surpasses his father in "fatherliness," as does his chief, and the Emir surpasses all. And to all these (superiors) he must use some aspect of *barzum* or disciplined respect.

Culture influences behavior through the use of language to codify environment. Members of different cultures usually codify their environments and experiences. Therefore, the language spoken by people in different cultures may differ in regard to particular content areas. Furthermore, some concepts that people in one culture find "natural" in their own language are not necessarily universal or "natural" to people in other cultures. Some concepts may be absent in a culture not because the people do not have the biological structures or genes to produce those concepts, or because parents failed to teach their children the "missing concepts," or because individuals in that culture lag in psychobiological "development." The concepts are "missing" because they are not functional and have not been coded in the language of the people.

Fishman (1964), writing about the Whorfian hypothesis, provides several examples of cultural differences in the codification of environments. He shows how one culture may have several terms for a given phenomenon, while another culture has only one term for the same phenomenon; and still, a third culture has no concept at all for it. Examples of variation in the codification of a given phenomenon include the following:

fly: English speakers have several terms for ideas and objects associated with flying, such as *fly* (noun), *fly* (verb) pilot, airplane. Hopi Speakers, on the other hand, have only one term for the idea and object: *fly.*

snow: English speakers have two terms for snow; Eskimos have several terms for snow; the Ibos of Nigeria have none.

color: English speakers distinguish between blue and green but lump shades of black to gray; Navajo speakers lump "blue" and "green" together but have no terms for different shades of black.

Culture also influences the social meaning of language or communication. Hymes (1971) has introduced the notion of "a speech community," which allows us to understand cultural influences on communication. A speech community is made up of a population whose members share a common language and a common "theory of speaking" or a common understanding of what it means to be a good or bad speaker, an effective or ineffective speaker – in short, the meaning of "communicative competence." Within a speech community there are:

speech situations: situations which are considered appropriate for certain types of speeches (e.g., speeches in connection with parties, lovemaking, election campaigns, etc.)

speech events: culturally defined events, such as conversation, debate, lecture, confession, and job interview, that are governed by cultural rules learned and known to members of a speech population, e.g., the speech event of conversation can take place at a party, a memorial service, a campaign rally, during a grocery shopping, or other speech situations.

nonverbal codes: gestures, facial expressions, postures, paralinguisitc sounds like intonation, loudness, distance maintained from others in interaction, clothing, deodorants and scents

communication channels: verbal channels or forms of verbal expressions; kinetics and body movements, proxemics or culturally patterned use of space.

Hymes defines competence in communication within a speech population as knowing when it is appropriate to speak and when to remain silent, which communicative code to use, where, when, and to whom. Thus, communicative competence in a speech population involves not only the ability to convey information in one or more available channels but also the ability to match channel, form, content, and style to specific contexts and situations —in other words, to use communicative skills appropriately (Hansen 1979). As children mature, they learn the language (e.g., vocabulary and grammar) of their speech population as well as their population's "theory of speaking." That is, they learn both their language and the habits, attitudes, and rules associated with the value and use of that language. Every normal child usually successfully learns both the language and the theory of speaking of his or her speech population.

In a plural society like the United States, there are several speech populations, even among those whose "mother tongue" is English. Communication in these speech populations is influenced in different ways by their cultures and often results in cross-cultural miscommunication (see Becknell 1987; Kochman 1981).

Differences in mathematical concepts and behaviors constitute another example. Such differences exist between people in the United States and the Kpelle of Liberia in West Africa, according to Gay and Cole (1967) who studied the Kpelle. I will briefly summarize some of their findings.

The Kpelle and Americans have similar concepts in arithmetic because both people classify things: they add, subtract, and so forth. But they also differ because the Kpelle do not carry out such an activity explicitly or consciously like the Americans. The Kpelle also differ from Americans because their counting system does not have the concepts of zero or number. Neither do the Kpelle recognize or have concepts for abstract operations like addition, subtraction, multiplication, and division, even though in their customary mathematical behaviors they add, subtract, multiply, and divide things.

The Kpelle have fewer geometric concepts than Americans. Furthermore, they use their concepts less precisely than Americans. For example, in describing a circle they point to shapes of a pot, a frog, a sledgehammer, a tortoise, a water turtle, or a rice fanner, all of which represent a circle to them. When asked to describe a triangle they point to a tortoise shell, an arrowhead, a monkey's elbow, a drum, and a bow. Finally, while, like Americans, the Kpelle measure length, time, volume, and money, the Kpelle do not measure weight, area, speed, or temperature, while Americans do. Similar differences are found between other non-Western peoples and Americans. These cultural differences, in turn, affect the learning of mathematics by members of the two cultures.

Edward Hall showed with great skill how culture influences behaviors with respect to time, space, and social context behaviors. The following explanations are taken from Brislin's summary of Hall's work (Brislin 1993; see Hall 1959, 1966).

Time Orientation

To mainstream white Americans, punctuality is important. This value is readily observed at a scheduled business meeting, say, at 10:00 a.m. People attending the meeting expect that the meeting will start promptly, or at least before 10:10 a.m. If it does not start by 10:12 a.m., some people will be heard to say that the meeting should start because some of them have other appointments at 11:00 a.m. or some other specific time. This time awareness contrasts sharply with what happens in some other countries, such as those in South America. There a meeting scheduled for 10:00 a.m. may start at 11:15 a.m. or even later. Latin American cultures clearly place different values on time. While mainstream white Americans place more emphasis on "clock time," Latin Americans and other peoples place more emphasis on "event time" (Brislin 1993, p. 20-21).

Spatial Orientation

Mainstream white Americans differ from Latin Americans in use of space during social interaction. At an informal social interaction, mainstream white Americans tend to maintain a distance of "approximately the length of a tall man's arm: three feet" between two people. If the distance is closer, one or both parties may begin to feel uncomfortable; and if the interacting parties are male and female, a closer distance may be interpreted as implying "sexual advances." In Latin America, the distance between two people in an informal interaction may be closer, about two and one-half feet. Cultural conflict will arise if the distance is closer, especially if the interacting parties are a male and a female: both parties may begin to feel uncomfortable. On the other hand, if the distance is more than two and one-half feet the intentions of the interacting parties may be questioned and the interacting parties may feel uncomfortable (Brislin 1993, p. 21).

Social Contexts

Japanese and some other cultures are considered "high-context" cultures. In this type of culture, everyone clearly knows the rules, norms, and guidelines for various types of social encounters. Everyone knows exactly how to behave in a given situation. For example, at a meeting of an organization, people know who is the first to speak; a speaker knows how to introduce his or her topic; people meeting for the first time know how to introduce a topic of conversation; they also know who will take credit for successful outcomes accomplished through team effort. In "low-context" cultures, the rules and norms are not clear to everyone. At organizational meetings, people invest a great deal of time and energy trying to formulate ad hoc rules.

The difference between high- and low-context cultures can be seen during a large company meeting to introduce a new plan for future business venture in Japan, a high-context culture, compared to such a meeting in the United States, a low-context culture. Brislin (1993, p. 22) describes the difference of cultural influence as follows:

> *In Japan* people know the rules: The person (introducing the plan) goes around to the offices of all the individuals who might be affected by the proposal. After these one-on-one meetings,

the concerns of others are integrated into a final draft. This is also "cleared" with the people affected. Then, during a formal meeting of company executives the new proposal is put on the table. In actuality, this step is a formality because by this time everyone present knows a great deal about the proposal. The proposal is then approved by consensus, with a formal voice vote rarely taken. This is a high context behavior. Everyone knows what to do!

> *In the United States,* a low-context culture, it is different. There are many ways to accomplish one's goals, and Americans feel constrained if there are too many rules. For example, there are a number of ways to introduce a proposal in one's organization. A person can follow the typically Japanese route as outlined. Or, the person can introduce the proposal at a meeting even if the people present have not heard about the ideas involved. Or, the person can ask a highly respected executive to introduce the proposal, and in so doing communicate a willingness to share the credit for any eventual success . . . The important point for the present discussion is that the exact guidelines for behavior are not clear: the behavior is low context.

Comparative work on cultural influence on behavior is a fast-growing business because current international economic and technological relations promote contacts between members of different cultures and nations. Books on cultural influence on behavior have been published for visitors to the United States (Althen 1988; Lanier 1988) and for Americans going to China (Wenzhong and Grove 1991), France, or Germany (Carroll 1990; Hall and Hall 1990), Japan (Condon 1984; Finkelstein, Imamura, and Tobin 1991), the Philippines (Gochenour 1990), Mexico (Condon 1985), the Middle East (Nydell 1987), Russia (Richmond 1992), Thailand (Mortlock 1989), and Vietnam (Bache 1989).

Cultural Frame of Reference and Behavior

Another aspect of cultural influence on behavior is not well recognized and yet very important in culture contact and learning situations. This is cultural frame of reference. A cultural frame of reference refers to the correct or ideal way to behave within a culture. It encompasses the attitudes, beliefs, preferences, and practices considered appropriate by members of the culture or population. A population's cultural frame of reference may be oppositional to the cultural frame of reference of another population, depending on the relationship between the two populations. When cultural frames of reference are not in opposition interacting parties from the populations usually interpret the cultural and language differences between them as barriers to be overcome. They also usually consciously strive to overcome these initial cultural differences and thus are able to cross cultural boundaries. In contrast, when cultural frames of reference are in opposition, the interacting parties tend to perceive the cultural and language differences between them as markers of group identity and boundary maintaining. They are less motivated to overcome the initial cultural differences and thus have greater difficulty crossing cultural boundaries.

The influence of cultural frame of reference can be observed in the interaction between members of subordinate or minority groups and members of the dominant groups in plural societies. In the United States the cultural frames of reference of some nonwhite immigrant minority groups, such as the Chinese (ARC 1984) and the Punjabis (Gibson 1988) were formed prior to their emigration. Their cultural frames of reference are different from, but are not necessarily oppositional to, the cultural frame of reference of mainstream white Americans. Often these minorities consider not knowing how to behave like mainstream white Americans (i.e., according to mainstream white American cultural frame of reference) in certain situations (e.g., in school and the workplace) as barriers to the attainment of the goals of their emigration. Thus they strive to learn how to behave according to the cultural frame of reference of mainstream white American in the selected domains.

In contrast, the cultural frames of reference of some nonimmigrant or involuntary minorities, such as black Americans (Luster 1992; Ogbu 1988) and Native Americans (Kramer 1991) appear to have developed as oppositional responses to subordination by mainstream white Americans. Involuntary minorities do not usually think that barriers to their economic and social well-being are due to their not knowing how to behave like mainstream white Americans in school and workplace. Compounding the situation is the fact that they tend to interpret the cultural differences as symbols of their group identity; for them, learning to behave according to mainstream white American cultural frame of reference requires that they abandon behaving like minorities, an action that may result in a loss of their minority cultural identity. Therefore, nonimmigrant minorities are less motivated and may be afraid or unable to try to behave according to mainstream white American cultural frame of reference in the selected domains.

Unwillingness or inability to cross cultural boundaries occurs in other situations, outside minority-majority relations in the United States, and for a variety of reasons. It can be found in the interactions between the Walloons and the Flemings in Belgium (Irving 1980; Lijphart 1981), between the Tewa and the Hopi in the United States (Dozier 1951), and between the Basques and mainstream white Americans (Petrissans 1991). Spicer has reviewed other cases of cultural persistence or opposition involving the Jews, Irish, Welsh, Catalans, Mayas, Yaquis, Senecas, Cherokees, and Navajos (Spicer 1966, 1971; see also Castile and Kushner 1981).

Culture is a concept that enables us to understand people's behavior. It is, as Bohannan (1992) notes, a phenomenon both inside the minds of the members of a population and in their environment as acts, artifacts, and institutions. People behave in cultural ways because their culture provides for them to be brought up in their cultural worlds.

Culture and Learning

Learning is behavior. As such, learning is influenced by culture. Perhaps, because they assume that learning is behavior influenced by culture, anthropologists who study learning have not usually focused on what goes on inside the head of the learner. Cross-cultural studies provide enough evidence to suggest understandings of perception, memory, and logical thinking differ culturally because they are culturally constructed (Cole and Scribner 1974; Ogbu 1988; Segall, Campbell, and Herskovits 1966; Segall et al. 1990; Vernon 1969). This is not to deny that there are individual differences in perception, memory, and logical thinking within culture. There is a genetic basis of perception, memory, logical thinking and language in all human populations. However, while genetic factors may explain some individual differences in learning within a culture, the genetic argument provides no adequate guide to our understanding of group differences.

In the next section on evolution of human learning, I will endorse Fishbein's argument that, based on paleoanthropological records, primate studies, and ethnographic data, human learning evolved as a distinct form of learning. I will also suggest that all human groups have the genetic and psychobiological capacities for learning anything they have to learn for their physical and social survival.

In this section I will discuss how human learning evolved; how culture determines what children learn (i.e., enculturation), and differences between learning outside school and cultural influence on school learning, including cultural frame of reference.

Evolution of Human Learning

From an evolutionary point of view, physical anthropologists have studied the biological foundations of human learning (Bogin 1994); primatology anthropologists and sociocultural anthropologists specializing in foraging populations have investigated the sociocultural foundations of human learning (Fishbein 1976; Herzog 1976; Kimball 1973; Ogbu 1994a; Porier and Hussey 1982). These studies show that learning among human populations is different from learning in nonhuman animal populations. The difference is due to differences in biological equipments for learning, the nature of sociocultural adaptations of human populations, and the amount and complexity of what has to be learned and the time required to learn it.

Most nonhuman animals are born with extensive genetically programmed behaviors. They possess at birth instincts genetically transmitted for dealing with many situations. For this reason, what young nonhuman animals have to learn to survive and behave as competent adults is relatively small (Hansen 1979, p. 2) By contrast, the human child has more extensive and more complex things to learn to survive physically and socially. Furthermore, the human child is not equipped with genetically transmitted instincts for requisite behaviors. But the human child is able to learn the extensive and complex things because he or she possesses anatomical features (especially in the brain) beyond those of the nonhumans and has a long period of dependency because of being comparatively more immature at birth. Moreover, the sociocultural organization of human groups provides both the context and the formula for the learning (Hansen 1979; see also Bruner 1974).

A brief examination of changes in learning from nonhuman primates to the human primate will show how and why human learning is different. The general pattern during the evolution of learning was that changes in anatomical features led to changes in sociocultural adaptation. The latter, in turn, resulted in changes in the "curriculum" to be learned, namely, the new sociocultural adaptation. Thus, in the pre-Catarrhini primate stage, humans and other pre-Catarrhini primates had similar anatomical features; their brain structures, for example, were similar. At that stage, humans and other pre-catarrhini primates made similar sociocultural adaptations and learned the same sociocultural adaptations, namely, arboreal living. Anatomical changes during this period, notably the emergence of new brain structures, resulted in the emergence of catarrhini primates who made a new sociocultural adaptation. The latter took the form of terrestrial or ground living. This adaption brought about the necessity to learn how to live and survive on the ground.

Sometime after the terrestrial adaptation, other anatomical changes occurred, making possible the transition to the hunter-gatherer stage among human primates. The important anatomical changes include increase in brain size, which further slowed down maturation rate, and increase in the extraneurons of the nerves for storing and processing information. The neocortex region of the brain became more differentiated and specialized as the region of the brain that formed the foundations for human capacities for language, nonverbal ideation, spatial understanding, memory, motor skills, analytical ability, and planning

(Fishbein 1976). These anatomical changes led to a new form of social and cultural adaptations – sociocultural adaptation characterized by hunting and gathering. These and other changes had specific effects on the adaptation to the hunter-gatherer way of life and the learning of the hunter-gatherer child. For example, changes in the limbic region of the brain made possible the capacity for empathy, what Fishbein (1976, pp. 17, 151) calls "the glue of social life," and for self-awareness. Both, in turn, made possible the evolution of reciprocal obligation. Other changes increased the human capacity for spatial understanding —a very important ability for successful hunting and other subsistence activities. These changes also resulted in the development of the unique human language. In general, these biological developments facilitated the evolution of higher sociocultural adaptation among hunter-gatherer peoples and the evolution of learning.

The new sociocultural adaptation —the hunter-gatherer way of life—made possible by the biological changes led to further increases in the amount and complexity of what the human child had to learn. At the same time the twin developments provided him or her with the biological and social foundations for learning the new curriculum in order to become socially competent in hunter-gatherer population. Social competence in a hunter-gatherer population included knowing cooperative hunting, reciprocity, food sharing, tool making, roles in husband-wife relationship, symbolic communication, and rule making and rule following. Thus there was more to learn than at the previous phases (Fishbein 1976).

Among the biological changes that equipped the hunter-gatherer child with the capacities to learn the increased and complex knowledge and skills was, first, an increased period of immaturity that ensured a long period of dependency for learning. The increased period of immaturity was due to increased brain size. The human brain is designed to reach its full size after birth; human children were (and are) born prior to the full maturity of their brain. In addition, the period of physical immaturity in other areas also increased, so that it took (and still takes) humans much longer period to reach adulthood. For example, among Macaca monkeys, infancy lasts 0-1.5 years, juvenile period 1.5-4 years and adolescence 4-7.5 years. In human, by contrast, infancy lasts 0-6 years; the juvenile period is from 6 to 13 years; and adolescence is from 13 to 18 years (Jolly 1972, cited in Fishbein 1976, p. 124; see also Bruner 1974).

Human sociocultural adaptation continued to change in magnitude and complexity in the course of cultural evolution beyond the hunter-gatherer phase. And so did the human children's capacities to learn their culture. This point is well illustrated by Wilson's (1972) study of the evolution of learning. Wilson employed a unilinear evolutionary scheme that arranged human societies from "simple, restricted wandering" (i.e., foraging societies of hunter-gatherers) to "advanced supranuclear integrated" societies (i.e., contemporary urban industrial societies). He found that as sociocultural adaptation became more advanced at each subsequent level of the seven evolutionary stages, the attendant "education" was characterized by increased differentiation and greater specialization of functions to meet the needs of that level. Wilson argues that formal schooling developed as appropriate to an industrial economy and its concomitant social organization. Formal schooling meets the functional requisite for training occupational specialists in this type of society. In general, a strong relationship exists among level of formal education, degree of occupational specialization, and the social ranking of modern industrial cultures.

I want to conclude this section by noting that by the stage of hunter-gatherer adaptation, human populations were equipped with all the necessary psychobiological structures for learning adaptive curriculum, no matter how large and complex the material is that has to be learned. I assume that the capacities for the learning are universal on the basis of the observation by Scribner and Cole (1973). According to these cognitive and cross-cultural psychologists, people in all known human populations have the cognitive capacities to remember, generalize, form concepts, operate with abstractions, and reason logically. However, each population may perform these functions differently. In any case, each population has a culturally organized system of thought developed out of its historical experience.

Enculturation

Children in all human populations thus have the capacities to learn their cultures and seem to do so successfully through what anthropologists call enculturation or cultural transmission. When anthropologists study particular populations, they usually collect data on enculturation as a part of general ethnography (Juan 1994; Middleton 1970). However, they began to study enculturation systematically from the late 1920s in response to some generalizations about human development by Western psychologists, especially Freudians.

This response led to a new anthropology subfield, culture-and-personality, which, in turn, promoted more systematic study of enculturation. A major concern of culture-and-personality anthropologists was the influence of social institutions (or culture, broadly speaking) on enculturation or childrearing practices and, in turn, the influence of enculturation on personality formation (Barnouw 1963; Du Bois 1944; Kardiner 1939; Linton 1945; Whiting and Child 1953). Culture-and-personality anthropologists

assumed that culture exerted influence in molding its members through enculturation. That is, the way members of a population raised their children would be expected to produce certain types of personality attributes and distinct patterns of roles played by adults. It was to determine if this was the case that anthropologists began to collect data on enculturation systematically and to collect personality data with the Rorschach and other projective instruments. Both sets of data were analyzed blind by psychoanalysts. Eventually, the study of enculturation became an important subfield in its own right.

The work of Margaret Mead will illustrate how anthropologists demonstrated that cultural values, roles, and behaviors were taught and learned. In the first study, *The Manus: Growing Up in New Guinea – Explorations in the Study of Primitive Education* (1928), Mead depicted the qualities or attributes valued by the Manus, that is, attributes functional in their culture. Manus culture valued property, hard work, and financial success; the people were characteristically hearty, self-confident, and alert. Mead found that these value attributes influenced the way the Manus trained their children. For example, they trained their children early, starting about the age of three, to learn to swim, to respect property, and to mingle with peers; they avoided indoctrinating their children through folklore, songs, and myths. As a result, Manus children grow up to be hardworking, valuing property, and self-confident.

In another study, *Sex and Temperament in Three Primitive Societies* (1935), Mead sought to discover how cultures influenced sex roles and attitudes toward sex roles in three New Guinea societies as well as how the sex roles and attitudes were transmitted. She found that among the Arapesh, men and women acted in a mild, maternal, and cooperative manner, just like American women were traditionally expected to behave. Both Mundugumor men and women were aggressive and fierce, in the manner traditionally expected of American males. Neither the Arapesh nor the Mundugumor assumed that there were temperamental differences between men and women. Such an assumption was, however, found among the Tchambuli. They had a clear-cut idea of differences between male and female societal roles, but these roles were the opposite of the male-female roles in the United States. Among the Tchambuli, the women were the food providers or food gatherers – the "bread winners." Mead described them as hearty, efficient, and comradely among themselves. The men, on the other hand, were concerned mostly with art, hairdos, and their relationship with women. In summary, enculturation in each of the three cultures was tailored to transmit to the next generation the prevalent pattern of sex roles and sex role attitudes.

Enculturation research focused on the influence of

culture on what children learned, not on how children learned what they were taught. But these studies more or less indirectly provided some insights on cultural influences on how children learned (see Kneller 1965 for a summary of "universal principles" of enculturation). Comparative studies of cultural transmission suggest that children are capable of learning to behave in many different ways and to perform many different cultural tasks. However, each culture or population seems to "guide [children] away" from learning the total set of human behaviors. Each culture encourages children to learn the more limited set of behaviors considered by members of that culture acceptable and important (Brislin 1993, p. 95; see also Child 1954; Segall et al. 1990, cited in Brislin 1993). What members of a culture or population consider acceptable and important constitutes the curriculum for children's upbringing or education, and their learning is intended to ensure that they will grow up as competent adults in the way defined by their population.

Learning outside School versus Learning in School:
Generally speaking, the way children learn outside Western-type schools, especially in nonliterate populations is different from the way they learn in school. Based on comparative analysis, both Cohen (1971) and Scribner and Cole (1973) distinguish three types of teaching and learning in order to understand what is distinctive about learning in school. These are informal education or enculturation in kin-based societies; noninstitutional formal education; and institutional formal education or schooling.

Learning In Informal Education:
Informal education, according to Scribner and Cole (1973), is the learning that takes place in the course of mundane adult activities in which children participate according to their abilities. There is no activity set aside solely to "educate" the child. Social processes and institutions are structured to permit the child's acquisition of the basic skills, values, attitudes, and customs that define appropriate adult behaviors in the culture. This is what is called "enculturation" in anthropology (see also Cohen 1971; Ruddle and Chesterfield 1977).

Learning in informal education is particularistic, in the sense that it occurs in the family or among related individuals. It also fosters traditionalism and fuses emotional and intellectual domains, so that it is highly charged affectively. What is learned is not easily separated from the identity of the learner. The main technique of learning is observation: children learn by observing what adults or their teachers do rather than by following verbal instructions. Consistent with observation technique, teachers or adult models do not formulate explicit rules of how to learn a body of

knowledge or practical skills; instead, they rely on demonstration. Usually, verbal formulation of the problem on the part of the learner is not encouraged or required.

It is necessary to point that the limited verbal interaction in teaching and learning in informal education is not a deficiency. From my personal experience in growing up in an African village and from my anthropological study of funeral ceremonies, title taking, and other activities, it seems that children do not need "instructions" to learn the roles they have to play as adults in these matters. These and other important events occur in the full view of children, who are not excluded. They witness adults enact their roles, and they participate in the roles expected of them as children, according to age. When I took a title in my village in the summer of 1993, children were present in every phase of the ceremony. They ran errands and took part in the ceremonial dance. I also found children present in nearly every phase of two funeral ceremonies that I recently studied in Ibo culture. When interviewed, the children were able to describe these events and what was required of different categories of adults involved.

Learning in Noninstitutional Formal Education
Formal education is a deliberately organized process of transmitting knowledge or practical skills. It is usually removed from the manifold tasks of daily life, placed in a special setting, and carried out according specific routines. It is controlled by or is the responsibility of a group larger than the family or kin group (Cohen 1971; Scribner and Cole 1973).

Formal education may be either institutional or noninstitutional. Noninstitutional formal education is found among some non-literate societies with secret societies and initiation rites. The main functions of formal education in such societies appear to be to inculcate appropriate values and attitudes as well as knowledge and skills in such areas as military training, music, geography, totemic names, secret language, and the like. Children may be taken to a special setting for instruction (e.g., the "bush school" in West Africa), but what they learn is not entirely discontinuous with their culture. The learners acquire traditional knowledge and skills valued in the population; learning is not depersonalized but continues to be bound up with the status of their teacher. It is "bounded learning" in the sense that how children learn one set of activities or skills is not necessarily transferred to learning or understanding other sets of activities

Examples of noninstitutional formal education are the "bush schools" of the Kpelle, Mende, and other "tribes" in Gambia, Liberia, and Sierra Leone in West African (Cohen 1971; Gibbs 1965; Little 1951; Watkins 1943). In these societies, "schooling" was not compulsory, but it was nearly universal: every youth, male or female, attended a special training under the sponsorship of the poro society (for boys) or sande society (for girls) before assuming adult responsibilities. Teachers were specialists in their subjects. The curriculum covered activities for physical development (e.g., swimming, hunting, dancing, wrestling), technical skills (e.g., construction of building, crafts, etc.), and tribal laws and tradition. Participants took "tests" at the beginning of the session to determine their aptitudes and interests. Those who demonstrated special knowledge, skills, or interests in weaving, leatherwork, dancing, or medicine were encouraged to participate in activities that would further their interests and skills in those subjects.

An example of how culture influences the way children learn in noninstitutional formal education comes from Forge's study (1970) of the way the Abelam of New Guinea learned to perceive two-dimensional paintings. The Abelam are a patrilineal people. They base patri-clan/village organization on the concept of nggwalndu spirits. Intermarriages between villages or patri-clans form the basis of ceremonial exchange, during which male children of exchange partners are initiated. Art is very highly valued in the Abelam culture and plays a very important part in the ritual exchange ceremony.

According to Forge, the Abelam environment lacks many two-dimensional visual images. The only flat surfaces are the highly prominent and very powerful ritual paintings, the amei (i.e., the yard outside the ceremonial house) and the gray thatched sides of the houses. Forge studied how the Abelam learn the two-dimensional imagery in the ritual ceremony and the Abelam ability to transfer the two-dimensional perception to other forms of two-dimensional imagery, such as photography. Abelam youth learn the two-dimensional imagery during initiation ceremonies that have a cycle of twenty to thirty years. During this length of time the male Abelam youth is exposed to eight displays of nggwalndu and other artworks in the ceremonial ground. The ceremonial house is covered with carved and painted images of nggwalndu. The images are the same at each ceremonial occasion. The youth are told on the first occasion that they are being shown the nggwalndu; then on next ceremonial occasion they are told that they were tricked last time but this time they will really see the nggwalndu. This continues until the final ceremony, when the youth are shown the "real" nggwalndu in the form of huge carved figures.

Forge interviewed those who had completed their initiation ceremonial cycle and found that they had indeed learned the two-dimensional representation of the nggwalndu imagery. A number of factors seem to facilitate this learning. One is the importance of the imagery in Abelam culture. It serves as a compelling,

nonverbal text to communicate social relations and expected behavior. The youth recognize this and thus make efforts to learn it. Furthermore, because the images probably do not vary from one viewing to the next (except for the final viewing), repeated viewing enhances learning them. It also appears that telling the initiates during each ceremony that they would see the "true" nggwalndu served to increase their expectations, which they may have transferred to the nggwalndu images. In this way they kept the effects of the recurring visual stimulus from diminishing over subsequent viewing. In other words, the initiates were more or less being asked to see more in each viewing of nggwalndu than they had before or to transcend previous readings and understand the nggwalndu, the ritual, and the social relationships it supports, in a deeper way (Charland 1994).

Learning in Institutional Formal Education
Learning in school is different from the two types of learning previously discussed because formal education in modern Western-type schools introduces a new system of teaching and learning (Cohen 1971; Scribner and Cole 1973). Let me summarize distinctive features of school learning, as presented by Scribner and Cole. First, it enhances the role of language in learning in at least three ways:

• language is used in school learning as an explicit means of information exchange

• school learning restricts the amount of information exchanged or imparted

• school learning proceeds from verbal formulation to empirical evidence or referents—that is, learning ideally starts with verbal description and is eventually connected with the empirical referents from which it has been abstracted.

Second, the new use of language develops or encourages a scientific approach to learning because it teaches concepts like generalized rules and verbal descriptions. For example, the learner begins with a verbal definition, and the process of learning consists of overcoming his or her ignorance about specific aspects of reality to which the definition applies. In this way the child learns concept formation. Furthermore, the way language is used in school promotes acquisition of competence in the use of language to describe behavior, to classify and to perform; it also enhances learning rules for solutions to problems. Finally, it promotes the acquisition of more accuracy in description.

Third, learning in school is decontextualized. This means that a child is asked to learn materials that have no natural or symbolic context. Thus, in learning mathematics a child is asked to learn numbers the operation of which is different from that of nonformal education. He is not being asked to use numbers to manipulate particular things; rather, he is asked to learn to manipulate numbers *qua* numbers. He is learning that numbers are things in themselves.

Fourth, learning in school involves acquisition of symbol systems as tools for other learning. School teaches people to become competent in the use of symbols, such as numbers in mathematics. It also teaches them information processing as instrumental techniques for further learning. Examples of these instrumental techniques are how to read, how to write, how to figure. These instrumental techniques have no parallel in learning outside school.

Finally, learning in school results in the acquisition of a new functional learning system or "learning-to-learn." According to Scribner and Cole (1973, pp. 55-7), learning-to-learn "occurs when people are repeatedly presented with 'problems of the same type' and learn to apply the solution to different problems." It is through this kind of learning that children acquire generalized rules or the ability to generalize and to treat a wide range of problems as examples of some general class or rules. Children thus acquire common operational rules that they apply over a wide range of tasks and contents: how one operates with a book or a ruler is not much affected by the subject matter or goal, so that an inch of cloth is equivalent to an inch of wood in a special sense. The consequence of these activities is the acquisition of the ability to generalize rules. The authors suggest that "learning-to-learn" is one of the reasons cross-cultural studies often find that school populations tend to generalize rules and operations across a number of problems, in contrast to nonschool populations. The implications will be seen when we examine cultural influences on school learning below.

Cultural Influences on Learning in School

The school may be regarded as having its own culture. What I have just summarized is the learning style of the school. Children attending school come with other styles of learning they acquired in their respective cultures. The various styles usually result in some learning "discontinuities" (Ogbu 1982). It is in this context that anthropologists have been studying cultural influences on school learning.

Anthropologists began to write about cultural influence on learning in school at the turn of the century in an effort to refute false notions about the intellectual status and learning abilities of colonial peoples, minority groups, immigrant groups and lower-class people in the United States and other Western societies, (see Boas 1928; Hewitt [1905] 1976; Malinowski [1943] 1976; Roberts 1976). Early anthropological writings were not based on ethnographic studies of actual learning situations in school. Beginning in the 1960s, however, anthropologists have taken two research approaches to show that culture influences school learning. In the first approach they have studied teaching and learning among minority and lower-class children and found that children do not learn successfully in school when provided with education that is discontinuous with their cultures. In the second approach they showed that children learn more successfully when provided with education compatible with their cultures (Lee 1993; Moll 1994; Moll and Diaz 1987; Vogt, Jordan, and Tharp 1987).

As defined by Philips (1976), cultural discontinuities in schooling occur when children with different cultural backgrounds or different cultural environments attend school or are educated in a different culture – that is, receive their education in a culturally different learning environment. In such a situation the children from the different cultural background have difficulty acquiring the content and style of learning presupposed by the curriculum material and teaching methods. The result is often school failure. Such cultural discontinuities and learning difficulties occur both in transitional populations in developing nations and in contemporary plural societies like the United States. Spindler (1987) has summarized some of the problems as follows: In transitional societies the curricular content is often alien to the existing culture; there is little or no reinforcement to what is learned in school in the home or population; the school is isolated from the children's cultural system; and the teaching method is alien to the children. In the United States immigrants, minorities, and lower-class children face cultural discontinuities in school learning. The teachers as members of the dominant mainstream white society are alien to these children. The children experience discontinuities with respect to values, expectations, and behaviors (LaBelle 1976).

Anthropologists have identified and described specific types of cultural discontinuities that make learning difficult. One is the mismatch between the "cognitive maps" of teachers and students. The teachers' cognitive maps eventually dominate, forcing students to comply, a result that apparently sometimes discourages students from participating.

Another source of discontinuity is the distinctive features of school learning discussed above. To recapitulate, there is a discontinuity between children's cultural knowledge and school knowledge. In some subjects children are asked to learn materials that contradict the commonly held or accepted knowledge and beliefs in their cultures; they are presented with new subjects (e.g., grammar) that have no cultural counterparts or direct referents. Students may be made to "know" the "words" but not the external referents. Learning is usually out of context, so that students are asked to learn materials devoid of natural (nonsymbolic) contexts (e.g., numbers). Finally, students are taught things that are to be used later in life but have no parallel in their everyday life (Scribner and Cole 1973).

Cross-cultural misunderstandings also influence learning among nonmainstream children. An example is the different interpretations of eye contact between members of the opposite sex by Punjabi Indian Americans and their white American teachers (see Byers and Byers 1974; Gibson 1988). Another example of cross-cultural misunderstanding is found among black American students. Blacks have many "code words" and use "code talk" in many areas of life (e.g., money, toughness, beauty, dressing, work, intelligence, smartness, mental health, etc.) that are not understood by white Americans and are misinterpreted by white teachers when used by black students (Becknell 1987; Hale-Benson 1986).

Cultural differences in teaching and learning styles have been found to contribute to learning problems among nonmainstream children. Immigrant children from Asia come from cultures in which lecture is the primary teaching method. The immigrant students were brought up to expect considerable structure in their education. Such children are initially baffled by assignments involving group activities in the U.S. public schools. Team teaching and "open classroom" approaches to instruction in U.S. schools may seem disorganized to some immigrant students. Their learning style may be different. For example, among the Chinese, the traditional learning style placed emphasis on memorization, rather than observation, analysis, or comprehension that is favored in U.S. schools. The nonanalytic approach to learning may be manifested in the styles of thinking of these students (Ogbu 1983; Ogbu and Matute-Bianchi 1986).

In some nonimmigrant minority cultures, such as black American and Native Hawaiian cultures, children are also socialized into learning styles different from the one expected in the public schools. Shade (1982, p. 232) suggests that black Americans use somatic or kinesthetic perceptions to process information, an approach that she says is not particularly conducive to learning in the public schools, where students are expected to process information visually and aurally (see also Boykin 1986; Hale-Benson 1986).

Several case studies of cultural discontinuities and learning have been conducted in transitional societies and in the United States. One study of a transitional society focused on the mathematical knowledge and behaviors of the Kpelle of Liberia (Gay and Cole 1967). In the United States, studies investigated include the study of miscommunication in the classrooms of Oglala Sioux Indians (Dumont 1972); participant structure and miscommunication in the classrooms of Warm Spring Indian children in Oregon (Philips 1972, 1983); and incongruity between indigenous learning structure and school learning structure among Native Hawaiian children (Au 1980; Vogt, Jordan, and Tharp 1987).

The other approach, which is basically the other side of the coin, consists of studies showing that when teaching, learning style, or school curriculum is compatible with that of the children's culture, the children tend to learn more successfully. The assumption behind this approach is that some classroom practices (teaching and learning) do not enhance classroom learning for some nonmainstream children. Researchers, therefore, would first study the children's culture and then search for meaningful matches between the knowledge they generated within their study of the minority culture and the knowledge or practices expected in the classroom or school contexts. Here are three examples of such study of cultural influences on learning.

The best-known example of this approach is the work of anthropologists among Native Hawaiian students. The problem was that Hawaiian children had difficulty learning to read through conventional reading lessons structure. Anthropological study of native Hawaiian culture led to the discovery of a speech event, "talk story," that was later used to reorganize reading lessons for the children. The reorganization enabled the children to use their prior experience or familiarity with the indigenous storytelling format in dealing with reading texts and viceversa. In other words, building upon research on Hawaiian culture, anthropologists and teachers deliberately created a classroom structure that enhanced the children school success (Vogt, Jordan, and Tharp 1987).

In the second example, anthropologists studied "population fund knowledge" in a Mexican-American population in Arizona. This concept included household knowledge about agriculture (e.g., ranching, farming, hunting, tracking, animal husbandry), and repair (e.g., automobiles, airplanes, household appliances, tractors, fences). The cultural knowledge was used to help the children develop an understanding of the knowledge intended for them in the classroom (Moll 1994).

Our last example is Lee's (1993) study of the strategies that black children use when they interpret "signifying." The latter is a form of social discourse in black culture. Lee argues that the strategies black students use in interpreting "signifying" are similar to the strategies readers use in interpreting genres in literature. She therefore devised an instructional model that permitted black children to transfer their culturally based skills to school-required tasks. The experiment was successful.

In each of these examples researchers first had to study children's population or culture to look for a cultural practice and knowledge that could be used to reorganize classroom practice. Sometimes the anthropologists worked in collaboration with teachers. The assumption is that there is a causal relationship between school achievement and the opportunity for young children to build upon the skills they bring to school from their families and cultures.

Cultural Frame of Reference and School Learning

There is no question that cultural discontinuities are real and cause real difficulties in school learning for non-Western children in Western-type schools and for lower-class and minority children in the public schools in the United States (Gay and Cole 1967; Lancy 1983; LaBelle 1976; Musgrove 1953; Ogbu 1988). But there is some reason to be skeptical about any generalization attributing the persistent dispro-portionate school failure rates of some minorities to cultural discontinuities. Comparative research shows that some minority groups do well in school even though they do not share the language and cultural backgrounds of the dominant group that are reflected in the curriculum, instructional style, and other prac-tices of the schools. Such minorities may initially experience learning problems due to the cultural and language differences, but the problems do not persist (Ogbu 1992, In press). Furthermore, the reasons some minorities learn successfully in school is not necessari-ly because their cultures or learning styles are similar to the mainstream culture or learning style. For example, Punjabi Indians are successful students in California schools even though judged by mainstream culture they would be regarded as being academically at risk (Gibson 1988). Studies in Britain (Ogbu 1978; Taylor and Hegarty 1985) and Japan (DeVos and Lee 1981; Ogbu 1978; Shimahara 1991) also show that minority children do not fail to learn merely because they do not share the culture and language of the dominant group reflected in school environment and practices.

I have suggested two prerequisites for understand-ing why learning problems due to cultural and lan-guage differences are more enduring among some groups than among others. One prerequisite is to clas-sify minority groups into immigrant or voluntary minorities and nonimmigrant or involuntary minori-ties. The different histories of the two types of minori-ties – voluntary incorporation and involuntary incor-poration into the U.S. society (or any other society) – affect how minorities interpret the cultural and lan-guage differences they encounter in society at large and in school learning situation.

The other prerequisite is to adopt the concept of cultural frame of reference for analyzing the interpre-tations of the cultural and language differences in learning situations of minorities and other nonmain-stream peoples. As explained earlier in this paper, a cultural frame of reference can be oppositional or nonoppositional vis-á-vis mainstream white American (or school) cultural frame of reference.

With the two prerequisites in mind, I think that something more is involved in the school learning

problems faced by minority children than merely cul-tural and language differences, although these differ-ences are important. That something more, which is thus far not generally recognized, is the nature of the relationship between the cultures and languages of the minorities and the culture and language of main-stream white Americans (as reflected in the public schools). The nature of that relationship is qualitative-ly different for the two types of minorities, voluntary and involuntary. Specifically, I suggest that the two types of minorities tend to invest or ascribe different secondary meanings to the cultural differences: immi-grant minorities define the cultural differences in learning situations as barriers to be overcome and try to overcome them; nonimmigrant minorities define the cultural differences in learning situations as mark-ers or symbols of group identity to be maintained and are unwilling or unable to cross cultural boundaries in learning situations (Ogbu 1994a). This type of cultural influence on learning deserves more attention from researchers. Children do not usually describe their school learning behaviors in terms oppositional or nonoppositional cultural frames of reference and may not be aware that their behaviors involve opposition or nonopposition. Likewise, parents will generally deny the oppositional behaviors when questioned directly and will genuinely say that they want their children to learn to read and so forth. Nevertheless, ethnographic study of the cultural frames of reference of minorities strongly suggests that there exists among some groups embedded opposition to crossing cultural boundaries.

Ethnography of Learning in Science Museums

Learning behavior, like other forms of behavior, is influenced by culture. Culture defines what is to be learned and how it is learned (i.e., perceived, inter-preted, retained in memory or eliminated). For a pop-ulation, as for its individual members, what is learned successfully is what is culturally valued and endorsed.

It is in cross-cultural learning that problems of nonlearning arise (DeVos 1984). Nonlearning often occurs when subordinate populations go to learn in schools established by the dominant group. It can also happen when people learn in other societal institu-tions, such as museums. The relevant questions in such situations are: Are things to be learned valued and recognized as necessary? Are they meaningful? Does the learning situation and/or teacher evoke pos-itive or negative responses? For what reasons? It depends on the meaning of what has to be learned and on what the situation and teachers represent to the learners.

From an anthropological perspective, the museum is one of the societal agencies for the transmission of knowledge to children and adults in modern urban industrial societies such as the United States. It serves the same functions as the public schools, although it differs from the latter in the process of teaching and learning. It also differs from the public schools in the sense that "the students" of the museums are not constant. Nevertheless, teaching and learning in the museums can be studied ethnographically, just as they have been in the school.

There are many good texts providing general guides to qualitative research in educational settings (see Fetterman 1989; Glesne and Peshkin 1992; Goetz and LeCompte 1984; Marshall and Rossman 1989; Miles and Huberman 1994; van Maanen 1983; Wolcott 1990). It is not possible in this paper to provide a general guideline for ethnographic research in museums. The nature of a specific ethnographic research depends on the research question or "research problem."

Acknowledgments:

The preparation of this essay was supported by the University of California faculty research funds and grants from California Policy Seminsar, Carnegie Corporation of New York, the Ford Foundation, W. T. Grant Foundation, the Rockefeller Foundation, the Russell Sage foundation, and the Spencer Foundation. I wish to thank Sara D. Haessler and Marcellina A. Ogbu for their editorial assistance.

References

ARC. 1984. *Bilingual education in a Chinese population: Final research report*. Contract 400-80-0013. Washington, D.C.: National Institute of Education.

Althen, G. 1988. *American ways: A guide for foreigners in the United States*. Yarmouth, Maine: Intercultural Press.

Au, K. H. 1980. Participant structure in a reading lesson with Hawaiian children: Analysis of a culturally appropriate Instructional event. *Anthropology and Education Quarterly* 11, no. 2:91-115.

Bache, E. 1989. *Culture clash*. Yarmouth, Maine: Intercultural Press.

Barnouw, V. 1963. *Culture and personality*. Homewood, Ill.: Dorsey Press.

Becknell, C. E. 1987. *Blacks in the workforce: A black manager's perspective*. Albuquerque, N.M.: Horizon Communications.

Boas, F. 1928. *Anthropology and modern life*. New York: Norton.

Bogin, B. 1994. "Anthropological perspectives on evolution of human learning." *International Encyclopedia of Education*. 2nd ed. Oxford: Pergamon Press.

Bohannan, P. 1992. *We, the alien: An introduction to cultural anthropology*. Prospect Heights, Ill.: Waveland Press.

Boykin, A. W. 1986. "The triple quandary and the schooling of Afro-American children." In. *The school achievement of minority children: New perspectives*, ed. U. Neisser, pp.57-92.Hillsdale, N.J.: Erlbaum.

Brislin, R. 1993. *Understanding culture's influence on behavior*. New York: Harcourt, Brace College Press.

Bruner, J. S. 1974. "Nature and the uses of immaturity." In *The Growth of Competence*, ed. K. J. Connolly and J. S. Bruner, pp. 11-48. New York: Academic Press.

Byers, P. and H. Byers. 1972. "Non-verbal communication and the education of children." In *Functions of language in the classroom*, ed. C. B. Cazden, V. P. John, and D. Hymes, pp. 3-31. New York: Teachers College Press.

Carroll, R. 1990. *Cultural misunderstanding: The French-American experience*. Chicago: University of Chicago Press.

Carroll, T. G. and J. J. Schensul, eds. 1990. Cultural diversity and American education: Visions of the future. *Education and Urban Society* 22, no. 4: special issue.

Castile, G. P. and G. Kushner, eds. 1981. *Persistent peoples: Cultural enclaves in perspective*. Tucson: University of Arizona Press.

Charland, W. 1994. Learning to see in New Guinea: A review. Department of Anthropology, University of California, Berkeley.

Child, I. L. 1954. Socialization. In *Handbook of social psychology*, ed. G. Lindzey, 2: 655-92. Cambridge, Mass.: Addison-Wesley.

Cohen, R. 1965. Some aspects of institutionalized exchange: A Kanuri example. *Cahiers d'Etudes Africaine* 5:353-69.

Cohen, Y. A. 1971. "The shaping of men's minds: Adaptations to the imperatives of culture." In *Anthropological perspectives on education*, ed. M. L. Wax, S. Diamond and F. O. Gearing, pp. 19-50. New York: Basic Books.

Cole, M. and S. Scribner. 1974. *Culture and thought: A psychological introduction*. New York: Wiley.

Condon, J. C. 1984. *With respect to the Japanese*. Yarmouth, Maine: Intercultural Press.

———. 1985. *Good neighbors: Communicating with the Mexicans*. Yarmouth, Maine: Intercultural Press.

De Vos, G. A. 1984. *Ethnic persistence and role degradation: An illustration from Japan*. Paper presented at the American-Soviet Symposium on Contemporary Ethnic Processes in the USA and USSR, New Orleans, LA, 14-16 April.

Dozier, E. 1951. Resistance to acculturation and assimilation in an Indian pueblo. *American Anthropologist* 53:56-66.

Du Bois, C. 1944. *The people of Alor: A social-psychological study of an East Indian island*. Minneapolis: University of Minnesota Press.

Dumont, R. V., Jr. 1972. "Learning English and how to be silent: Studies in Sioux and Cherokee classrooms." In *Functions of language in the classroom*, ed. C. B. Cazden, D. Hymes, and V. John pp. 344-69. New York: Teachers College Press.

Edgerton, R. B. and L. L. Langness. 1968. *Methods and style in the study of culture*. San Francisco: Chandler & Sharp.

Fetterman, D. M. 1989. *Ethnography: Step by step*. Newbury Park, Calif.: Sage Publications.

Finkelstein, B., A. E. Immamura and J. J. Tobin, eds. 1991. *Transcending stereotypes: Discovering Japanese culture and education*. Yarmouth, Maine: Intercultural Press.

Fishman, J. A. 1964. A systematization of the Whorfian Hypothesis. In *Approaches, contexts, and problems of social psychology*, ed. G. G. Sampson, pp. 27-43. Englewood Cliffs, N.J.: Prentice-Hall.

Fishbein, H. D. 1976. *Evolution, development, and children's learning.* Pacific Palisades, Calif: Goodyear.

Forge, A. 1970. Learning to see in New Guinea. In *Socialization and social anthropology,* ed. P. Mayer, pp. 269-91. London: Tavistock Publications.

Freilich, M. 1989. Introduction: Is culture still relevant? In *The relevance of culture,* ed. M. Freilich, pp. 2-26. New York: Bergin & Garvey.

Gay, J. and M. Cole. 1967. *The new mathematics and an old culture: Learning among the Kpelle of Liberia.* New York: Holt.

Gearing, F. O. 1976. "Where we are and where we might go from here: Steps toward a general theory of cultural Transmission." In *Educational patterns and cultural configurations: The anthropology of education,* ed. J. I. Roberts and S. Akinsanya, pp. 183-94. New York: David McKay.

Gibbs, J. L., Jr. 1965. "The Kpelle of Liberia." In *Peoples of Africa,* ed. J. L. Gibbs. New York: Holt.

Gibson, M. A. 1987. Playing by the rules. In *Education and the cultural process: Anthropological approaches,* ed. G. D.Spindler, pp. 274-84. Prospect Heights: Waveland Press.

———.1988. *Accommodation without assimilation: Punjabi Sikhs in an American high school and population.* Ithaca: Cornell University Press.

Glesne, C. and A. Peshkin. 1992. *Becoming qualitative researchers: An introduction.* New York: Longman.

Gochenour, T. 1990. *Considering Filipinos.* Yarmouth, Maine: Intercultural Press.

Goetz, J. P. and M. D. LeCompte. 1984. *Ethnography and qualitative design in educational research.* New York: Academic Press.

Hale-Benson, J. E. 1986. *Black children: Their roots, culture, and learning styles.* Rev. ed. Baltimore: Johns Hopkins University Press.

Hall, E. T. 1959. *The silent language.* Garden City, N.Y.: Doubleday.

———. 1966. *The hidden dimension.* Garden City, N.Y.: Doubleday.

Hall, E. T. and M. R. Hall. 1990. *Understanding cultural differences: Germans, French and Americans.* Yarmouth, Maine: Intercultural Press.

Hansen, J. F. 1979. *Sociocultural perspectives on human learning: An introduction to educational anthropology.* Englewood Cliffs, N.J.: Prentice-Hall.

Herzog, J. D. 1976. The socialization of juveniles in primate and foraging societies: Implications for contemporary education. In *Educational patterns and cultural configurations: The anthropology of education,* ed. J. I. Roberts and S. Akinsanya, pp. 170-77). New York: David McKay.

Hewitt, E. L. [1905] 1976. "Ethnic factors in education." In *Educational patterns and cultural configurations: The anthropology of education,* ed. J. I. Roberts and S. Akinsanya, pp. 27-36. New York: David McKay.

Holt, G. S. 1972. "'Stylin' Outta' the black pulpit." In *Rappin' and stylin' out,* ed. T. Kochman, pp. 189-204. Urbana: University of Illinois Press.

Hymes, D. 1971. On linguistic theory, communicative competence, and the education of disadvantaged children. In *Anthropological perspectives on education,* ed. M. L. Wax, S. Diamond, and F. O. Gearing, pp. 51-66. New York: Basic Books.

Irving, R. E. M. 1980. *The Flemings and Walloons of Belgium.*

Report 46. London: Minority Rights Group.

Jolly, A. 1972. *The evolution of primate behavior.* New York: Macmillan.

Juan, S. 1994. Education of indigenous peoples: Anthropological study. *International Encyclopedia of Education* 3:1750-56. Oxford: Pergamon Press.

Kardiner, A. 1939. *The individual and his society: The psychodynamics of primitive social organizations.* New York: Columbia University Press.

Kimball, S. T. 1973. "An anthropological view of social system and learning." In *Cultural relevance and educational issues: Readings in anthropology and education,* ed. F. A. J. Ianni and E. Storey. Boston: Little, Brown & Co.

Kneller, G. 1965. *Educational anthropology: An introduction.* New York: Wiley.

Kochman, T. 1981. *Black and white styles in conflict.* Chicago: University of Chicago Press.

Kramer, B. J. 1991. Education and American Indians: The experience of the Ute Indian tribe. In *Minority status and schooling,* ed. M. A. Gibson and J. U. Ogbu, pp. 287-308. New York: Garland Publishing Co.

Kroeber, A. L. and C. Kluckhohn. 1952. *Culture: A critical review of concepts and definitions.* Cambridge, Mass.: Harvard University Press.

LaBelle, T. J. 1976. Anthropological framework for studying education. In *Educational patterns and cultural configuration: The anthropology of education,* ed. J. I. Roberts and S. Akinsanya, pp. 67-82. New York: David McKay.

Lancy, D. F. 1983. *Cross-cultural study of cognition and mathematics.* New York: Academic Press.

Lanier, A. R. 1988. *Living in the U.S.A.* 4th ed. Yarmouth, Maine: Intercultural Press.

Lee, C. and De Vos, G. 1981. *Koreans in Japan: Ethnic conflict and accommodation.* Berkeley: University of California Press.

Lee, C. D. 1993. *Signifying as a scaffold for literary interpretation: The pedagogical implications of an African American discourse genre.* Urbana, Ill.: National Council of Teachers of English.

LeVine, R. A. 1967. *Dreams and deeds: Achievement motivation in Nigeria.* Chicago: University of Chicago Press.

LeVine, R. A. 1973. *Culture, behavior and personality.* Chicago: Aldine.

Lijphart, A. ed. 1981. *Conflict and coexistence in Belgium: The dynamics of a culturally divided society.* Berkeley: Institute of International Studies, University of California, Berkeley.

Little, K. 1951. "The social cycle and initiation among the mende," in *The Mende of Sierra Leone,* ed. K. Little, pp. 113-130. London: Routledge and Kegan Paul.

Linton, R. 1945. *The cultural background of personality.* New York: Appleton-Century-Croft.

Luster, L. 1992. Schooling, survival, and struggle: Black women and the GED. Ph.D. diss., Stanford University.

Malinowski, B. [1943]1976. "Native education and culture contact." In *Educational patterns and cultural configuration: The anthropology of education,* ed. J. I. Roberts and S. Akinsanya, pp. 42-61. New York: David McKay.

Marshall, C. and G. B. Rossman. 1989. *Designing qualitative research.* Newbury Park, Calif.: Sage.

Mead, M. 1928. *Coming of age in Samoa.* New York: William Morrow.

Mead, M. 1935. *Sex and temperament in three primitive societies.*

New York: William Morrow.

Middleton, J., ed. 1970. *From child to adult: Studies in the anthropology of education.* Garden City, N.Y.: Natural History Press.

Miles, M. B., and A. M. Huberman. 1994. *Qualitative data analysis.* 2nd ed. Thousand Oaks, Calif.: Sage.

Miner, H. 1956. "Body ritual among the Nacirema." *American Anthropologist* 58:503-7.

Moll, L. C. 1994. "Mediating knowledge between homes and classrooms." In *Literacy: Interdisciplinary conversations,* ed. Deborah Keller-Cohen, pp. 385-410. Cresskill, N.J.: Hampton Press.

Moll, L. C., and S. E. Diaz. 1987. Change as the goal of educational research. *Anthropology and Education Quarterly* 18, no. 3:300-311.

Mortlock, E. 1989. *A common core: Thais and Americans.* Intercultural Press.

Musgrove, F. 1953. "Education and the culture concept." *Africa* 23:110-26.

Nydell, M. K. 1987. *Understanding Arabs: A guide for Westerners.* Yarmouth, Maine: Intercultural Press.

Ogbu, J. U. 1978. *Minority education and caste: The American system in cross-cultural perspective.* New York: Academic Press.

———. 1981. Origins of human competence: A cultural-ecological perspective. *Child Development* 52:413-29.

———. 1982. Cultural discontinuities and schooling. *Anthropology and Education Quarterly* 13, no. 3:290-307.

———. 1983. Minority status and schooling in plural society. *Comparative Education Review* 27:168-390.

———. 1987. Cultural influences on plasticity in human development. In *The malleability of children,* ed. J. J. Gallagher and C. T. Ramey, pp. 155-169. Baltimore: Paul Brooks.

———. 1988. Diversity and equity in public education: Population forces and minority school adjustment and performance. In *Policies for America's public schools: Teachers, equity, and indicators,* ed. R. Haskins and D. McRae, pp. 127-70. Norwood, N.J.: Ablex.

———. 1990. Understanding diversity: Summary and comments. *Education and Urban Society* 22, no. 4:425-9.

———. 1992. Understanding cultural diversity and learning. *Educational Researcher* 21, no. 8:5-14.

———. 1994a. Anthropology of education: History and overview. *International Encyclopedia of Education.* 2nd ed. London: Pergamon Press.

———. 1994b. Minority Status, Cultural Frame of Reference, and Schooling. In *Literacy: Interdisciplinary conversations,* ed. Deborah Keller-Cohen, pp. 361-84. Creskill, N.J.: Hampton Press.

———. (In press). "Cultural problems in minority education: Their interpretations and consequences—Part Two: Case Studies." *The Urban Review* 27, no. 4.

Ogbu, J. U., and G. E. Matute-Bianchi. 1986. "Understanding sociocultural factors in education: Knowledge, identity, and adjustment." In *Beyond language: Social and cultural factors in schooling of language minorities,* pp. 73-142. Sacramento, Calif.: California Deptartment of Education.

Petrissans, C. M. 1991. When ethnic groups do not assimilate: The case of Basque Americans resistance. *Ethnic Groups* 9:61-81.

Philips, S. U. 1972. Participant structure and communicative competence: Warm Springs children in community and classroom. In *Functions of language in the classroom,* ed. C. B. Cazden, D. Hymes, and V. John, pp.370-94. New York: Teachers College Press.

———. 1976. Commentary: Access to power and maintenance of ethnic identity as goals of multicultural education. *Anthropology and Education Quarterly* 7, no. 4:30-32.

———. 1983. *The invisible culture: Communication in classroom and population on the Warm Springs Indian Reservation.* New York: Longman.

Porier, F. and L. K. Hussey. 1982. Nonhuman primate learning: The importance of an evolutionary perspective. *Anthropology and Education Quarterly* 13, no. 2:133-48.

Richmond, Y. 1992. *From Nyet To Da: Understanding the Russians.* Yarmouth, Maine: Intercultural Press.

Roberts, J. I. 1976. Introduction. In *Educational patterns and cultural configurations: Anthropological studies of education,* ed. J. I. Roberts and S. Akinsanya, pp. 1-21. New York: David McKay.

Ruddle, K., and R. Chesterfield. 1977. *Education for traditional food procurement in the Orinoco delta.* Berkeley: University of California Press.

Scribner, S., and M. Cole. 1973. Cognitive consequences of formal and informal education. *Science* 182:553-9.

Segall, M. H., D. T. Campbell, and M. J. Herskovits. 1966. *The influence of culture on visual perception.* Indianapolis: Bobbs Merrill.

Segall, M. H., P. R. Dasen, J. W. Berry, and Y. H. Poortinga. 1990. *Human behavior in global perspective: An introduction to cross-cultural psychology.* Boston: Allyn & Bacon.

Shade, B. J. 1982. *Afro-American patterns of cognition.* Madison, WI: Wisconsin Center for Educational Research, University of Wisconsin.

Shimahara, N. K. 1991. Social mobility and education: Burakumin in Japan. In *Minority status and schooling: A comparative study of immigrant and involuntary minorities,* ed. M.A. Gibson and J. U. Ogbu, pp. 327-53. New York: Garland.

Spicer, E. H. 1966. The process of enclavement in middle America. 36th Congress of International de Americanistas Seville 3:267-279.

———. 1971. Persistent cultural systems: A comparative study of identity systems that can adapt to contrasting environments. *Science* 174:795-800.

Spindler, G. D., ed. 1987. *Education and cultural process: Anthropological approaches.* 2d ed. Prospect Heights, Ill.: Waveland Press.

Spradley, J. P. 1979. The concept of culture. In *Ethnographic Interviews,* ed. J. P. Spradley, pp.7-9. New York: Holt.

Taylor, R. B. 1988. *Cultural ways: A concise introduction to cultural anthropology.* Prospect Heights, Ill.: Waveland Press.

Taylor, M. J. and S. Hegarty. 1985. *The best of both worlds...? A review of research into the education of pupils of South Asian origin.*Windsor, U.K.: NFER-Nelson.

van Maanen, J., ed. 1983. *Qualitative methodology.* Beverly Hills, Calif.: Sage.

Vernon, P. E. 1969. *Intgelligence and cultural environment.* London: Methuen & Co.

Vogt, L. A., C. Jordan, and R. G. Tharp. 1987. Explaining school failure, producing school success: Two cases. *Anthropology and Education Quarterly* 18, no. 4:300-11.

Watkins, M. H. 1943. The West African Bush school. *The American Journal of Sociology* 48:666-75.

Wenzhong, H., and C. L. Grove. 1991. *Encountering the Chinese: A guide for Americans.* Yarmouth, Maine: Intercultural Press.

Whiting, J. W. M. and L. L. Child. 1953. Child training and personality. New Haven: Yale University Press.

Wilson, H. C. 1972. On the evolution of education. In *Learning and culture,* ed. K S. T. Kimball and H. J. Burnett. Seattle: University of Washington Press.

Wolcott, H. F. 1990. *Writing up qualitative research.* Newbury Park, Calif.: Sage.

Further Readings:

1. On Culture And Learning

Middleton, J. 1970. *From child to adult: Studies in the anthropology of education.* New York: Natural History Press.

Roberts, J. I., and S. K. Akinsanya, eds. 1976a. *Educational patterns and cultural configuration: The anthropology of education.* New York: David McKay.

Roberts, J. I. and S. K. Akinsanya, eds. 1976b. *Schooling in the cultural context: Anthropological studies of education.* New York: David McKay.

Sspindkler, G. D. 1987. *Education and cultural process: Anthropological approaches.* 2d ed. Prospect Heights, Ill.: Waveland Press.

Williams, R. T. 1972. *Introduction to socialization: Human culture transmitted.* St. Louis, Missouri: C.V. Mosby Company.

2. On ethnographic/qualitative research methods

Fetterman, D. M. 1989. *Ethnography step by step.* Newbury Park, Calif.: Sage.

Glesne, C., and A. Peshkin. 1992. *Becoming qualitative researchers: An introduction.* New York: Longman.

Leedy, P. D. 1993. *Practical research: Planning and design.* 5th Ed. New York: Macmillan.

Miles, M. B., and A. M. Huberman. 1994. *Qualitiative data analysis.* 2d. ed. Thousand Oaks, Calif.: Sage.

Spradley, J . P. 1979. *Ethnographic interviews.* New York: Holt.

Wolcott, H. F. 1990. *Writing up qualitative research.* Newbury Park, Calif.: Sage.

Evidence of Development from People's Participation in Communities of Learners

Eugene Matusov
and
Barbara Rogoff
University of California at Santa Cruz

The educational function of museums results from a blending of efforts of many people participating in a process of social mediation that goes far beyond face-to-face interaction of people present in a museum. The process includes the museum staff, those whose ideas and artifacts are represented in the museum, those who prepare and fund the exhibits, and those who visit the museum. The sociocultural process of learning from visits to a museum involves the content and organization of the exhibition, the architecture of a museum building, gift shops, and companionship at a display. The issue of assessing the long-term impact of this socially mediated learning relies on consideration of the conceptual relationship between socially mediated learning and individual development.

This paper describes the implications of four conceptions of how the social world relates to individual learning for the organization of museums and the study of their long-term effects on learning and development. We focus on a conceptual view of development as mutual participation in communities of learners and contrast this view with three one-sided approaches in which either only the learner or the social world is conceived as active (or they alternate). The three one-sided approaches portray learning as solo discovery, as transmission of knowledge, or as transfer of control over the curriculum. The participation model considers development as transformation of participation in a community of practice. Participation in a community of learners involves participation in specific institutions (e.g., schools, museums) in which people pursue inquiries, make connections among various contexts, share interests with others, and learn how to learn and how to assist and collaborate with others. Evidence of learning in the participation model involves transformations of people's participation in sociocultural activities as they assume more responsibility for an activity.

Each philosophy of learning assigns specific roles to the participants. For example, in the solo discovery philosophy of learning, a museum visitor is considered as an active learner who is involved in discovering essential relations in the environment. In the transmission philosophy of learning, a visitor is considered as a passive receiver of a body of knowledge provided by the museum organizers. Here only one "side" of the exchange between participants is considered to be active in the organization of the learning processes. The transfer of control philosophy is a compromise in that first the educators (e.g., parents, teachers, museum staff) are responsible for structuring the learning situation, and then the learners (e.g., children, students, museum visitors) are responsible for active learning in one-sided succession.

Our own preference and commitment are to the participation philosophy of learning, which treats learning as participation in a community of learners. This philosophy corresponds to a sociocultural approach in psychology, which assumes that socially mediated education and psychological development mutually constitute each other. In contrast with the three one-sided approaches — rather popular among educators — in which responsibility for the learning process is either assigned to educators or to learners, the participation approach treats all the participants in an educational institution as learners who share interests and expertise. Educational leaders have the responsibility to guide this process, while children, students, and visitors have the responsibility to contribute to their own learning and, given the opportunity, to assist the educational leaders in developing their roles. Our goal in this paper is to describe the four approaches and their underlying philosophies of learning, their implications for the organization of museums, and how to assess the long-term impact of museums on learning within each of the approaches.

There have been many discussions about how to organize museums in manners that provide more effective learning. These discussions are often focused around specific organizational elements of museum activity such as how much text should accompany an exhibit or whether "hands-on" and "hands-off" exhibits are better (Falk and Dierking 1992). Although all these questions are important, our focus has been on the learning philosophies that underlie many of those discussions. This paper examines the following four learning philosophies and their implications for the promotion and evaluation of learning in museums.

The *traditional transmission* model treats visitors as receptacles for the knowledge provided by the museum staff. This model of learning requires a visitor to attend to the exhibit and digest the information provided by the exhibit designer. Of course this process is complicated; museum staff must find ways to attract and maintain visitors' attention to the exhibit and to control how the visitors use the exhibit.

In reaction to the transmission model of learning, some educational institutions employ the *solo discovery* approach, which treats the visitor as an isolated active constructor of knowledge. Involvement by the museum staff (beyond provision of raw materials) is seen as a potential hindrance, limiting the visitor's creativity and exploration. It is assumed that the visitor has self-motivation for learning that is based on a stimulating, enriched environment provided by the museum. This model calls for the museum staff to avoid active guidance and involvement in the activities and limit their assistance to providing minimal guidance when asked for help.

The *transfer* approach attempts to combine the two previous approaches and design the educational curriculum in a way that chains tasks so visitors have the opportunity to discover essential relations between exhibited objects. It is based on a division of labor in which the museum staff are fully responsible for defining the learning curriculum and defining the educational tasks, while visitors are responsible for engaging in and solving the tasks. The problem in the learning process arises when visitors have their own educational agenda or their own tasks that are not addressed by the exhibits. Moreover, like the transmission approach, it requires visitors to move sequentially from one educational task designed by the museum staff to another, a requirement that is often difficult in museum settings in which visitors have freedom to move in various directions.

The *community of learners* approach goes beyond the transmission, solo discovery, or transfer alternatives because it focuses on mutuality in joint activity and guidance rather than on control by one side or the other. In a community of learners, both the visitors and museum staff are seen as active in structuring the inquiry, with museum staff assuming responsibility for guiding the process and visitors learning to participate in the management of their own learning (Dewey [1916] 1944; Newman, Griffin, and Cole 1989; Rogoff, Matusov, and White, forthcoming; Tharp and Gallimore 1988; Wells, Chang, and Maher 1990).

The remainder of this paper provides a brief orientation to the transmission, solo discovery, and transfer alternatives, with their implications for museums, and then turns to develop the community of learners approach in more detail.

Learning as Transmission of Information

According to the transmission approach, development involves a process of internal restructuring or encoding of information transmitted from external sources. Often a learner is treated as a "black box," a device that changes its internal state and outcome according to external input and its previous internal state. Teaching is regarded as a series of unilateral interventions in the learner's mental processes aiming to change the learner's internal state and his or her output.

In the transmission model, the purpose of educational institutions is to "design" development by defining systems of teaching interventions that add to learners' knowledge and skills. From this approach, educational institutions should choose what kind of facts and skills they want people to learn and implement instruction on the basis of the learner's previous knowledge. This model considers the long-term impact of learning as etching of transmitted facts, skills, and behavior in the learner.

The transmission model focuses on six major issues for the implementation of unilateral teaching.

1. How to define the learner's current knowledge — an issue of finding a genuine test of competence.

2. How to provide the right amount of guidance necessary to change the learner's internal state in accord with the desired plan — an issue of the optimal pedagogical technique.

3. How to make the learner accept and be ready for the teaching interventions — an issue of the learner's motivation.

4. How to schedule the teaching interventions for many learners at once — an issue of the effective management and organization of the educational process.

5. What the learner should learn — an issue of the curriculum.

6. How to engrave the transmitted skills so they stay forever with the learner — an issue of the long-term impact of learning.

The key recommendations that this approach might give to museums include:

• Clearly define pieces of information that visitors have to know after visiting a museum.

• Repeat this information to the visitors as much as necessary to imprint it in the visitors.

• Make the visitors responsive to the information and the repetitions.

In this approach, the evidence of the long-term impact of museum learning can be obtained from testing recall of the information to which individuals are exposed in a museum after a lapse of time.

We consider the transmission approach as one-sided because it gives full responsibility for the learning processes to educational leaders and assigns the learner a passive role, as the receptacle of externally transmitted knowledge (see also Rogoff, 1994, and Rogoff, Matusov, and White, forthcoming).

Learning as Solo Discovery

According to the solo discovery approach to learning inspired by the work of Jean Piaget (1970) among others, the role of education is to diagnose and facilitate ongoing processes in the universal sequence of development of children's concepts of causality, reasoning, and mastery of logical forms of thought. The child is viewed as active in developing an understanding of the world through experimenting with the environment in order to discover the logical relations among her or his own actions. Piaget attempted to study the child's "genuine" thinking apart from any knowledge that was uncritically absorbed by or imposed on the child in school or other educational institutions.

From the perspective of the solo discovery approach, educational institutions should assess developmental readiness and capitalize on development by providing a schedule for teaching subject matter that copies and nudges the universal sequence of developmental processes. For example, because, according to Piaget's findings, the concept of speed precedes the concept of time, the notion of speed should be taught before the notion of time. Capitalizing on developmental achievements involves teaching the subject material that can be assimilated by the child because development can be facilitated at the point when the child is ready to progress. For example, teaching metric units of volume measurement would be considered developmentally appropriate only for the child who has already developed the notion of volume conservation (i.e., that the volume of liquid remains the same even when its shape is changed by pouring it into another vessel).

The proponents of the solo discovery approach argue that educational institutions can speed up developmental processes by providing opportunities for a child to participate in activities that promote the child's development through enriching the child's physical and social environment. For example, many kindergartens provide opportunities to work with clay and liquid to facilitate the development of the notion of conservation of volume and mass. In the Piagetian view, such enriched physical environments provide opportunities for a child to apply his or her cognitive schemes, find discrepancies between expectations and the outcome of actions, experiment with actions and

expectations, and, finally, discover new and better cognitive schemes for actions.

According to Piaget, certain social interactions can also push children's development (Tudge and Rogoff 1989). Development occurs in situations of open dialogue when a child encounters the views of other children that, even if they are limited and incorrect, provide different perspectives on the topic. For example, two children who have not yet fully developed the notion of conservation of volume might notice different kinds of changes when a liquid is poured from a wider vessel into a thinner vessel. One child might notice that the level of the liquid is higher and conclude that the volume of the liquid has increased. The other child might notice that the vessel is thinner and conclude that the volume of the liquid has decreased. The children's attempts to argue their positions with each other as equal partners — with no special social status predefining which perspective is right — is considered to promote cognitive development. (This process is contrasted with superficial acceptance of an adult's opinion). The children have to accommodate their partner's perspective and find new schemes of actions that incorporate all the perspectives. Thus, according to the solo discovery approach to learning, the task of educational institutions is to provide opportunities for such discussions among socially equal partners.

If we apply the solo discovery approach to designing museums for optimal learning, this approach would recommend:

• Define developmentally appropriate content for museum exhibitions that can be easily assimilated by visitors on the basis of a diagnostic study of the current level of understanding of the target population of visitors

• Provide opportunities and choices for visitors to work actively with physical and symbolic objects

• Provide opportunities for visitors to be involved in open discussions with socially equal partners.

Although this approach has much to recommend it, we consider it to be one-sided, giving full responsibility for learning processes to the learner.

A Compromise:
Learning as Transfer of Control over the Curriculum

A third approach involves sequentially active roles for both educational leaders and learners, with education redirecting developmental processes in a transfer of control over the educational curriculum from educators to the learners. Unlike proponents of the solo discovery model, proponents of the transfer approach put strong emphasis on guidance. Unlike proponents of the transmission model, they emphasize the active role of learners in problem solving and are careful in choosing educational curricula in order to, on the one hand, foresee and allow learners' active engagement in the task and, on the other hand, lead them in a socially desired direction.

Proponents of the transfer of control approach (e.g., Davydov and Markova 1982; Davydov 1980) believe that educational curricula should be highly structured to allow the child to learn tasks successfully in a step-by-step fashion. First, each task has to be analyzed to extract the essential relations between the cognitive actions it requires. Second, the hierarchy between the relations has to be built to define the most effective learning schedule for these relations, which is nothing less than an integrated teaching curriculum. This stage involves developing a chain of the tasks carrying the essential relations leading to learning.

With regard to museums, this approach can offer the following recommendations.

• Define the desired tasks that visitors have to learn in a museum.

• Extract the tasks' underlying essential relations.

• Design tasks that carry the essential relations.

In the transfer of control approach, there is an attempt to overcome the differing one-sided approaches of both the solo discovery and the transmission philosophies of learning by appreciating the child's active role in the educational tasks fully defined by educational leaders. The solo discovery philosophy is one-sided because the responsibility for the educational agenda is fully assigned to the child, while the transmission philosophy is one-sided because the responsibility for the educational curriculum is assigned to educational leaders such as parents, teachers, and museum staff. The transfer approach, however, is sequentially one-sided because it involves switching from one type of one-sidedness during the phase when the task is designed by educators and professionals (without any involvement of the child in the curriculum definition process) to the other type of one-sidedness during the phase when the task is solved by the learners. In the transfer of control philosophy, it is first the educators' and then the learner's responsibility to be active in arranging for and engaging in learning, transferring responsibility for learning from one side to the other.

Learning as Participation in a Community of Learners

The participation approach is not one-sided but is mutual, based on shared engagement among the participants with an educational agenda emerging in collaboration (with potentially differing responsibilities) among the participants. This approach was inspired by Lev Vygotsky (see Vygotsky, 1978) and his students and has been expanded by researchers from different social science disciplines (Heath 1991; Lave and Wenger 1991; Newman, Griffin, and Cole 1989;

Rogoff 1990, 1995; Tharp and Gallimore 1988; Wertsch 1991). According to the participation approach, education, learning, and development cannot be separated. Psychological development, defined as mastery of participation in communities of practice, includes formal and informal educational processes.

Vygotsky (1978) noted that the level of mastery observed as a child works individually on a task (as in traditional assessments of development) does not provide a full picture of the child's psychological development. Two children demonstrating similar outcomes on a battery of individual psychological tests might behave differently in a situation in which assistance by a more knowledgeable partner is offered. One child, with the help of the more knowledgeable partner, might easily solve the tasks that she could not solve before; the other child still might demonstrate difficulties in problem solving. Vygotsky defined accomplishing the tasks which the child could not solve alone but could accomplish with the help of a more knowledgeable partner as working in the child's zone of proximal development (ZPD). This concept redefines development as involving collaborative efforts of people rather than as an individual endeavor. From this perspective, what develops is not a child's mastery of more complex tasks on an individual basis, but a child's participation in sociocultural activities that involves collaboration and, in some cases, temporarily working alone as well. According to Vygotsky (1978), sociocultural teaching[1] creates the zone of proximal development and thus guides developmental pathways.

Because of the diversity of sociocultural practices, children in different communities have different developmental pathways. Tharp and Gallimore (1988, p. 31) report, "Boys in Micronesia, where sailing a canoe is a fundamental skill, will have a ZPD for the skills of navigation, created in interaction with the sailing masters. A girl in the Navajo weaving community will have experiences in a zone not quite like any ever encountered by the daughters of Philadelphia." The diversity of goals of different communities necessitates defining development in terms of progress toward more responsible participation in specific communities of practice rather than assuming that development is a generic process independent of the goals and institutions of the communities in which an individual develops. At the same time, the developing individual contributes to the further development of the practices (and goals and institutions) of the community.

Development involves not only the content of sociocultural practice in differing communities but also the ways that learning occurs. That is, in varying communities of practice, learners participate in different activities explicitly or less deliberately designed for their learning. The learners' development includes not only what they are learning how to do but also how they are participating in the community using (and demonstrating) their developing skills and knowledge.

For example, Matusov, Bell, and Rogoff (forthcoming) suggest that children learn more than curriculum content through their involvement in the teaching and learning practices of their school. Participation in different school institutions (e.g., stressing collaboration or stressing individual competition) shapes the formats of children's interaction in guidance and joint problem solving. We found that in joint problem solving, third- and fourth-grade children experienced with cooperative schooling built on each other's ideas in a collaborative way and embedded their instruction in collaboration more often than did children from a traditional schooling background. Children with a traditional schooling background emphasizing individual competitive performance predominantly used guidance based on withholding of information, consistent with known-answer questions used by teachers in traditional schools.

According to the participation approach, development occurs as people change responsibilities for and membership in communities of practice and when they transform sociocultural tools that they use in the activity. For example, when people visit a museum for the first time they try to construct its meaning and relate it to known institutions and experiences, and later they may orient other new visitors to an exhibit.

The new experience allows individuals to build new relations with other people and with the subject matter, and to redefine old relations. A person's orienting of a newcomer may occur within familiar relationships (as when parents who have just become familiar with an exhibit orient a child to it in the same manner that they help the child with homework) or within transformed relationships (as when a child who has become familiar with an exhibit orients a parent to it).

New practices can be embedded in other practices, using or transforming practices from other settings. For example, didactic formats from school or more collaborative exploration from scouts can be used in the museum, involving development of ways of learning that bridge across different institutions as people participate in a new setting on the basis of their involvement. Their participation may also contribute to changing practices in other settings, as when involvement in museum learning sparks ideas for curriculum and for ways to approach it in schools.

The Museum as a Bridge between Communities of Learners

Museums, as educational institutions, provide opportunities for people to bridge different sociocultural practices and, through this process, to bridge different institutions and communities. John Dewey ([1916] 1944, p. 20) argued that one of the main functions of educational institutions is to give an individual "an opportunity to escape from the limitations of the social group in which he was born, and to come into living contact with a broader environment." According to this definition, an educational institution is a crossroad of a great variety of communities of practice. Visitors of museums are past, present, and future participants of different communities of practice, including professional, religious, political, recreational, ethnic, and other communities. Thus learning that is involved in museums begins before and continues after the physical visit to a museum.

The contact among these communities provides the ground for both creativity in the design of museums and the development of visitors as participants in them. Museums can be considered as places where different practices and their participants can meet, learn from each other as peripheral members in different communities, and contribute to each other's practices (Falk and Dierking 1992; Lave and Wenger 1991). For example, such a sociocultural practice as scuba diving (see Lagache 1994) has become known to the broader public through exciting documentaries of the underwater world. The success of those documentaries has transformed scuba diving as well: a new scuba diving practice of making underwater documentaries has developed. The relationship between the three communities of the museum's exhibits, museum staff, and museum visitors is not hierarchical and one-sided. Through negotiation and mutual contributions, people constitute a new type of practice and new type of community — a community of learners making individual and shared contributions to understanding. In museums, visitors usually encounter three other kinds of communities of practice:

1. communities of practice that are represented by the museum (e.g., in a museum of the history of aviation, visitors have an opportunity to meet with practices of professional aviators and designers of aircraft)

2. communities of practice that organize the museum (involving not only educational staff at the museum but also historians of flight, former professional aviators and designers of aircraft, as well as indirect contributors such as business people, educators, psychologists, economists, and so on)

3. communities of practice of other visitors who might deliberately accompany each other or just meet in the museum.

The social mediation provides complex negotiation among communities having different — complementary and/or contradictory — agendas, goals, and stakes in the institution. Very often a sociocultural practice involves different definitions of what an object and goal of the activity might be even if the participants deal with the same physical materials. Consequently, the negotiation between the participants about the object of museum learning is a dynamic process.

Diversity of communities of practice that are directly or indirectly involved in the museum generates a diversity of agendas that shapes the museum as practice and institution. For example, donor business communities (and government agencies) want to know why they should finance museums over other social programs, including how museums contribute to a local community and address their social issues in the long run. Schoolteachers want to know how museums can help them in developing and teaching the school curricula. Educators want to know the specifics of learning in museums in comparison to other educational institutions and how they complement each other. Visitors want to know how well they can socialize, learn, relax, and engage in interesting activities in museums. Disciplinary communities (e.g., rocket engineers, space scientists, astronauts for a museum of space exploration) want to know how well the museum informs their field and the public about their practices and propagates their goals. Museum administrators want to see museums as organizationally and economically sustained institutions. This diversity of agendas makes assessment of learning in museums a complex endeavor. It involves a dialogue among the communities to spell out their agendas, concerns, and goals.

Visiting a museum involves opportunities for visitors to participate in different practices and communities. For example, a visit to some museums offers many visitors an unusual opportunity to participate in a model of learning that contrasts with their contact with similar concepts in other settings, such as schools. Participation in museums often requires more contribution from visitors to the organization of the learning event (i.e., the museum visit) and provides more leeway than participation in schools usually allows for students. Newcomers have the opportunity to approach the concept, learning how to manage their own participation in ways different from those required or allowed in many schools. Their development in the museum setting includes learning how to make use of the available resources (written explanations on walls, lectures from museum docents, and so on), which differ from the resources in many schools (such as textbooks and teachers). Visitors have greater freedom (and responsibility) to manage their own choices about where to go first, how long to spend, which aspects of the exhibit to explore, and how to do so. Thus, the museum is not only a crossroad of different practices and communities; it also guides visitors in how to bridge different practices and communities.

Evaluating Long-term Learning in Museums

In one-sided approaches, learning is usually assessed by isolating the individual and applying a standard procedure to "measure" competence that tests original knowledge, applies a treatment, and again tests the resulting change in knowledge gained. Competence is regarded as obtaining pieces of knowledge.

In contrast, the participation model assesses learning by analyzing individuals' changing roles in the context of their participation — how they coordinate with others in shared endeavors — with attention to the dynamic nature of the activity itself and its meaning in the community (Rogoff forthcoming). In the participation approach, evidence of learning in different educational institutions is not independent of the learning philosophy of the institution. Assessment of long-term museum learning requires attention to the institution's goals; there is no value-free, universal scale or method for assessment. Each of the four philosophies of learning defines its own educational values and ways of assessment, and these vary from institution to institution.

For example, in the study mentioned above involving children and schools with different learning philosophies (Matusov, Bell, and Rogoff, forthcoming), the researchers' attempts to measure the correctness of problem solutions of two children working on a few math problems illustrate how the definition of an appropriate solution varied in the two school programs. The two schools differed in the philosophies of learning in deep ways. In the cooperative school, instruction focused on *processes* of solution and involved collaborative problem solving, whereas in the traditional program, instruction focused on the correctness of *products* made on an individual basis. In the traditional school, learning was considered successful when a student demonstrated increasing mastery of working alone, whereas in the cooperative school, learning was considered successful when a student demonstrated increasing mastery of managing learning in collaboration with other people. The children from the traditional school tried to do the problems as much as they could and then turned to the experimenter to announce either their solution or their failure to solve the problem. In many cases, the children from the cooperative school tried to involve the experimenter in their collaborative work on the problems the experimenter gave them, but he did not cooperate. Attributing correctness of problem solution to the children alone would be inconsistent with the cooperative school's emphasis on children making use of available adult (and child) resources in solving problems.

The traditional methodology for measuring learning (e.g., individual pretest, treatment, individual posttest) fits the traditional school's philosophy and definition of learning, but not that of the cooperative school. Moreover, even if an institutionally appropriate measurement of cognitive development for each school were designed (e.g., portfolios with narratives of students' progress in classroom collaborative activities in the cooperative school and testing of individual skills in the traditional school), it would be impossible to compare developmental outcomes based on these different measurements. This is the issue of cultural equivalence of measurement (Cole, Gay, Glick, and Sharp 1971; Cole and Means 1986). The comparison of effectiveness of approaches requires judgments of quality tied to sociocultural values.

According to the participation model, the learning process is easy to observe. Parents assess their children's learning all the time by observing changes in their children's participation in home activities. For example, a mother notices progress of her child in reading by observing changes in the child's participation in reading activities: mastery of the child's retelling stories, increases in the child's attention to the text, the child's desire to read and hear reading, and so on. Learning is a lifelong activity (and a way of life) rather than a one-time event. If we consider Dewey's definition of an educational institution as an opener of the sociocultural environment of its participants, who are, otherwise, "locked" in their immediate surroundings, we can also assess visitors' learning by observing changes in their participation in different communities and practices. The more an individual learns, the more he or she gets access to diverse practices of a society, and vice versa. Getting access to societal practices and learning how to get such access should be the core of assessment of learning in museums.

According to a sociocultural approach, cultural development involves individuals becoming members of communities of practice. It focuses on how, through incorporation of new community members, people, their relations, and the community are changed. Rogoff (1995) suggested that this process involves three aspects: transformation of individual participation in joint activity (i.e., personal plane of development), transformation of interpersonal relations (i.e., interpersonal plane of development), and transformation of community practices themselves (i.e., community plane of development). To study evidence of learning in a museum as a community of learners, it is necessary to focus on how people change their participation in museum activities (defined in a broad sense). Rogoff (forthcoming) identified the following aspects of transformation in participation as central to the evaluation of individuals' learning and development:

• individuals' contributions to the endeavor (their roles and the responsibilities with which they engage in the endeavor)

• their initiative or need for support in becoming involved and sustaining involvement (their commitment)

• their leadership and support of others' roles

• their attitude toward change in involvement (a learning attitude)

• their understanding of (and flexible readiness to fill) complementary roles in the endeavor

• their understanding of the relations with other activities (extension to other activities as appropriate; comfort in switching to different modes of involvement as appropriate)

• their flexibility and vision in revising ongoing community practices.

Study of the long-term effects of museums on development also includes how innovations and changes are brought about in the museum itself (in Rogoff's community plane of analysis), since according to the participation approach, developmental processes of individual and institutional development mutually constitute each other. To examine the community plane of development, it is necessary to focus on historical development of practices and institutions and their relationship.

Based on the view that the goals of an institution itself are an aspect of sociocultural activity that can be coordinated more successfully given participants' awareness of their values and philosophies, the participation approach can offer the following recommendations for studying learning in museums:

• Define the goals and philosophy of learning for the specific museum — how staff and visitors of a specific museum define learning, what they value, what is involved in the museum's practices, and how the purposes of the museum are negotiated by its constituents

• Define relations among different communities that are directly or indirectly involved in museum practice and their changes over time

• Define the roles of each community involved (e.g., visitors, educators, professionals, business associates) in each phase of the decision-making process in museum practices (from determining the purpose of the museum to the content of exhibition labels and locations for gift shops)

• Define how practices of the museum relate to other educational and noneducational practices of other institutions.

In sum, according to the participation approach, socioculturally mediated education and development mutually constitute each other through the community practices in which people are involved. Learning is based on mutuality in guidance and goes beyond processes defined by the three one-sided approaches described above. It is defined as transformations of people's participation in sociocultural activities.

Acknowledgments

We are grateful to Lori Felton, Cathy Angelillo, and Edouard Lagache for their excellent comments on earlier drafts of this paper.

References

Cole, M., and B. Means 1986. *Comparative studies of how people think: An introduction.* Cambridge, Mass.: Harvard University Press.

Cole, M., J. Gay, J. Glick, and D. Sharp 1971. *The cultural context of learning and thinking.* New York: Basic Books.

Davydov, V. V., and A. K. Markova, 1982. A concept of educational activity for schoolchildren. *Soviet Psychology* 21: 50-76.

Davydov, V. V. 1980. Analysis of psychologico-pedagogical principles of learning. *Studia Psychologica* 22: 41-50.

Dewey, J. [1916] 1944. *Democracy and education.* New York: Macmillan.

Falk, J. H., and L. D. Dierking 1992. *The museum experience.* Washington, D.C.: Whalesback Books.

Heath, S. B. 1991. The sense of being literate: Historical and cross-cultural features. In *Handbook of reading research,* ed. R. Barr, M. L. Kamil, P. B. Mosenthal, and P.D. Pearson, pp. 3-25, New York: Longman.

Lagache, E. 1994. Diving into communities of learning: Existential perspectives on communities of practice and zones of proximal development. Ph. D. diss. University of California, Berkeley.

Lave, J., and E. Wenger 1991. *Situated learning: Legitimate peripheral participation.* Cambridge, Eng.: Cambridge University Press.

Matusov, E., N. Bell, and B. Rogoff. Forthcoming. *Assistance in joint problem solving by children differing in cooperative schooling backgrounds.*

Newman, D., P. Griffin, and M. Cole 1989. *The construction zone: Working for cognitive change in school.* Cambridge, Eng.: Cambridge University Press.

Piaget, J. 1970. Extracts from Piaget's theory. In *Manual of child psychology,* ed. P. H. Mussen pp. 703-732. London: Wiley.

Rogoff, B. 1990. *Apprenticeship in thinking: Cognitive development in social context.* New York: Oxford University Press.

Rogoff, B. 1994. Developing understanding of the idea of communities of learners. *Mind, Culture, and Activity, 1,* 209-229.

Rogoff, B. Forthcoming. Evaluating development in the process of participation: Theory, methods, and practice building on each other. In *Change and development: Issues of theory, application, and method.* ed. E. Amsel & A. Renninger. Hillsdale, NJ: Erlbaum.

Rogoff, B. 1995. Observing sociocultural activity on three planes: Participatory appropriation, guided participation, and apprenticeship. In *Sociocultural studies of mind,* ed. J. V. Wertsch, P. del Rio, and A. Alvarez, pp. 139-164. Cambridge, Eng.: Cambridge University Press.

Rogoff, B., E. Matusov, and C. White. Forthcoming. Models of teaching and learning: Participation in a community of learners. In *Handbook of education and human development: New models of learning, teaching, and schooling,* ed. D. Olson and N. Torrance. London: Basil Blackwell.

Tharp, R. G., and R. Gallimore 1988. *Rousing minds to life: Teaching, learning, and schooling in social context.* Cambridge, Eng.: Cambridge University Press.

Tudge, J., and B. Rogoff 1989. Peer influences on cognitive development: Piagetian and Vygotskian perspectives. In *Interaction in human development,* ed. M. Bornstein and J. Bruner. pp. 17-40. Hillsdale, NJ: Erlbaum.

Vygotsky, L. 1978. *Mind in society: The development of higher psychological processes,* ed. M. Cole, V. John-Steiner, S. Scribner, and E. Souberman. Cambridge, Mass.: Harvard University Press.

Wells, G., G. L. Chang, and A. Maher 1990. Creating classroom communities of literate thinkers. In *Cooperative learning: Theory and research,* ed. S. Sharan, pp. 95-121. New York: Praeger.

Wertsch, J. 1991. *Voices of the mind: A sociocultural approach to mediated action.* Cambridge, Mass.: Harvard University Press.

Note

1. Vygotsky used the Russian word obuchenie, which connotes both formal intentional and informal unintentional teaching (or instruction, or guidance); literally, it means learning from somebody else who is supposed to be more knowledgable.

Human–Factor Considerations in the Design of Museums to Optimize their Impact on Learning

Alan Hedge

Human factors, and its European equivalent, ergonomics, is a problem oriented discipline that focuses on the application of scientific knowledge about human capabilities and behavior to design. To do this, the discipline draws on information from many different fields, such as psychology, biology, anthropometry, biomechanics, anatomy, medicine, engineering, physics, computer science, and management sciences. The goal of human factors analysis of any problem usually is to improve human performance, which includes improving learning, by increasing accuracy and reducing errors. A frequent corollary of this performance improvement is a reduction in discomfort and adverse health effects. The combined effects of consequent improvements in performance and health result in optimization of the design of a system, setting, or product (Sanders and McCormick 1993).

Where possible, human factors approaches problem situations in a systematic way by trying to conceptually define the components of the problem and frame them as what is termed a person-technology system (see fig. 1). In this framework I use the term "exhibit" to refer to the display of immediate information to the user (e.g., a display case, a hands-on exhibit such as a computer, etc.). The definition of "technology" is broad: any object in the environment with which a person must interact to achieve the goal of the system. The approach, then, is to analyze behavior into time-delimited slices, called "tasks," which are defined as purposeful activities directed toward achieving the system's goal. These tasks, in turn, are analyzed to determine what the information-processing requirements and limitations are and also what corresponding responses or control actions need to be executed. This analysis often reveals sources of inefficiencies and errors in the design of the system, which can be rectified to optimize the performance of the person-technology system.

But what does all of this have to do with the design of museums? A quick search of the human factors literature reveals few answers to this question. Museums do not seem to have been studied in any detail by human factors specialists. This paper seeks to demonstrate the value of a human factors analysis of museums.

The Museum as a Person-Technology System

The first step in conducting a human factors analysis of any person-technology system is to define the system objectives and the system components. Webster's dictionary defines a "museum" as "an institution devoted to the procurement, care, study, and display of objects of lasting interest or value: a room, building, or locale where a collection of objects is put on exhibition." From Victorian times this view of the museum has been standard, and it remains widespread even today. The Victorians were enthusiastic museum visitors; they had no television to distract them, and the concept of the museums fitted well with prevailing social values of tidiness and order. Museum buildings were designed as great galleries; objects were separated from visitors by glass (touch was to be avoided in Victorian England), artifacts

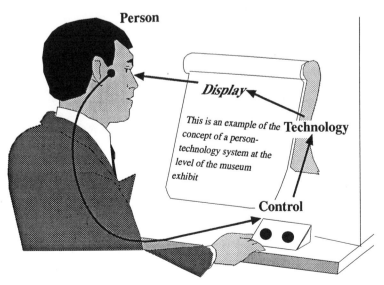

Figure 1. An example of a person-technology system

were organized into taxonomic displays, and people were expected to pass through the space in an orderly manner. Victorian museums were places of learning, but the learning appealed primarily to amateur experts (e.g., naturalists, geologists, scientists).

Today these values still are reflected in the ways in which museums organize and exhibit artifacts. But, unlike their Victorian predecessors, modern museums have diversified. Their orientation has shifted from passive display to active learning. Moreover, the social norms of visitors have changed drastically. The power of television has increased visitor awareness of the world—and consequently decreased some of the curiosity value of artifacts—and museums have become business enterprises. To better understand visitor expectations and the impact of museums on learning experiences Donald (1991) groups museums into four different categories based on their topic domains:

fine arts museums: Many of these still are designed to epitomize the Victorian ideal: exhibits are displayed for visitor admiration. But methods for presenting information have expanded in recent years, and many fine arts museums regularly organize tours, workshops, lectures, performances, and other activities.

natural history museums: Many of these similarly follow the Victorian ideal, presenting exhibits in huge cases containing a plethora of artifacts. In presenting informaiton, many try to combine narrative with the displayed objects (e.g., through read-along visitor guides, push-button audiotapes, interactive computerized displays, and docent tours). Often a favorite with schools, these museums frequently try to increase visitor involvement by treasure-hunt-type questionnaires. A recent trend has been the periodic use of thematic animated exhibits, such as dinosaur automatons.

science museums: Generally these take one of two forms. The traditional science museum exhibits the history of science, examples of scientific principles, and the development of technology in traditional forms as well as some hands-on, interactive exhibits. Here the focus is on things rather than people. Sometimes the display of technology combines peacetime exhibits with wartime exhibits. In the last twenty to thirty years, a new type of science museum, often called a science center, has emerged. These differ from the traditional science museum by emphasizing their role in learning and presenting almost exclusively hands on, interactive exhibits to display scientific principles.

park museums: Another recent development, park museums try to raise visitor awareness of natural, ecological, or social issues pertinent to a specific geographical locale. Typically these adopt a thematic approach to guiding the visitor through, say, an ecosystem, and along the way using a variety of modes of exhibiting information, such as traditional passive displays, hands-on or interactive exhibits, audiotape loops, and videotape loops.

In addition to Donald's four categories, I propose adding at least four other types of museums that can be visited today and that, in terms of their human factors design, offer different opportunities for learning:

social history museums: Here the focus of the museum is the display of artifacts that illustrate social conditions pertinent to a specific time, such as items of clothing or everyday life. A recent trend is to create settings using wax models or automatons that simulate how life was lived in a particular era. Displays are designed to focus attention on the human dimensions of the artifacts being displayed (i.e., how they were used, why they were used, who used them) rather than the technology or design of the artifacts. Some museums focus solely on a specialist theme, such as a museum of torture.

place museums: Geographical locale is all-important in these museums because the museum building and/or its location are, in fact, the primary object of interest (e.g., Gettysburg battlefield, frontier forts). To convey a sense of realism to the visitor, these museums often have staff dressed in the attire of the period, sometimes even speaking in the tongue of that time. Although there may be little remaining of the original place or location (Gettysburg, for example, looks like any other group of agricultural fields) experiential information is of paramount importance, and museum exhibits are designed to stimulate imagination and often to encourage some role-playing to give the visitor a better sense of the time and place of interest.

aquariums, botanical gardens and zoos: although not traditionally considered museums, perhaps because of their grander scale and outdoor nature, from a human factors perspective aquariums, botanical gardens and zoos are functionally almost identical to other types of museums. The primary difference is that the exhibits in these settings usually are alive rather than dead or inanimate. The intent is much the same as that of any museum: to display living species to visitors so that they will learn about them. Other concepts, such as conservation, evolution, and extinction, are frequently woven into the themes being illustrated.

entertainment museums: With advances in technology over the past twenty years, the differences between museums and traditional places of entertainment are blurring. Visitors go to places like Epcot or Disneyland primarily for entertainment. The design of exhibits in this style of theme park is such that, incidentally, the visitor learns a great deal of information about a range of issues, including social and political history, technological developments, agriculture, wildlife, evolution, conservation, cultural diversity, and futuristic possibilities. The Walt Disney company uses the term "imagineering" to describe what it is attempting to achieve with its exhibits, and, while the goal may sound fanciful, it parallels what many museum exhibit designers try to achieve.

Thinking about classifications of museums is an important first step in developing relevant human factors principles, because the development of a taxonomy provides a framework within which we can better comprehend possible relationships between existing concepts and see the gaps in our knowledge. For example, Dmitry Mendeleyev's development of the periodic table allowed a clearer picture of the relationships between elements to emerge and also predicted missing elements based on their properties, which then were searched for and identified. Research on the relevant conceptual dimensions that visitors use to differentiate different types of museums will help in developing a descriptive taxonomy and may reveal some unique opportunities for new forms to emerge. Dodds (1992) has attempted a typology of museums. Based on her review of the literature, Dodds defined the functions of a museum as to collect, conserve, research, exhibit, educate, serve the community, and define self and culture. A questionnaire was developed and a random sample of directors of institutions accredited by the American Association of Museums was surveyed. Respondents rated each of twenty-seven hypothetical scenarios using these functional components. Museum work was rated as comprised equally of collection, conservation, research, exhibition, and education. Thus there is consistency in the ways in which museum professionals categorize their work. What remains unknown is how visitors view the same places and the degree of congruence between visitor and professional views. In this particular study the dimensions for comparison were predefined based on a literature review, and therefore they may have constrained opportunities for respondents to offer other, unique expressions.

It may be interesting to explore further taxonomic possibilities using other ideographic methods, such as repertory grid techniques (Fransella and Bannister 1977), to reveal the underlying constructs that professionals and visitors use to develop conceptual frameworks for museums. Repertory grid methods allow researchers to uncover the constructs that people use to frame other people, objects, situations, and places. Constructs are dimensions we use to arrive at decisions (e.g., good-bad, nice-nasty, beautiful-ugly, interesting-boring). Repertory grid studies can reveal which constructs are shared among others and which are unique to individuals, which are of core importance and which are more peripheral, and so on. Knowledge of these constructs gives a means of gauging how a person or a situation has changed an indi-

vidual's conceptual framework. The same type approach can also be applied to classifying the types of exhibits displayed within a museum setting, and again it may reveal some new and hitherto unforeseen opportunities. Future research on the development of a taxonomy of museums and exhibits may also help designers meet the expectations of visitors and may reveal some new design opportunities.

With the sophistication of late twentieth-century life, any modern museum must strive to satisfy a diverse array of objectives. Although museum buildings and their contents may differ enormously, the ways in which the people who visit and work in museums experience the environment and process information are remarkably consistent. Thus it is possible for a human factors analysis to derive a common set of requirements that apply to all museum settings in order to facilitate learning. In terms of human experience these consistent objectives include at least the following:

• Museums should be places of learning.
• Museums should be repositories for artifacts and exhibits.
• Museums should satisfy the expectations and needs of staff and visitors.
• Museums should be places of optimal experiences and change.

Meeting these objectives can be challenging, because sometimes there are inherently conflicts between objectives (e.g., between the needs of staff who must keep the museum in working order and visitors who expect everything to be functioning smoothly). All these objectives have implications for museum design and the visitor experience. This paper, however, will not attempt to deal comprehensively with each of these objectives; rather, it will focus on the human factors design implication of museums as places of learning, wonder and curiosity, entertainment, and change.

Museums as Places of Learning

Human factors specialists typically analyze the learning process by studying the ways in which information from the environment is assimilated and processed by human beings. Unlike behavioral models of learning, which focus on the role of reinforcement schedules, this approach decomposes information processing into its functionally discrete sensory, perceptual, cognitive, memory, and attention processes and then examines the demands that the task places on the person who will be learning in terms of each of these functionally discrete processes. Figure 2 summarizes this basic model of information processing. This approach treats the brain as an abstract system, but it also recognizes that it is one with finite limits and definite requirements. In functional terms, museums can

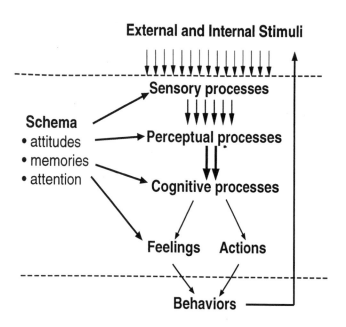

External and Internal Stimuli

Sensory processes

Schema
- attitudes
- memories
- attention

Perceptual processes

Cognitive processes

Feelings   **Actions**

Behaviors

Figure 2. Simplified diagram of the functional flow of information through the brain.

be thought of as vast information warehouses that differ from other information warehouses, such as libraries, because they usually display physical objects and processes, or facsimiles of these, along with associated text and/or graphics identifying and describing these objects or processes. Vision is the dominant sensory modality in most museums, and most exhibits are designed to appeal to experiential learning through seeing and reading information. Exhibits can be viewed as discrete person-technology systems. In a passive exhibit the user may simply internalize information displayed in the exhibit. In an active exhibit, users may interact with the display by some type of hands-on control. As with all person-technology systems, the design of the interface is a prime determinant of the success of the system and the extent of learning. Improving the design of the interface requires a more detailed understanding of the mental processes that govern our ability to acquire, analyze, and assimilate information.

Sensory Processes: The Beginnings of All Awareness
Before any learning can take place, information must be input into the nervous system via one or more of the five senses. For brevity, the discussion that follows will focus on the acquisition of visual information because vision is the dominant sense for most people. The brain cannot knowingly respond to that which the senses cannot detect. This statement may sound trite, but visits to museums reveal that often it is overlooked. If, for example, a museum exhibit is displayed where there is insufficient light to clearly see the

exhibit items, then learning cannot occur because information cannot be input into the system. If an exhibit is displayed in, say, a glass case where reflected glare makes it difficult see the exhibit item, then learning is suboptimal. If an exhibit is placed too high for a child or a wheelchair user to see its contents, or too low for an adult to see, then pertinent information cannot be input into the nervous system and appropriate learning cannot occur. When more than one modality is needed to process information from an exhibit, such as when viewing a video projection that requires sight and sound, then information must be presented in congruence and modalities must not be in conflict. Consider the difficulty of watching, for example, an audiovisual tape-slide show in which the projection of the visual image and the narrative on the audiotape are out of synchrony, or think about the annoyance of watching a movie where the movements of the lips and the audio dialogue are not in synchrony. Detailed consideration of the sensory modalities involved in processing information about an exhibit is a critical first step to maximizing the chances that the exhibit will successfully facilitate learning.

The nervous system is never inactive while we are alive, and all sensory judgments about external conditions (i.e., impulses from sensory receptors called signals) are made relative to this background nervous activity (called noise). Thus all of our sensory systems operate as relative rather than absolute detectors of the environment. This relative performance can be elegantly described by signal detection theory (SDT). In SDT, the learner can make only one of four judgments about information being transmitted from the senses to the central nervous system. A hit describes the situation in which something has happened in the environment (called a signal) the senses have detected this, and the person has correctly identified the signal (e.g., the person correctly sees the name of an exhibit). A miss describes the situation in which a signal has happened but the person fails to detect it (e.g., the person misses seeing a sign to an exhibit that he or she may have been looking for). A false alarm describes the situation in which the person thinks a signal has happened but it hasn't (e.g., the person thinks he or she sees the sign to an exhibit but actually misread another sign). A correct rejection describes the situation in which the person correctly rejects the signal (e.g., the person sees that something is not the sign to an exhibit that he or she is looking for). For any information display, each of these four outcomes can be represented by two probability curves, one curve representing that the person will interpret firing of the receptors as noise (correct rejection), and one representing interpretation of firing of the receptors as a signal (hit). These two curves overlap to yield the miss and false alarm probability regions (see fig. 3).

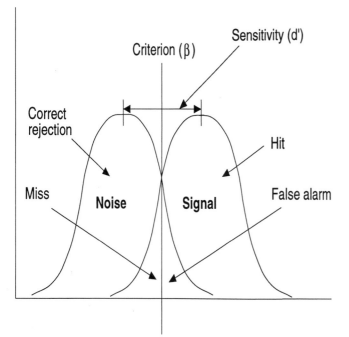

Figure 3. Signal detection theory.

We can calculate all of the required performance measures necessary to evaluate a display from knowing the probability of a hit (p[miss] = 1 - p[hit]) and the probability of a false alarm (p[correct rejection] = 1- p[false alarm]). The magnitude of the distance between the peaks of the signal and noise distributions influences detectability and is the sensitivity measure, called d-prime (d1). When the sensitivity is high, there is a large signal-to-noise ratio. As we increase the ratio of signal-to-noise, we improve the chances of the senses detecting the signal (McNicol 1984). For example, it is easier to read black text on a white background under adequate lighting because this combination has a high contrast (i.e., high signal-to-noise ratio) than it is to read black text on an orange background under the same lighting because this combination will have a lower signal-to-noise ratio. Thus for visual information, the lighting design for a museum exhibit can either enhance or impair sensory input by either increasing or decreasing the signal-to-noise ratios of text and figures against the background.

From personal experience, I suspect that many exhibit labels and descriptions are written, viewed, and approved as adequately discriminable under more optimal lighting conditions than those present in many museum galleries, because all too often I have found that it is difficult to read artifact descriptions because of poor lighting and poor display design. It is worthwhile remembering that maximizing the signal-to-noise in exhibits assumes increased importance for elderly visitors because their sensory systems lose sensitivity with age. Other important aspects of maximizing the signal-to-noise ratio of exhibited visual information must also include considerations of figure-background color discriminability, choice of text font, use of appropriate line weights, and choice of appropriate font sizes for the likely viewing distance and angle of gaze. Highly discriminable signals will grab and hold attention, thus facilitating learning. One other concept in signal detection theory is that of the criterion (() or cutoff point for a sensation level. Users can adjust the criterion they apply to any given display situation (this will be considered in greater detail in the next section).

An observer's response to an information display can be represented by plotting the proportions of hits and false alarms separately for signals of different probabilities to obtain what is called a receiver operating characteristics (ROC) curve. The ROC curve is, in effect, an isosensitivity curve for signals of different probabilities for a given level of sensitivity and a given signal strength. We can apply signal detection theory to compare the performance of different ways of exhibiting information in terms of the discriminability of this information for users.This approach has been applied to studying information displayed in chest x-rays and related medical decision making (Lusted 1968). Poor environmental conditions in a museum (e.g., low ambient illuminance, high noise) can reduce the signal-to-noise ratio, making it more difficult to detect information that is being presented. For example, auditory presentations that sound excellent in an empty gallery may be drowned in a cacophony of noise from children and foot traffic when the museum is in operation. Museum guides speaking in different languages, and sometimes shouting to be heard, may create acoustic interference problems. Exploring the sensory consequences of worst-case situations in a museum may reveal useful design insights to improve the detectability of salient information. In this way, future research could usefully explore the application of signal detection theory to improving the design of museum exhibits and associated information displays.

Other considerations that determine the success of sensory processing include the time available to register a signal, the direction of gaze (for visual information), and familiarity or expectancies about the information to be acquired. If the input occurs too briefly, for example we run past displays or are moved quickly past displays on some form of people mover, then we will fail to register the pertinent information and therefore cannot learn it. If we look in the wrong direction or in the wrong places, we will fail to acquire the relevant information (these processes will be considered in more detail later in this paper). If we are unfamiliar with the information to be acquired, we may fail to fully assimilate it after an initial encounter (e.g., when we read a book or watch a movie for a second time we often see things that we missed the first time around). This failure may lead either to motivation to return to review the information again, or it may lead us to conclude that something just was not worthwhile.

Perception and Cognition: Awareness Acquires Form and Meaning

The distinction among sensation, perception, and cognition is a conceptual convenience that we make because it is important to separate out the conditions necessary for a sensory receptor to detect an environmental stimulus from what may subsequently happen to this information prior to conscious consideration. Assuming that sensory information has been registered successfully, the brain then attempts to interpret this information in some way, to filter out the less-relevant cues, and to retain the more-relevant cues. This process, termed perception, is the stage at which we begin to weigh information by attaching some level of meaning to it. The filtering process depends on how we direct our attention and on what we store in our shorter-term memory systems. Information that passes into these memory systems has a chance of being retained over longer time periods—in other words, of being learned. Cognition works as a higher-level executive controlling perceptual processes through mental schemata, such as those we commonly think of as beliefs and attitudes. Because the focus of this paper is on the more immediate human factors issues concerning the design and presentation of information, the main focus will be on functional perceptual and cognitive considerations; higher-level cognitive and social influences on information processing will be only briefly considered.

As we have seen in the previous section, signal detection theory utilizes information about the probability of choices to evaluate the discriminability of information displays. Another virtue of this theory is that it can readily account for the facts that different users may respond in different ways because of personal differences in sensitivity (d1) and that the same user may respond in different ways at different times because of changes in sensitivity. These same processes shape how we may change sensitivity (d1) to information displays. For example, if we are looking for a specific artifact in a museum exhibit we may walk past other exhibits, dismissing them with only a cursory glance (correct rejections); we may think we see the specific artifact, only to discover that it is something that looks similar but is not the desired artifact (false alarm); we may see the desired artifact (hit); or we may fail to see the desired artifact even though it is there (miss). If the museum contains relatively few exhibits, our search task will be relatively easy (d1), but if it is very crowded our task will be much more difficult (small d1). If when we visit the museum we are expecting to see a specific artifact (e.g., King Tutankhamen's burial mask) we will scan exhibit cases searching for that item and probably experience more false alarms (less-strict criterion) by reacting to every exhibit case with a similar gold mask than if we have no prior expectations about what we will see (stricter criterion).

Other perceptual effects influence information acquisition. The number of choices with which we are presented imposes an information-processing load on the brain. The $\log2$ of the number of choices represents this information load in bits (binary digits). Thus, a display with two choices represents 1 bit to be processed, with 4 choices it is 2 bits, with 8 it is 3 bits, and so on. Studies suggest that the brain is capable of simultaneously handling about 7 bits (128 choices) across all senses. Given that the shortest time to discriminate between any two sequential stimuli is about one-eighth of a second, the brain can process about 126 bits per second (Csikszentmihalyi 1990). Although this capacity seems quite formidable, studies show that simply trying to understand someone who is speaking requires about 40 bits per second of processing. Thus it is relatively easy for the environment to overload the senses and for us to fail to detect appropriate information.

Several perceptual processes help us in trying to minimize the risks of information overload. First, the limitations on the perceptual system appear to relate to so-called chunks of information, which can be thought of as the greatest units of perceptual meaning rather than individual items of information. In early studies, Miller (1956) found that the capacity of short-term memory was about 7 ± 2 chunks, where the size of the chunks can differ. For example, if presented with a randomly organized list of, say, 20 letters, people can recall about 7 of these (± 2), and if presented with a randomly organized list of 20 words they recall 7 ± 2 words, not 7 ± 2 letters. If you saw the following numbers 011447135839724315, you probably could recall any 7 of these after a single presentation, whereas if these are organized for you as chunks, as in an international phone number in the UK (i.e., 01144-71-358-3972 x4315), then recall is more accurate and learning is faster. Without chunking, modern phone systems, credit card numbers, social security numbers, and so forth. would pose a learning nightmare to many people!

These same principles of chunking should be applied to the design of exhibit displays to facilitate learning. Designers should think about meaningful chunks and then organize the information so that the chunking is obvious and so that people are not faced with displays that present them with more than seven chunks to assimilate.

Other perceptual phenomena related to chunking

include the way in which our brain makes associative links between chunks. The use of mnemonic aids is an excellent example of this. Learning the seven colors of the spectrum can be a difficult task, especially for children, because seven is about our maximum capacity for chunking. It is easier to learn seven letters that make a word (however nonsensical) like ROYGBIV, together the letters represent a single chunk that can readily be recalled. This word, in turn, can act as a skeleton for associative links to the color names red, orange, yellow, green, blue, indigo and violet, all correctly sequenced as the spectral colors. For children especially, learning rhymes, such as "Richard Of York Gave Battle In Vain," often are even easier than learning the word ROYGBIV. There is something about tempo which we do not yet understand that further facilitates chunking abilities. Later in this paper you will learn the mnemonic PACIFICS. When you reach that section see if you can recall having read this. Designers of museum exhibits often present information about artifacts in a correct and factual manner, but fail to use mnemonic devices to maximize the chances of significant recall (i.e., what has been learned) in the brief time available to most visitors.

Most museums possess many more artifacts than are actually on display. The tendency to want to display as much as can be fitted into the space is high. I suspect that museum professionals may even judge the quality of a museum by the number of artifacts that are or can be exhibited. Consequently, many museums contain exhibits comprised of cases bulging with artifacts, which to the naive observer may appear very similar. Often these objects are displayed simply with name labels or dates attached, and the naive user is given no clues about what salient cues differentiate between, say, an Etruscan and a Greek urn. Not surprisingly, most museum visitors, who may start a visit by viewing exhibit cases with great intensity, quickly become either overloaded with apparently dissimilar artifacts, or underloaded (bored) with apparently similar artifacts, which they cannot fit into a meaningful conceptual framework. Overload and underload problems are exacerbated if there is time pressure, and for many visitors who begin with the best of intentions, museum behavior quickly degenerates into increasingly brief skirmishes with additional exhibit cases as they head for the cafe, shop, or exit. From a human factors perspective this response is a problem of information overload or underload coupled with a lack of appreciation in the information design of the varying levels of user sophistication.

To illustrate how these problems might be minimized, think about how we teach children. Early learning consists of presentations of a restricted range of concepts in simple ways. As the child progresses through the education system, the range of concepts is broadened and levels of sophistication increase. We would never expect to confront children at school with the range and complexity of information presented to students in universities, because their level of understanding would be insufficient and they would soon be overloaded. Unlike schools, however, museums seem to assume a shared level of reasonable competence among visitors, and all visitors are expected to follow a common route through exhibit space. In a children's museum, parents may gain little additional insight because the level of presentation may be too simple (an underload problem). In an adult museum, then children may gain few insights because information may be too complex (an overload problem). Yet I know of no museums that explicitly design exhibits to minimize overload or underload problems, (e.g., by using principles of chunking, mnemonics, and salient cues). Especially with the advent of new multimedia technologies, there are tremendous opportunities to think of ways of designing museum exhibits in which information is layered in increasing levels of complexity so that on a first encounter the naive user is not daunted and overloaded or underloaded, but on repeated visits as the user becomes increasingly sophisticated he or she can interact with increasingly complex levels of information.

Another way in which perception allows us to cope with the vast array of potential information inputs is via the processes of selective attention. Selective attention allows perception to function as an active rather than passive process. Neisser (1976) proposed an elegantly simple concept, the perceptual cycle, to describe how selective attention processes guide the acquisition of sensory information (see fig. 4). Neisser argued that the brain implements higher-level structures, called cognitive schemata (these will be further considered later), which prepare the senses for the reception of anticipated sensory information. For example, when we look at a book, we expect to start at the front and read through to the back page, and on each page of text written in English our expectation is that we should scan this text from left to right, top to bottom. This learned scanning pattern is reinforced every time we successfully read something. Interestingly, in other cultures this scanning pattern can be very different. Text in Hebrew or Arabic is read from right to left, top to bottom. In Japanese a book is read from the back page (according to English bookbinding conventions) progressing through to the front page, and characters written vertically on a page are read from top to bottom, right to left, whereas those written horizontally are read from top to bottom, left to right. These learned scanning patterns may transfer to the order in which people from different cultural backgrounds scan more complex visual information displays, such as looking from one object to the next

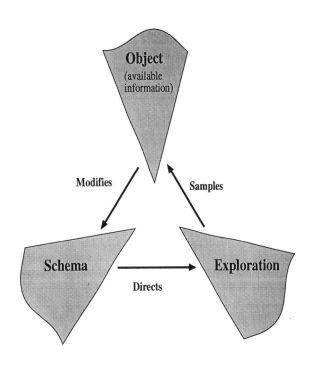

Object
(available
information)

Modifies   Samples

Schema ———→ **Exploration**

Directs

Figure 4. The perceptual cycle (Neisser 1976).

in a cased exhibit or trying to follow a theme where text is linked to describe a process that flows from left to right. Patterns of eye movement also vary depending on the observer's intentions at the time of viewing. As a recent study has shown, these patterns differ systematically among observers asked to estimate either the ages or wealth of individuals in the same scene (Coren, Ward, and Enns 1994). Learning to scan a scene by inspecting spatial locations in a systematic order is an eye movement skill acquired by the age of six or seven years, and the length of time we spend fixating on specific locations in the scene depends on their features, such as how unusual or how desirable they are. This finding means that in designing the layout of exhibits, designers need to consider the cultural and age mix of their visitors and try to match the layout to predicted patterns of visual search to facilitate information acquisition.

Researchers who evaluate museum exhibits use the concept of holding power (time the person stays at an exhibit divided by the minimum time it takes to read an exhibit) as a measure of the time on task, which may indirectly measure the amount of learning (Donald 1991). By itself, this measure can be very misleading, because even a brief glance at a well-designed and familiar exhibit may be sufficient to reinforce learning, whereas a person may ponder a

complex exhibit for much longer without ever figuring out its information content and therefore learning little of use. In addition, the degree to which the visitor can interact with the exhibit affects holding power. In a study of a science museum, mineral and fossil exhibits were viewed on average for forty seconds, puzzle tablets for almost five minutes, and computer terminals were used for an average of sixteen minutes (Linn 1976).

Other expectancy effects that influence the success of the perceptual cycle include expectations about language structure, redundancy and context. We expect words to appear in certain orders to make phrases, and phrases to appear in certain orders to make sentences, changes in this order make comprehension difficult. Language structure can be used to estimate the perceptual demands of a display. The difficulty of perception, and therefore learning, can be gauged by the amount of verbal description required to specify an object or process unambiguously for the level of understanding that is required (Welford 1984). Related to language structure is the way in which the information is visually presented to visitors, which has been studied by research work on the legibility of printed text. This work has embraced a number of interrelated issues, and detailed human factors guidelines for character size, font, weight, italics, uppercase versus lowercase, interletter spacing, interline spacing, and line length are available (Reynolds 1984; Sanders and McCormic, 1993).

Redundancy refers to the fact that only about 20 percent of written language is actually required for us to extract meaning (i.e., the essence of a conversation or a good book), but the rest of the text provides additional contextual cues that help to shape and reinforce the correct interpretation of the linguistic message. Without appropriate contextual cues language can be ambiguous. For example, interpretation of the sentence, "They are eating apples," depends on whether the speaker is describing what people are doing or which objects are being viewed. Redundancy should be built into the often terse descriptive prose used in exhibit design to reinforce the contextual interpretation. Where language differences between visitors may create barriers to learning, recognized graphics, such as symbols and pictograms, often can be used to overcome these barriers.

Contextual cues allow us to anticipate the outcome of the experience, and perhaps even imagine and mentally rehearse this outcome prior to actual information input. If the page of text we are presented with is the last page of a gripping murder "whodunit" we have been reading, we expect the identity of the murderer to be revealed, and we may read this page with great fervor, whereas if the page we are presented with is the first page of a book we have been told is tedious, we will approach it with reluctance.

Advertisers use anticipatory information to hype the release of many kinds of products and experiences, such as movies. In the same vein museum visitors can be primed to anticipate certain experiences prior to entering different parts of a museum or a traveling exhibition. This type of anticipatory publicity sometimes accompanies the arrival of a special exhibition at a museum, but it seldom seems to be used to structure visitor expectations as they pass from gallery to gallery or exhibit to exhibit. This type of priming is, however, used to great success by some entertainment organizations. The Disney company employs priming techniques at Epcot and Disneyland to create appropriate expectations while people are waiting in line to enter exhibits. Future research might profitably explore the benefits to learning of developing methods of museum foreplay, which could shape anticipations of perceptual information.

From this brief overview of basic perceptual requirements, an obvious prerequisite of any museum experience is that the information to be learned must be displayed in a way that is accessible to the learner. Yet in spite of the obviousness of this requirement, it is surprising how frequently the environment is designed in ways that do not facilitate information acquisition.

Museums as Places of Optimal Experience and Change

So far we have considered some of the basic pitfalls in the ways in which information presentation can inhibit learning. Considerable psychological research points to the fact that learning occurs more easily when one is interested and motivated to acquire information. This motivation depends on either extrinsic contingencies, such as the need to acquire and retain information to pass an examination, or intrinsic contingencies, such as the joy of learning for the sake of satisfying one's curiosity, or both. For most visitors, museums are informal places without structured lessons and examinations, and therefore to a great degree learning occurs because of the level of intrinsic motivation to acquire and retain information. Part of this intrinsic motivation derives from the total experience that is felt when information actually reframes and restructures our cognitive schemata. Exclamations such as "eureka," "now I get it," "then the penny dropped," "I didn t see it before but now I do," "it was like a veil being lifted from my eyes," and "suddenly I could see everything in a different light," all describe the outcome of the reframing of cognitive schemata. Such experiences invariably are pleasant, and sometimes they are exhilarating. In fact, reaching a new level of understanding about the world represents an optimal experience. Csikszentmihalyi (1990, p. 3) describes optimal experience as follows: The best

moments usually occur when a person's body or mind is stretched to its limit in a voluntary effort to accomplish something difficult and worthwhile. Optimal experience is thus something that we make happen. People who frequently have had such experiences know how self-reinforcing these are, creating an internal excitement, a buzz without resorting to any external psychoactive agents. Optimal experiences are both enjoyable and memorable, and therefore they represent a situation of peak awareness and learning, a feeling of inner order in consciousness. Csikszentmihalyi invokes the concept of flow to denote situations in which there is a confluence of mental and/or physical processes that produce optimal experiences, such as joy, creativity, and a total involvement in life. Optimal experiences do, of course, differ from one person to another, but studies of hundreds of people of different ages, with different backgrounds, from different cultures, have revealed that the basic requirements remain invariant. Fortunately, settings can be designed to create situations in which these basic requirements of flow are provided, thereby maximizing the likelihood of people achieving their own unique optimal experiences.

PACIFICS
Csikszentmihalyi lists eight fundamental requirements for enjoyable optimal experiences. These requirements do not proceed in a strict sequence, and I have reorganized Csikszentmihalyi's list and renamed some of his stages (original names given in parentheses in the titles) into the acronym PACIFICS (do you recall having already read this acronym?). PACIFICS refers to the following requirements for any situation: purpose, attention, challenge, involvement, feedback, immersion, control, and sense of time. Each of these requirements for creating an optimal experience is described below:

Purpose (Goal-oriented)
The activity in which a person is engaged must have some meaning to him or her. The goal or goals of the activity must be clearly articulated at the outset. When we do not know why we are doing something, we are less likely to do a good job and use our full capabilities. In a museum, it is not uncommon to hear a child ask a parent questions such as, Why are we looking at this? What does this do? How does this work? and often receiving curt replies from parents who also may be mystified but unwilling to admit it. Designers should repeatedly ask themselves, What do I expect the visitor to do when he is here in the museum? What do I expect the visitor to do when she interacts with this hands-on exhibit? Without purpose, without clear, unambiguous goals, ultimately we lose all motivation and are unable to learn anything effectively.

Attention (Concentration)

The ability to concentrate on the task at hand is a fundamental requirement for learning. When we are distracted or under stress we are less able to retain information in memory and less able to formulate strategies that allow us to plan ahead. Museums, when crowded, can be highly distracting places because of high ambient noise levels, large numbers of people, frequent confusing movements, and the sheer enormity of the number of artifacts being exhibited. If the visitors are in a family, the environmental stressors of the museum are amplified by parental concerns over the location and behavior of children. In such situations museums will be experienced by visitors as stressful settings, and enjoyment and learning will be minimal.

Exhibit designers need to consider such worst-case scenarios in their design. If an exhibit is too complex (i.e., demands too much attention) for the prevailing conditions, then it will most likely be ignored. Conversely, if it is too simple, it may not have sufficient attention holding power for effective learning. The complexity of an exhibit should be related to where the exhibit is placed in the layout of the museum relative to anticipated visitor routes. For example, less complex exhibits should be more centrally located in galleries, and more complex exhibits should be located in more peripheral settings, such as quieter corners or side galleries. Alternatively, if there is a need to place a complex exhibit in a more central location where there will be a high traffic volume, the detailed design of the exhibit should be reviewed, and, if possible, ways of simplifying exhibit information should be implemented.

Challenge

Once a person realizes the purpose of a task and is prepared to devote attention to performing it, he or she must have the necessary skills required to enable them to complete the task. Once people believe that they have little if any chance of successfully completing the task, they will quickly abandon this and will only learn failure. Witness the rapid abandonment of the infamous Rubik's cube by all but the most persistent of children.

Incongruences between user abilities and task demands are common in many museums. In natural history museums the correct labeling of exhibits with lengthy Latin names is appropriate if the visitors are zoologists but distinctly offputting to those barely able to pronounce or read these labels. Similarly, visitors will quickly move on when faced with a poorly labeled exhibit containing no functional information and a child's request, What does this do? Thus in the design of exhibits, whether passive or interactive, particular attention needs to be paid to the degree of challenge posed. Exhibits should not be designed sim-

ply to meet the capabilities of the least-able visitor. Perhaps they should be organized or layered so that they reveal progressively more complex information and difficult challenges as the visitor's skills improve, much like a modern video game has numerous levels of challenge as the player's skill improves. With a fixed exhibit, such as a cased display, applying this principle may mean presenting the simplest information and challenges at the lowest-height level so that these can be tackled by children, while the more complex challenges are placed at a higher level so that these can be tackled by adults. Another way of varying challenges may be to create zones of increasing complexity within a museum space organized in such a way that visitors can move to more complex zones only upon completion of some challenge. Varying the challenges appropriately will not only increase motivation and learning but will also encourage visitors to revisit a museum. Conversely, once something can easily be mastered, it usually ceases to be motivating.

Involvement (Engrossing)

Successful tasks are those that are sufficiently involving for visitors to lose awareness of their everyday worries and frustrations. This quality characterizes successful movies, in which viewers become so engrossed in the story that they forget about daily problems.

The more involved a person has to be in a museum exhibit, the greater his or her motivation and memories of the experience. In traditional museums, where exibits are predominantly passive, engagement is difficult to achieve because the visitor must navigate through the place, and consciously has to divide his or her attention between navigation demands and reading or listening about the exhibits. In entertainment museums, such as many of the exhibits at Epcot, direct involvement with exhibit items is passive, but overall involvement with the exhibit is greater because people are moved through the exhibit and can concentrate on the narrative. It may be possible to create similar situations in linear galleries by providing moving walkways, or perhaps people can be stationery while the exhibits move past them. Simpler forms of involvement in traditional museums include tactics such as giving visitors treasure-hunt-type questionnaires to complete. Anything that increases involvement will increase opportunities for learning.

Feedback

Lack of feedback or inappropriate feedback are demotivating conditions. A person faced with an interactive exhibit must receive immediate and appropriate feedback on his or her performance, either in terms of a score, or in terms of skill level or spatial position relative to the task goal. A wide variety of forms of feedback can be used. For example, if the visitor has been given a treasure-hunt-type questionnaire, there should be some way of having the accuracy of the answers checked and of receiving a reward, however small, for successful completion of the challenge. Visitors could be given treasure-hunt-type challenge cards designed to be read optically by hand-fed readers or easily checked by staff. Small but memorable items could be dispensed for successful completion of the challenge. The experience of winning something for effort expended in this way is highly motivating.

Immersion

Total immersion in the task at hand is commonly reported by those questioned about optimal experiences. Total immersion represents more than full involvement. Involvement refers to the mental resources required to complete the task, immersion refers to the experience of involvement to a level at which the person becomes oblivious to external events and may even become so completely absorbed as to lose consciousness of self. Techniques for encouraging feelings of immersion include lowering lighting levels and passively transporting people through the exhibition space. The success with which the challenge of a task matches the level of involvement also improves feelings of immersion, which in turn improve enjoyment and facilitate learning. Again, the Walt Disney company is skillful at creating exhibits in which visitors become totally immersed as they are transported through darkened spaces while spot-lights or luminous objects direct attention to relevant items.

Control

Learning is facilitated when people feel that they have some degree of control over the flow of information. In a traditional museum control is exercised by the choice of exhibits visited. In a passive ride through an exhibit a sense of control can be given by offering people choices. In active exhibits a sense of control can be given by allowing users to select among alternative scenarios. An example of this approach is illustrated at the end of one of the exhibits in Epcot in which the visitor is given a choice from a small number of alternatives (e.g., underwater, land, space, desert) of the final scenes of the planet earth to view as the ride is about to finish. The fact that different alternatives are offered also encourages people to revisit the exhibit to make different choices. Leading edge interactive TV programs allow users to select from alternative endings. New multimedia technologies can facilitate a visitor's ability to control the nature, pace, and outcome of information being presented.

Sense of Time (Duration)

When people are immersed in a challenging task their perception of time is altered. It may be accelerated, so that minutes may seem like seconds, hours like minutes, and so on. When the task is not challenging, the reverse may happen, and time passage will appear to be decelerated, with seconds seeming like minutes, and minutes like hours. Relating a visitor's estimate of the time spent involved with an exhibit to the actual chronological time may be a much better measure of the degree of interest, challenge, and involvement provided by an exhibit than a measure such as holding power.

Variety

Exhibits or museum settings that score high on each of the PACIFICS dimensions should prove enjoyable and memorable and therefore facilitate learning; they should more frequently evoke optimum experience feelings. However, even the most highly rated situational experiences will lose their appeal when they repeatedly occur in the same predictable way. Consequently, museums need to consider ways of facilitating feelings of change with time by creating different opportunities for visitors. In a traditional museum the layout generally remains fairly fixed, and variations can only occur in the nature of the exhibits or by visitors' changing their routes through the museums. In other types of museums there may be greater opportunities for modifying the layout of the spaces to change the experiences of exhibits upon repeat visits by the same people. However, I do not know of any museums, other than park museums, that advise visitors to vary their routes through the space. Parks usually have trails that differ in terms of their length, difficulty, types of scenery, and so on. Many museum visitors attempt to do this type of variation themselves by selectively choosing to view only particular exhibits if they have the opportunity to return over several days. Museums could, however, offer visitors a variety of suggested routes through their exhibits depending on the nature of the visitor (adult, child, first-time visitor, repeat visitor, naive visitor, professional visitor), the visitor's interests, and time available for the visit. Customized route planning, such as that sometimes used in major exhibitions, could be provided with a computerized system. This type of system could also help museums to keep track of the exhibit preferences and interests of their visitors, and allow them to profile types of visitors. Where possible, museums could also use mobile exhibits and vary the internal layout so that repeat visitors probably would not receive precisely the same experience on consecutive visits.

Experiential learning: the essence of the museum experience

Thus far this paper has examined some of the human factors aspects of exhibit design. Museum learning is not, however, a simple consequence of the experience of exhibits. Exhibits may be designed based on their attracting power, but when the visitor is surrounded by multiple exhibits he or she can become overloaded (Falk and Dierking 1992). In many instances, visitors are drawn to exhibits that they find intrinsically interesting or visually compelling, and most will spend less than one minute reading exhibit labels. Given this situation, it is unreasonable to expect museum learning to occur as a form of rote learning of information, and it is inappropriate to measure this reading as the acquisition of content information. Museum learning consists of much more than simply the recall of information about artifacts, and the museum experience perhaps is best conceptualized as a gestalt , that is greater than the sum of the individual exhibit experiences. For many, visiting a museum may be motivated primarily by a desire for an enjoyable experience in a setting associated with learning, not a desire to acquire specific information. Learning is a continuous process of information flow through the brain, and, to the extent that any part of experience is recalled, it has been learned. In any learning situation some specific elements will be retained for later recall (e.g. the names of famous people presented in an exhibit), while others will be lost (e.g., perhaps the birth and death dates of these same people); yet overall, all of the elements, both remembered and forgotten, will have contributed to the recall of the experience, (as worthwhile and enjoyable, or worthless and boring). It is this overall recall of the situation that will shape behavioral intentions. If, for example, a museum visit is remembered as being enjoyable, then it is likely to occur again.

Several important considerations follow from this view of museum learning. First, conceptualizing the museum experience merely as what has been learned in conventional terms, as the acquisition of information, may be less important than focusing on what has been forgotten. Riccio, Rabinowitz and Axelrod (1994) have argued that forgetting, which involves the loss of memory for specific stimulus attributes, is actually a positive process that serves to encourage future behaviors rather than discourage them. Thus, the reason we may read a book more than once or watch a movie more than once is that we will have recalled enjoying the experience but will have forgotten the details. Even when exhibits have not been changed, museum visitors may undertake repeat visits to a museum for precisely the same reasons—that is, they may have enjoyed the overall experience of being in an environment that they associate with

learning but may have forgotten most of the detailed information about specific exhibits. From this assumption it follows that if one could design a museum which facilitated perfect learning—by which I mean perfect recall of information—it would actually discourage rather than encourage repeat visits. The experience of directly visiting a museum is the most important aspect of all museum learning. Even though museum contents can be indirectly experienced through books and television, and with modern technologies, such as CD-ROM, people still visit museums. Fazio, Zanna, and Cooper (1978) have shown that attitudes formed through direct behavioral experience are a better predictor of later behaviors than attitudes formed through indirect experience. They attributed this effect to a crucial difference in information processing between direct and indirect experience. With indirect experience, which always involves some medium, such as a book, both the medium and the description of the behavior are salient, whereas with direct experience it is the behavior itself that is salient to the person. The example of the behavioral difference between a child listening to a friend describing a toy and the child actually playing with the toy illustrates this difference. In an experimental test, Fazio, Zanna, and Cooper (1978) were able to show that direct experience had a more salient effect on attitudes, even though the recall of information was comparable between direct and indirect experience groups.

Other studies have confirmed the importance of direct experience. Kilduff and Regan (1988) investigated the differential effects of informational cues on the choice of work tasks, and found that direct experience has a greater effect on behavioral choices than does indirect experience through information provided by others. Sherman et al. (1982) found a similar powerful effect of direct experience on smoking intentions in adolescents. Salomon and Koppelman (1992) compared the differences between "teleshopping" (i.e. shopping via TV) and actually going shopping. They concluded that direct experience is the reason that many people still prefer to go shopping. The activity of shopping, especially nondirected shopping, shows many similarities with browsing and grazing behaviors seen in other species; it is motivating in itself. The same kind of browsing activity can be observed in museums. Salomon and Koppelman (1992) point out that shopping is a major recreational activity for many people, and the motivation for shopping as a recreational behavior probably stems from the ways in which the store and shopping mall environment provides shoppers with multisensory stimulation, which in turn supplies psychological gratification. These aspects of shopping are available only through direct experience. A museum can be viewed as a shopping mall, in which the exhibits are the equivalent of the individual stores that either grab and hold the person's attention or not. The experience of a shopping mall, however, is greater than that of any single store, and in the same way the experience of a museum is greater than that of any single exhibit.

Conclusions

This paper has presented an overview of some of the important considerations about the presentation of information as relevant to the design of museum exhibits. It also attempts to provide a succinct, yet provocative, account of some of the opportunities that may exist for applying a human factors analysis to improve the museum experience. Emphasis has been placed on the importance of creating appropriate environmental stimulus conditions to allow information to be acquired by the senses and analyzed by our perceptual and cognitive processes so that learning can occur. It has also been argued that motivation to learn information about exhibits and to optimize the museum experience follows from the success with which designs fulfill the PACIFICS requirements for flow.

It has also been suggested that the measurement of museum learning, using conventional approaches to the assessment of information recall, is an insufficient metric. Instead, it is proposed that the museum experience should be conceptualized and analyzed as a gestalt, a holistic experience. Investigating this holistic experience will necessitate a multimethods research approach capable of assessing affective dimensions, such as pleasure and enjoyment, as well as cognitive dimensions, such as information clarity and subsequent recall.

It is proposed that the social value of museums lies in their being places that provide people with a unique opportunity to experience artifacts directly in situations that would otherwise be unavailable to them. Indirect experience of artifacts—through books, television, video, CD-ROM—may prove to be an adequate substitute for the acquisition of information about these artifacts (i.e., the cognitive aspect of the museum experience), but indirect experiences cannot substitute for the additonal affective and behavioral benefits of direct experience. Direct experience is the fundamental reason why museums are visited and the foundation of their value to society.

References

Coren, S., L. M. Ward and J. T. Enns 1994. *Sensation and perception.* 4th Ed. Fort Worth, Tex.: Harcourt, Brace.

Csikszentmihalyi, M. 1990. *Flow: The psychology of optimal experience.* New York: Harper Collins.

Dodds, K. S. 1992. Toward a typology of museums: A multivariate analysis of museum functions and roles. *Dissertation Abstracts International* 53, no. 5: 1336A.

Donald, J. G. 1991. The measurement of learning in the museum. *Canadian Journal of Education* 16, no. 3: 371-82.

Falk, J. H. and L. D. Dierking. 1992. *The museum experience.* Washington, D.C.: Whalesback Books.

Fazio, R. H., M. P. Zanna and J. Cooper. 1978. Direct experience and attitude-behavior consistency: An information processing analysis. *Personality and Social Psychology Bulletin* 4, no. 1: 48-51.

Fransella, F. and D. Bannister. 1977. *A manual for repertory grid technique.* New York: Academic Press.

Kilduff, M., and D. T. Regan. 1988. What people say and what they do: The differential effects of informational cues and task design. *Organizational Behavior and Human Decision Processes* 41: 83-97.

Linn, M. 1976. Exhibit evaluation: Informed decision making. *Curator* 19: 291-302.

Lusted, L. B. 1968. *Introduction to medical decision making.* Springfield, Ill.: Thomas.

McNicol, D. 1984. The use of signal detection theory in the evaluation of information displays. In *Information design,* ed. R. Easterby, R. and H. Zwaga. Chap. 5, pp. 91-126. New York: John Wiley & Sons.

Miller, G. 1956. The magical number seven, plus or minus two: Some limits on our capacity for processing information. *Psychological Review* 63: 81-97.

Neisser, U. 1976. *Cognition and reality: Principles and implications of cognitive psychology.* San Franscisco, Calif.: W. H. Freeman.

Reynolds, L. 1984. The legibility of printed scientific and technical information. *Information design,* ed. R. Easterby and H. Zwaga, pp. 187-208. New York: Wiley.

Riccio, D.C., V. C. Rabinowitz, and S. Axelrod. 1994. Memory: When less is more. *American Psychologist* 49, no. 11: 917-26.

Salomon, I. and F. S. Koppelman. 1992. Teleshopping or going shopping? An information acquisition perspective. *Behavior and Information Technology* 11, no. 4: 189-198.

Sanders, M. S. and E. J. McCormick. 1993. Human factors in engineering and design. 7th ed. New York: McGraw-Hill.

Sherman, S. J., C. C. Presson, L. Chassin, M. Bensenberg, E. Corty, and R. W. Olshavsky. 1982. Smoking intentions in adolescents: direct experience and predictability. *Personality and Social Psychology Bulletin* 8, no. 2: 376-83.

Welford, A. T. 1984. Theory and application in visual displays. In *Information design,* ed. R. Easterby, and H. Zwaga. pp. 3-18. New York: Wiley.

Learning and the Physical Environment

Gary W. Evans
Cornell University

Although we take it for granted that the physical characteristics of settings can directly influence learning, there is remarkably little research on this topic. Moreover, what research does exist is devoted almost exclusively to the study of young children's environments, principally school and daycare settings. I draw on this literature wherever possible, but most of this paper builds a conceptual framework for thinking about how the physical environment could influence learning. I argue that there is evidence for linkages between physical setting characteristics and underlying psychological processes that directly affect learning. These processes include cognitive fatigue, distraction, motivation, emotional affect, anxiety, and communication. Many effects of the physical environment on learning occur indirectly, via these underlying, intervening psychological processes.

Cognitive Fatigue

Cognitive fatigue occurs whenever a person uses mental effort to sustain attention. Analyzing complex and difficult materials, writing about serious subjects, concentrating on ambiguous or complex signals, and puzzling through difficulties in wayfinding are examples of mental activities that can engender cognitive fatigue (Kaplan and Kaplan 1982, 1989). When cognitive fatigue occurs, it becomes extremely difficult to learn. One cannot pay attention, indeed, one typically is not motivated to engage in any higher order mental process. Under such conditions an individual is easily distracted and often irritable (Kaplan, Bardwell, and Slakter 1993). Although cognitive fatigue may co-occur with physical tiring or exhaustion, it is a distinct process brought about by sustained cognitive activities characterized by the expenditure of voluntary effort or directed attention.

The physical environment can influence cognitive fatigue in at least two direct ways. Setting characteristics can heighten cognitive fatigue when they are illegible or difficult to comprehend, to read, and to understand (Lynch 1960). Efforts to find one's way in an incoherent space or to make sense out of ambiguous or misleading cues about the meaning and/or function of objects contribute to cognitive fatigue.

Several physical features are known to support good orientation and wayfinding and thus contribute to enhanced legibility. These include interior settings that conform to relatively simple, overall geometric patterns; those that have well marked and bounded distinctive subsections or districts; interiors with views of the surrounding, external environment; and spaces with interior grid patterns (i.e., parallel interior hallways and 90 degree intersections) that indicate both direction of movement and extent of progress as the path is traversed, all contribute to enhanced legibility (Evans 1980; Garling, Book, and Lindberg 1989). Good signage and navigational aids such as maps may facilitate wayfinding, but they are limited in their ability to compensate for disorienting buildings (Talbot et al. 1993; Passini 1984).

Misaffordances or ambiguous affordances may also cause cognitive fatigue. Doors that we cannot determine how to open, controls that we cannot figure out, instructions that cannot be deciphered, the operation of devices that cannot be fathomed, or in extreme cases, objects whose very functions are indeterminant can all lead to cognitive fatigue (Norman 1989). Additional discussion of the role of cognitive ergonomics in learning can be found by Hedge in this volume. Other physical sources of ill affordance include conflicting perceptual cues (e.g., conflicting depth cues); sudden changes in light, color, or visual access as one moves across a sharp contour or edge; or requirements that one adopt a nonegocentric perspective when reading directional signage.

The other major way in which physical components of settings can contribute to cognitive fatigue is by providing restorative elements that help offset cognitive fatigue. The restoration of directed attention may be facilitated by the exercise of involuntary attention or fascination. Elements that elicit attention without effort (e.g., running water, plant life, artwork, animals in a healthy habitat) that elicit attention without effort are critical features of restorative environments (Kaplan and Kaplan 1989; Kaplan, Bardwell, and Slakter 1993). This description of environmental elements supportive of fascination or involuntary attention is similar to Csikszentmihalyi and Hermanson discussion in this volume of contextual characteristics that capture attention. They note the potential for stimuli that are novel, complex, surprising, or ambiguous to capture human curiosity.

Environments that extend in space and time, that envelope the individual, particularly when such spaces are compatible with current needs, are also likely to provide restoration (Kaplan 1983). For some people this setting might be a wilderness backpacking trek; for others it could be a visit to a living history exhibit. Some individuals can lose themselves in an engaging novel, play, or film. For still others, a drive along a country road is restorative. Finally, novel environments that provide a break from routines, that allow us to get away from some of the types of cognitive demands that induced cognitive fatigue in the first place, can be restorative.

Distraction

Environmental qualities that divert attention or make it difficult to focus can impede learning. Considerable evidence shows that both noise and crowding can serve as potent distractors, interfering with learning, especially on complex tasks (Evans and Cohen 1987). Task complexity is a function of the information rate of stimuli to be processed. Information rate is altered by the number of signal cues present, the certainty (probability) of cue occurrence, and the speed of signal cues to be processed. The rehearsal and encoding of materials in working memory also appear to be disrupted by noise. Noise stimuli that are unpredictable and crowding with strangers appear to be particularly potent distractors. Access to a stimulus shelter, where one can escape at least temporarily from crowded or noisy residential conditions, appears to buffer some of the harmful effects of these environmental conditions on children (Wachs and Gruen 1982).

Architectural complexity can also create distraction. Bright light and colors at the red end of the spectrum along with highly novel or unusual room decorations can heighten distractibility (Berlyne 1971; Kuller 1991). Certain floor plans can also influence distractibility. Open plan settings, with a minimum of partitioned space and barriers, create the potential for extremely high visual exposure. Visual exposure is the extent to which one can be seen from different vantage points in a space (Archea 1977). There is evidence both from children in open plan schools (Weinstein 1979) and from adults in residential spaces (Archea 1977) that high visual exposure causes distraction. Open plan schools are also associated with

higher levels of interruption and off-task behavior, particularly when they have few interior partitions (Gump 1987). Furthermore, modifications of open plan learning environments that provide better defined activity pockets or privacy nooks help prevent some of the distracting effects of these spaces on learning (Moore 1987; Weinstein 1977).

One's position in relation to circulation pathway systems is relevant here. Movement proximate to a person trying to concentrate is typically extremely distracting. Better shielding through barriers or relocation away from circulation patterns helps reduce this type of distraction. There is also some evidence indicating that the greater the width and extent of pathways, the greater the speed of movement through them, and presumably the higher the noise levels (Prescott 1987).

The distracting effects of stressors like noise, from arousing perceptual cues like bright light or certain colors, and from architectural features such as open plan designs with high visual exposure, describe the immediate or acute distraction potential of design elements. The long-term effects of living, working, or learning in highly distracting environments are not well understood. There is evidence that both adults and children adopt various cognitive strategies to tune out information overload when chronically exposed to high levels of perceptual stimulation (Cohen et al. 1986; Milgram 1970). One of the side effects of the adoption of such cognitive coping strategies may be overgeneralization of these strategies such that they are employed indiscriminately, even in situations where they are no longer adaptive. For example, children attending schools in noisy areas show several deficits in auditory processes related to speech perception (e.g., ability to discriminate similar phonemes) that appear to be caused by the overgeneralization of the tuning out strategies they utilize in their noisy schools (Cohen et al. 1986).

Motivation

Motivation is a central psychological process in learning. Three concepts linking the physical environment to motivation and learning are control, responsiveness, and predictability. Children and adults like to act on and manipulate their surroundings. When instrumental control over the environment becomes difficult or impossible, especially over long periods of time, motivational deficiencies may occur. For example both laboratory and fieldwork indicate that exposures to adverse, environmental conditions that are uncontrollable lead to reduced tolerance for frustration and less persistence on difficult, challenging tasks (Cohen 1980; Evans and Cohen 1987). Uncontrollable environmental stressors such as noise, crowding, temperature, and indoor air quality have all been shown to produce these effects. Experimental manipulations of the controllability of environmental stressors indicate that perceived control over the stressor is a critical component of these effects (Evans and Cohen 1987; Glass and Singer 1972).

Ergonomic factors can also play an important role in control. Scale, access and mobility, strength, and perceptual clarity are all salient features that may affect control. For example, there is evidence that in learning environments that child-scaled furniture, storage, and controls (e.g., light switches, water fountains) that are child-scaled are associated with greater independence and exploratory behavior (Weinstein 1987). Barriers to accessibility for the disabled or the frail may induce or accentuate feelings of helplessness.

Opportunities to explore the physical environment are an important element in the development of competency. Environmental barriers or social regulations that restrict movement can adversely affect learning, particularly in young children. For example, restrictions on exploratory behavior in infants are associated with delayed cognitive development (Wachs and Gruen 1982). Self-directed exploration is a critical component of spatial learning in young children and the extent of home range permitted is associated with the quality of adolescents' cognitive maps of their neighborhood (Evans 1980).

More indirectly, exploration can affect motivation because it is a component of effective interaction with the environment. Exploration allows young organisms to engage in a gradient of environmental challenges and experiences, thus learning how to self-regulate environmental exposure. Learning how to avoid or minimize exposure to noxious environmental conditions is a critical element in the development of a sense of personal self-efficacy (Seligman 1975).

Architectural elements can affect one's ability to function instrumentally in spaces. Doors and walls that are effective in shielding stimulation, semipublic spaces that are socially legible so one has a sense of who belongs, visual surveillance capabilities and regulation over ingress to private and community spaces all facilitate a sense of control (Sherrod and Cohen 1979; Newman 1972).

The size of an organization can also influence motivation vis-a-vis control related processes. Participants in larger organizations are much more likely to feel they are unimportant and cannot influence the direction or operation of the organization (Barker 1968; Wicker 1987). Children in larger daycare centers explore less, engage in less child-initiated activity, and suffer greater teacher control (Prescott 1987).

Interventions that alter the size of an organization one affiliates with, for example, by creating subunits within a previously large, single organization, facilitate a greater sense of belonging, participation, and identification with the organization (Wicker 1987). Some of these interventions can be architectural. Baum and his colleagues found that by dividing long corridor dormitories into two distinct wings, residents felt like they could control social interactions more effectively, perceived their dormitory as less crowded, and developed a more positive social climate in the dormitory (Baum et al. 1981).

Privacy, the ability to regulate social interaction (Altman 1975), is another component of control strongly influenced by architecture. Visual access describes one's ability to monitor a space visually. High visual access and low visual exposure, as well as the ability to establish, maintain, and mark a territory all contribute to privacy. So do low density living or working conditions. Privacy is also supported by a spatial hierarchy wherein spaces that support social interactions across a spectrum from solitude to large groups are present. Floor plans can also influence privacy. The degree of permeability between different rooms as well as the depth of a structure are physical features that may affect privacy (Hillier and Hanson 1984). Depth is defined as the number of spaces one must pass through in a structure to get from one room to another. Greater depth and lower permeability tend to be associated with ease of regulating social interaction.

Note that this conceptualization of privacy does not emphasize being alone or solitude. Rather, privacy is tied to the ability to regulate social interaction. Inadequate privacy is defined as the relationship between desired social interaction and achieved social interaction. Insufficient space can be determined, according to this model, in terms of the relationship between how much social interaction one desires and the amount of physical space available to accommodate that interaction (Altman 1975). Thus loneliness is a condition of inadequate privacy just as crowding is. It is worth noting briefly that although there are undoubtedly cultural differences in boundary maintenance mechanisms for regulating social interaction, anthropological research indicates that all cultural groups apparently have devised various mechanisms to regulate social interaction, particularly in the home.

A second set of environmental features related to control are responsive elements. Responsive elements can be manipulated and provide differential feedback. As one's actions on the environment change, the nature of the environmental response changes systematically. Moreover, the feedback that one receives about one's actions on the environment is relatively fast and clearcut. Competence, the ability to interact effectively with one's surroundings, is strongly determined by responsive environmental components, particularly during early human development (Wachs and Gruen 1982). The value of responsive design elements in toy design (Chase 1992) and in play settings (Weinstein 1987) has been emphasized in supporting healthy human development. Many different strands of research point toward strong human motivations to interact with environments that are responsive (White 1959).

A final environmental characteristic tied to motivation is predictability. Human beings are problem solvers; they like to be challenged by the environment. People like to make meaningful predictions, preferring situations in which prediction is possible but not trivial (Kaplan and Kaplan 1982). Roschelle in this volume describes how design can provide scaffolding to enable individuals to participate in more complex actions than they would could otherwise handle on their own. Design needs to provide moderate challenges, striking a balance between demands and personal abilities.

Moderate amounts of coherence, of underlying structure and regularity, enable people to make meaningful predictions. Coherence provides the necessary cognitive platform for estimating, testing, and subsequent revising predictions vis-a- vis environmental exploration. Structure also affords children opportunities to understand temporal and spatial continuities in sequential events that become the basis for comprehending abstractions such as cause and effect (Heft 1985).

Too much structure and regularity, however, render prediction trivial, and when problem-solving capabilities are not challenged, individuals become bored. Environmental complexity, the amount of information present as well as mystery, the promise of further information if one were to continue exploring a setting, are two key elements that can increase challenge by making environments interesting (Kaplan and Kaplan 1982). The tension between coherence or meaning on the one hand and complexity and mystery or interest on the other is related to intrinsic learning. Intrinsically motivated learning is supported by situations that are open and involve the opportunity to discover new things (Csikszentmihalyi and Hermanson in this volume). At the same time the individual must have sufficient environmental structure and personal ability to take advantage of the learning opportunities offered by the environment. A balance between underlying structure that provides coherence and legibility and elements that heighten interest, like complexity and mystery, is likely to motivate active problem solving in human beings.

Emotional Affect

The critical role of emotional affect in cognition provides a potentially powerful bridge between physical characteristics of settings and learning. Elevated negative affect can deter learning. Several features of the physical environment have been closely tied to negative affect. Windowless classrooms and offices are consistently rated negatively, although attempts to link this feature to productivity or learning have been unsuccessful (Ahrentzen et al. 1982; Sundstrom 1986). Some recent work, however, indicates an important role for natural lighting in the maintenance of hormonal balances in elementary school children (Kuller and Lindsten 1992).

Rooms that are ugly lead to increased negative affect. Messiness, drab colors, poor lighting, and little or no decoration are aspects of settings that contribute to perceived ugliness (Maslow and Mintz 1956). Institutional qualities are often associated with negative affect. Homogeneous surroundings, an absence of natural elements, large spaces with high ceilings and long hallways, the absence of chromatic colors, highly symmetrical spatial configurations and furniture treatments with a predominance of metal and plastic are specific qualities that invoke feelings of institutional space (Rivlin and Wolfe 1985). Some of the physical features discussed also contribute to negative affect. Not surprisingly members of smaller organizational structures are happier in comparison to members of larger units. This finding has been demonstrated in schools, churches, businesses, and other organizations (Wicker 1987). Poorly marked boundaries of behavioral settings as well as edges that do not align properly with the functional boundaries of specific activity spaces are major sources of conflict and dissatisfaction in organizations (Bechtel 1977). High levels of cognitive fatigue have been associated with negative affect, as have highly distracting situations, particularly when they occur in the context of learning tasks that demand concentration. People also report more comfort and relaxation in smaller, well- differentiated spaces where they are less visually exposed in comparison to large, open spaces (Holahan 1978). The frustration and confusion accompanying incoherent spaces and design elements with ambiguous affordances may also contribute to negative affect. Many behavior settings have prescriptive programs indicating desired and undesired behaviors. When prescriptive information about a behavior setting is unclear, people may react quite negatively (Wicker 1987).

Environmental stressors such as noise, crowding and congestion, and hot temperatures produce irritability and even hostility under specific circumstances (Evans and Cohen 1987). There is also evidence that poor indoor air quality, poor ventilation, and poor temperature conditions are associated with low job satisfaction and negative ratings of office environments (Hedge 1991).

The beneficial effects of positive affect on learning have been discussed by Isen and her colleagues (Isen, Daubman and Gorgoglione 1987). Positive affect may be invoked by homey elements that incorporate natural elements, personal memorabilia and objects, nonsymmetrical furniture arrangements, diminutive and embracing spaces (McCraken 1989). Limited evidence also suggests that learning settings that are comfortable and more informal are rated more favorably by students and, of particular interest, appear to support more student-initiated discussion (Sommer and Olsen 1980). The potent role of lighting, particularly natural light, to induce positive mood is well known as well (Kuller 1991).

Anxiety

When people are anxious or worried, particularly about important matters, learning is difficult. Thus environmental features that engender anxiety may interfere with learning. Disorientation or feeling lost is a good example of a state often associated with certain environmental characteristics that can interfere with learning. Until we find our destination, or at least orient ourselves with respect to our travel plans, few other problems will be solved; other tasks must wait until we get our bearings. Thus many of the physical features that contribute to legibility in the designed environment are likely to have an impact not only on spatial and geographic problem solving specifically but may interfere with problem solving in general because of their precedence in competing for personal attention. People do not like being disoriented under most circumstances, and disorientation interferes with learning. Since being disoriented may contribute if left unchecked to cognitive fatigue, it can also create a mental state inconducive to learning.

Although it is obvious, it is worth noting briefly that if people are afraid or perceive themselves in a risky or dangerous situation, their priorities for problem solving are likely to be totally fixated on dealing with the threat they face. Thus real or perceived hazards that threaten wellbeing are likely inhibitors to learning. Other types of information processing not directly related to the perceived hazards are going to receive little or no attention under such circumstances (Martin, Falk and Balling 1981). More subtly, anxiety can affect learning because it may change an individual's cognitive strategies for the handling of information. There is evidence, for example, that when people are anxious they push for rapid, possibly premature solutions to problems. Anxious persons also become less flexible, tending not to consider all options thoroughly before solving a problem. There is also suggestive evidence that when anxious, individuals tend to focus and rely heavily on one dominant cue (Janis 1982). Learning that requires attention and consideration of multiple sources of information may be seriously jeopardized under these circumstances.

Creative problem solving that requires the adoption of unique perspectives as well as problems entailing the consideration of complex and potentially conflicting or ambiguous information are probably quite vulnerable to high levels of anxiety. People's natural tendencies to see things through the schematic lens they have already developed for processing information are likely to become even more rigid in situations that make them feel anxious. Interest in new information or the ability to adopt new ways of looking at things are less likely under conditions of high anxiety.

Communication

The papers by Matusov and Rogoff and Roschelle in this volume note the critical importance of social interaction in knowledge acquisition, particularly as it enables participation in behaviors and problem-solving activities extending beyond the learner's current repertoire. A critical component of this socially supported learning is good communication. When communication is difficult or hindered, many forms of learning, particularly those dependent upon social interaction, are blocked.

Furniture arrangements can encourage or discourage social interaction. Sociopetal furniture arrangements cluster chairs so that people have easy eye contact, often around a table, and within a comfortable social interaction distance between two and one-half and four feet (Sommer 1969). Sociofugal furniture arrangements discourage social interaction by arranging chairs in a manner that makes eye contact difficult, often placing chairs side-by-side or in fixed rows and columns. In classroom settings, as one moves from the front to the rear, student participation decreases, grades decline, and more negative attitudes toward the class are evident (Gump 1987).

The ease with which people can physically see and talk with one another is a major component of neighboring. As distance increases social interaction, feelings of community, and attachment to place drop off. The association of neighboring with physical distance is particularly strong among the poor (Michelson 1976). The physical proximity of people in buildings can also influence communication, particularly unplanned, spontaneous interaction (Becker 1990). Typically people who do similar jobs are placed close to one another in offices. By creating functional inconvenience, Becker and his colleagues have shown that when people with different jobs are placed in close proximity, much more social interaction occurs among groups (e.g., sales and research and development personnel) than would otherwise be expected.

The above research has examined direct physical distance. Another element of distance is functional distance. Functional distance refers to the alignment of major pathways and entryways as they affect social interaction. The probability of social interaction increases as functional distance lessens. Two apartments may adjoin one another back to back and thus be physically close. However since one would have to walk around the building to get from one entry to the other, their functional distance might actually be quite far. Festinger, Schachter, and Back (1950) found that social interaction was considerably greater among people whose residences were in close functional proximity to one another, while direct physical distance had only weak effects.

Focal points are spaces that support informal, group interaction. In interior spaces focal points are centrally located, neutral territory, have visual prospect, are furnished with comfortable seating, and include activity generators (Bechtel 1977; Becker 1990). Visual prospect means that one can see what activities are going on in the focal point prior to making a behavioral commitment to enter the space. An activity generator might be a coffee pot or mailboxes-some activity or function that helps draw people to a specific space.

Noise and crowding can interfere with communication directly and indirectly. Most directly when a space is noisy or very crowded communication among people can be difficult because of speech interference. Indirectly, people appear to cope with noise and crowding by social withdrawal; they tune one another out as a means to reduce the plethora of stimulation or social interaction faced under such circumstances (Evans and Cohen 1987). As described above, this social withdrawal also makes people less inclined to interact socially, even when removed from the noise or crowding.

Both directly and indirectly, the physical environment can facilitate or inhibit the formulation and maintenance of social interaction. Such interaction plays a central role in knowledge acquisition.

Conclusions

There is evidence that the physical characteristics of settings can affect learning. However, the evidence for direct environmental effects on learning is limited. Instead, the physical environment is shown to influence various psychological processes that, in turn, are assumed to affect learning. Actual and speculative linkages between the physical environment and the psychological processes of cognitive fatigue, distraction, motivation, emotional affect, and communication have been discussed. For example, the reduction of cognitive fatigue through experience of restorative environmental elements (e.g., fascination) is hypothesized to enhance learning. Restorative, environmental elements themselves may not directly affect learning. However, by reducing cognitive fatigue, the restorative environmental elements enable better utilization of information-processing capabilities by the organism.

I am not arguing that the physical environment has no direct, unmediated linkages to learning. I am simply stating that to date we do not have much information about such direct effects. Where evidence does lie is primarily on the indirect, psychologically mediated processes described herein. My personal belief is that both types of effects-direct and indirect-probably operate in linking physical setting characteristics and human learning.

One limitation of the present analysis is its neglect of relevant personal characteristics that undoubtedly interact with some physical elements to affect the psychological processes linked to learning discussed herein. Two personal characteristics that seem particularly salient in thinking about learning and the physical environment are familiarity and age.

Designing learning environments that initiate the novice to new areas of knowledge and exploration while at the same time maintaining and enriching the interests of the more-seasoned learner presents a difficult and challenging issue that seems particularly germane to informal learning environments such as museums (Balling, Falk and Aronson 1979). Many of the effects of the physical environment described herein may be moderated by the level of museum visitor expertise and experience. For example, with a more seasoned learner. the balance between coherence and complexity would probably shift toward complexity.

The cognitive and social abilities of the human organism to take advantage of opportunities offered by the physical environment are key ingredients in the analysis of the physical environment and human learning. Thus we might expect that young children's needs for and reactions to some of the environmental characteristics described in this paper might be different from an adult's reactions. Privacy needs, sensitivity to distraction, or dependence upon physical cues for adequate wayfinding probably vary as a function of developmental status.

A second limitation of the present analysis of the physical environment and learning is the need to consider more carefully different types of learning. We know from research on stress and performance, for example, that task characteristics are central to understanding when and how stressors affect performance negatively. Some salient task characteristics that help determine the effects of stressors include information rate, working memory load, and strategy flexibility.

Museum settings provide an important and largely neglected scientific resource in the study of the physical environment and learning. They offer complex, realistic environmental arrays but also enable the imposition of important methodological tools such as random assignment and manipulation of independent variables.

As highly realistic, dynamic simulations of real

world settings, museums enable researchers and museum professionals to change components or bundles of the physical environment systematically. Self-reports of evaluation or cognitive responses (e.g., learning) as well as observations of engagement and interest can then be examined in response to manipulations of the physical environment. Many of the physical variables described in this paper could be systematically varied in museum displays or in some cases the museum building itself. For example with displays one could systematically alter complexity or information rate, change display placement vis a vis adjacent spaces or circulation systems, or manipulate visual access and responsiveness of display elements. Variables in the building could be altered as well. Examples include: design elements relevant to wayfinding, design features connoting homeyness—institutional dimensions, sociopetal elements (furniture, focal points) as well as restorative design elements (e.g., utilization of natural elements). There are very few actual settings where realism and experimental rigor can be combined; museums provide such an opportunity.

Additional Readings

Bell, P., J. Fisher, A. Baum and T. Greene. 1987. *Environmental psychology.* New York: Holt. *This is a thorough, well-documented textbook on the field of environmental psychology. Coverage of theoretical perspectives in the field and of environmental stressors like crowding, noise, temperature are particularly strong.*

Gifford, R. 1987. *Environmental psychology.* Boston: Allyn Bacon.
This excellent textbook has good coverage of architecture and behavior, especially schools, homes, and the work environment. It includes an in-depth analysis of how human attitudes and behavior influence environmental quality.

Hall, E. T. 1966. *The hidden dimension.* New York: Doubleday. *An anthropologist offers astute observations and a fascinating glimpse of human spatial behavior. The analysis of the role of culture in the human use of space is particularly incisive.*

Kaplan, S., and R. Kaplan. 1982. *Cognition and environment.* New York: Praeger. *This scholarly analysis of the role of the environment in human thinking and learning presents a creative integration of materials from cognitive psychology, computer science, ecology, and evolutionary theory.*

Sommer, R. 1969. *Personal space.* Englewood Cliffs, N.J.: Prentice Hall. *My favorite introduction to human behavior and the physical environment is unfortunately out of print but definitely worth the search. This book offers fascinating analyses of human spatial behavior and ways architecture promotes or inhibits human welfare.*

References

Ahrentzen, S., G. Jue, M. A. Skorpanich, and G. W. Evans. 1982.School environments and stress. In *Environmental stress*, ed. G. W. Evans, pp. 224–55. New York: Cambridge.

Altman, I. 1975. *Environment and social behavior.* Monterey, Calif.: Brooks/Cole.

Archea, J. 1977. The place of architectural factors inbehavioral theories of privacy. *Journal of Social Issues* 33: 116–37.

Balling, J. D., J. H. Falk, and R. Aronson. 1979. Pre-trip orientations: An exploration of their effect on learning from a single visit field trip to a zoological park. Final report, National Science Foundation Grant #SED77-18913.

Barker, R. 1968. *Ecological psychology.* Stanford, Calif.: Stanford University Press.

Baum, A., R. Gatchel, J. Aiello, and D. Thompson. 1981. Cognitive mediation of environmental stress. In *Cognition, social behavior, and the environment*, ed. J. Harvey, pp. 513–33. Hillsdale, N.J.: Erlbaum.

Bechtel, R. 1977. *Enclosing behavior.* Stroudsburg, Penn.: Dowden, Hutchinson, and Ross.

Becker, F.D. 1990. *The total workplace.* New York: Van Nostrand Reinhold.

Berlyne, D. E. 1971. *Aesthetics and psychobiology.* New York: Appleton Century Crofts.

Chase, R. 1992. Toys and infant development:Biological, psychological, and social factors. *Children's Environments* 9: 3–12.

Cohen, S. 1980. Aftereffects of stress on human performanceand social behavior: A review of research and theory. *Psychological Bulletin* 88: 82–108.

Cohen, S., G. W. Evans, D. Stokols, and D. S. Krantz. 1986. *Behavior, health, and environmental stress.* New York: Plenum.

Evans, G. W. 1980. Environmental cognition. *Psychological Bulletin* 88: 259–287.

Evans, G. W., and S. Cohen. 1987. Environmental stress. In *Handbook of environmental psychology,* ed. D. Stokols and I. Altman, pp. 571–610. New York: Wiley.

Festinger, L., S. Schacter, and K. Back. 1950. *Social pressures in informal groups.* New York: Harper.

Garling, T., A. Book, and E. Lindberg. 1986. Spatial orientation and wayfinding in the designed environment: A conceptual analysis and some suggestions for postoccupancy evaluation. *Journal of Architectural and Planning Research* 3: 55–64.

Glass, D. C., and J. E. Singer. 1972. *Urban stress.* New York: Academic.

Gump, P. 1987. School and classroom environments. In *Handbook of environmental psychology,* ed. D. Stokols and I. Altman, pp. 691–732. New York: Wiley.

Hedge, A. 1991. Design innovation in office environments. In *Design intervention,* ed. W. Preiser, J. Visher, and E. White, pp. 301–22. New York: Van Nostrand Reinhold.

Heft, H. 1985. High residential density and perceptual cognitive development:An examination of the effects of crowding and noise in the home. In *Habitats for children,* ed. J.F. Wohlwill and W. van Vliet, pp. 39–75. Hillsdale, N. J.: Erlbaum.

Hillier, W., and J. Hanson. 1984. *Social logic of space.* London:

Cambridge University Press.

Holahan, C. J. 1978. *Environment and behavior.* New York: Plenum.

Isen, A. M., K. Daubman, and J. Gorgoglione. 1987. The influence of positive affect on cognitive organization: Implications for education. In *Aptitude, learning, and instruction, Volume 3: Conative and affective processes,* ed. R. Snow and J. Farr, pp. 143–164. Hillsdale, N. J.: Erlbaum.

Janis, I. 1982. Decision making under stress. In *Handbook of stress,* ed. L. Goldberger and S. Breznitz, pp. 69–87. New York: Free Press.

Kaplan, R., and S. Kaplan. 1989. *The experience of nature.* New York: Cambridge University Press.

Kaplan, S. 1983. A model of person-environment compatibility. *Environment and Behavior* 15: 311–32.

Kaplan, S., L. Bardwell, and D. Slakter. 1993. The museum as a restorative environment. *Environment and Behavior* 25: 725 -42.

Kaplan, S., and R. Kaplan. 1982. *Cognition and environment.* New York: Praeger.

Kuller, R. 1991. Environmental assessment from a neuro-psychological perspective. In *Environment, cognition, and action,* ed. T. Garling & G.W. Evans, pp. 111–147. New York: Oxford University Press.

Kuller, R., and C. Lindsten. 1992. Health and behavior of children in classrooms with and without windows. *Journal of Environmental Psychology* 12: 305–17.

Lynch, K. 1960. *The image of the city.* Cambridge, Mass.: MIT Press.

Martin, W. W., J. H. Falk, and J. D. Balling. 1981. Environmental effects on learning: The outdoor field trip. *Science Education* 65: 301-9.

Maslow, A., and N. Mintz. 1956. Effects of aesthetic surroundings. *Journal of Psychology* 41: 247–54.

Mc Cracken, G. 1989. Homeyness: A cultural account of one constellation of consumer goods and meaning. In *Interpretive consumer culture,* ed. E. Hirschman, pp. 168–181. Provo, Utah: Association of Consumer Research.

Michelson, W. 1976. *Man and his urban setting.* Reading, Mass.: Addison-Wesley.

Milgram, S. 1970. The experience of living in cities. *Science* 167: 1461–68.

Moore, G. T. 1987. The physical environment and development in child care centers. In *Spaces for children,* ed. C. S. Weinstein and T. David, pp. 41–72. New York: Plenum.

Newman, O. 1972. *Defensible space.* New York: Macmillan.

Norman, D. 1989. *The psychology of everyday things.* New York: Basic.

Passini, R. 1984. *Wayfinding in architecture.* New York: Van Nostrand Reinhold.

Prescott, E. 1987. The environment as organizer of intent in child care settings. In *Spaces for children,* ed. C.S. Weinstein and T. David, pp. 73–88. New York: Plenum.

Rivlin, L. G., and M. Wolfe. 1985. *Institutional settings in children's lives.* New York: Wiley.

Seligman, M. E. P. 1975. *Helplessness.* San Francisco: Freeman.

Sherrod, D., and S. Cohen. 1979. Density, personal control, and design. In *Residential crowding and design,* ed. J. Aiello and A. Baum, pp. 217–28. New York: Plenum.

Sommer, R. 1969. *Personal space.* Englewood Cliffs, N. J.: Prentice Hall.

Sommer, R., and H. Olsen. 1980. The soft classroom. *Environment and Behavior* 12: 3-16.

Sundstrom, E. 1986. *Workplaces.* New York: Cambridge University Press.

Talbot, J., R. Kaplan, F. Kuo, and S. Kaplan. 1993. Factors that enhance effectiveness of visitor maps. *Environment and Behavior* 25: 743–60.

Wachs, T., and G. Gruen. 1982. *Early experience and human development.* New York: Plenum.

Weinstein, C. S. 1977. Modifying student behavior in an open classroom through changes in the physical design. *American Education Research Journal* 14: 249–62.

Weinstein, C. S. 1979. The physical environment of the school: A review of the research. *Review of Educational Research* 49: 577–610.

Weinstein, C. S. 1987. Designing preschool classrooms to support development. In *Spaces for children,* ed. C. S. Weinstein and T. David, pp. 159–86. New York: Plenum.

White, R. 1959. The concept of competence reconsidered. *Psychological Review* 66: 297–333.

Wicker, A. 1987. Behavior settings reconsidered: Temporal stages, resources, internal dynamics, context. In *Handbook of environmental psychology,* ed. D. Stokols and I. Altman, pp. 613–54. New York: Wiley.

Part 3

Further Reflections About Long-Term Learning Research in Museums

Mucking around in Museum Research

Deborah Edward
Austin Children's Museum

Discussions about establishing a museum research initiative are strikingly similar to processes in museum exhibit design. Consider, for example, current activities in our museum to design, prototype, and produce a hands-on exhibit about bats. We selected a "hot topic" to respond to our community's intense pride of being home to 1.5 million Mexican free-tail bats who live under a downtown bridge. We began the process by talking to our audiences, asking visitors and bat aficionados what they knew about bats and what they wanted to know more about. We collected source materials and resources about how bats had been studied and referenced in the sciences and in myth and folklore. We identified misconceptions about bats and looked at ways we could use the topic to explore themes in the arts, sciences, and humanities. We brought in the big guns – an international bat research institute – to inform our exhibit team. We initially "mucked around" with many directions for our exhibit and let the most vivid directions make themselves known. We eventually narrowed our focus to a few basic messages. Our choices reflected the interests of our exhibit team, the resources we had, and the interests, knowledge, misconceptions, and characteristics of our public. Secure in our direction, we prototyped a bat barn and an echolocation chamber; developed graphics and text; checked all aspects for accuracy; organized adjunct programs related to the exhibit for use in schools, teacher education, and family events; and sought funding to present the project. We were pleased with our construction and design – bringing in new tools and approaches to showcase the ways bats fly, find their pups, and seek their food. We sponsored a teen multimedia team to create a part of the exhibit. We evaluated activities at key milestones, and currently we are examining the way visitors are using our test edition exhibit, anticipating that revisions will occur as we prepare the exhibit for tour. We wanted to create an exhibit that is personally meaningful, at some level, to every visitor. As the exhibit begins its national tour the exhibit team will take use this experience to inform and set the stage for new exhibit designs.

The bats exhibit vignette has many parallels with what we are considering in creating a research agenda. We begin with an interest in exploring a topic— understanding what museum experiences provide individuals, groups, and society. We strive to find out all we can about what is known about museum experiences (and we find that the information is scattered —not like the international bat research organization we happened to have handy in our community). We ask our audiences – fellow museum professionals, colleagues in related academic fields, policy makers concerned about issues of culture and education – what they know and what they want to know about our theme. And we explore possible directions for our research—aware that there is not necessarily one right direction or one unique starting place or one basic format or theme that we need to start someplace with a good rationale for why we decided to start there. We look at our available methods and tools to see what will enable us to reach our goals. We envision our end product—a clearinghouse for research findings, a taxonomy to describe museum experiences, financial support for varied research efforts, a journal to disseminate information, a series of papers or seminars to help policy makers support our good work, a body of literature that informs the museum field, the development of a profession.

In terms of a national museum research agenda, we are only in the first stages of project development. We are in the "mucking around" stage. And like our exhibit, it is likely that the passion of the individuals on the team will play a significant role in determining direction, scope, resources and collaborations. This past year a number of think tanks have been organized to examine research issues and develop potential directions for museum research. Key themes and issues are becoming vivid:

• Exploring impact means looking at the level of individual and of the society. The question is not whether the visit has impact, but what impact the museum experience and the museum as a cultural and educational institution has on students, families, schools, communities, and society.

• We must define learning broadly, to embrace the potential of

museums to motivate, inspire, and have an enduring meaning

to visitors, beyond transmitting facts. Learning in museums includes learning values, appreciation and cultural icons.

• Defining and describing impact requires qualitative and quantitative methods and examination from various theoretical perspectives. The current emphasis on cognitive science, social anthropology, and educational psychology recognizes some but not all of the disciplines and perspectives that provide important lenses through which to view the museum and musuem experience.

• While much may already be known about museum learning, there is no one place or way to gain access to past, current, and future research activities. There is no one place to start or one way to go as we move forward en masse to encourage more research on museums.

• There are compelling and logical reasons to establish a broad based, multidisciplinary institute to coordinate, encourage, and disseminate research, but there is no one institution that is positioned to make this happen.

• Research on museum impact is more than a noble goal; it is a practical goal. Research can assist program designers, policy makers and funders in making decisions to improve and support activities.

• In current museum practice, it is still costly and risky for museum leaders to invest time and resources in research.

Developing a research agenda for museums must mean creating new tools, new language, and new alliances. Participants in the Annapolis conference touched on these needs often. Our task is to describe and document learning outcomes (broadly defined) from museum experiences. We explain that this task has multiple benefits: it will help designers make museum programs more effective; it will demonstrate to funders that museum programs are worthwhile investments; and it will provide a lens through which to observe and analyze the changing role of museums in society, in order to better understand human systems. We look at the task as one of mapping new territory—museum learning. As we define museum learning broadly – to include getting a sense of values, motivation, appreciation—we must by necessity move past traditional information-based assessment tools to more quantitative, descriptive methods. As we explore our definitions we must intrigue academicians in varied social science fields enough to have them share their conceptual frameworks that we may better understand our distinctive environment.

To an advocate for informal education, a national museum research agenda sounds like an idea worth endorsing. To a director concerned about funding, time allocation, and mission, it compels caution: What if the initiative does not provide evidence that museums are as meaningful and catalytic as we say? To someone in the children's museum field, the question is not whether we are meaningful institutions, but how we are meaningful. Understanding our role in the life of a child, a teacher, a community, and a family helps us become more effective, more powerful and more responsive. Explaining our impact helps us acquire funds to support our activities. Defining our unique and distinctive role helps us maintain an alliance (but not a blending) with schools. It is fine for our methods of presentation and our materials to be used in other educational contexts, but the power of a museum experience is special, and we should maintain this distinction with pride.

A national museum research agenda should promise enough of value to each individual museum to entice us to provide time and staff resources for this effort. The trends toward stronger educational roles in museums – as seen in the Excellence and Equity and related national initiatives by the American Association of Museums such as MAP III and the various foundation-funded public program expansions – are suggesting that museums are positioning themselves differently in the community. They are becoming centers not only of collection and research but of public education and discussion. As we emphasize this strength, we must provide evidence of the impact. Our collective voice – research across museums – can be a strong backdrop for individual efforts to quantify, describe, and critique the work within each institution.

Sometimes in the process of designing an exhibit a team member will complain that it takes too long to get started. As a naturally impatient person, I have to resist this tendency to criticize our field for taking so much time to get started. We probably need to take time to ensure that our work is thoughtful and appropriate. We do not have to find the "right" direction; we have to describe a realistic and meaningful set of first steps, one that researchers, practitioners, and policy makers will support and respect, within a larger vision. It will take time to coalesce on a direction, to attract funders, and to create a professional climate that understands that research is not a threat but a resource that can help museums improve their programs, understand their public, and provide evidence of their value. It is an endeavor well worth thought and action.

The value of the Annapolis Conference is its synergy. As a group we are identifying themes, creating shared language and vision, and keeping one another sensitive to issues. The dilemma posed by the conference is that we are all excited about making something happen but we are not sure what the something should be or who should be making it happen. Unlike the exhibit design process, no one person or team is empowered to create the research initiative. No one board of trustees provides the accountability and the conscience to ensure that the process is developing in accordance with high standards or a specific mission. Until we coalesce with a structure of some kind for support, direction, and action –a consortium of museums to conduct similar research or a group to get funds for commissioned papers and studies – or until a strong, appropriate agency or association takes a higher profile lead, we will continue to be "mucking around." It is not impossible for us to create our own independent research institute as a coalition of many groups — museums, research organizations, funders, and academic departments with similar missions. But one way or another, we need a stronger core to make a concerted, appropriate, systematic, long-term research agenda come to life. And like an exhibit-in-process, we need to know our audiences and ensure that our product is interesting and accurate, and that it evokes action.

The Need for Learning Research in Museums

Linda Downs
National Gallery of Art

Museums are now widely recognized for the learning about art, science, and history that takes place in them. After more than a century since their establishment as educational institutions, the concept of the museum as a place of learning is now recognized by the National Science Foundation, National Endowment for the Humanities, National Endowment for the Arts, National Art Education Association, as well as by some circles of academics and other professional agencies and organizations. While it is significant that professional organizations and academia officially identify museums as places of learning, it is also of concern that the type of learning recognized in museums is labeled "informal" as opposed to a "formal" academic model. This distinction may be used, in part, because museum professionals do not yet have the research data to build scientifically grounded practices acknowledged among academic institutions.

The conference, "Public Institutions for Personal Learning: Understanding the Long-Term Impact of Museums," examined the issue of museum learning from several perspectives. The learning theorists presented their latest findings and questions about the effects of learning in museums, which were distributed in draft form and read by all participants prior to the conference. For this museum educator who was well grounded in Jean Piaget from college years and had read the work of Rudolf Arnheim, Mihaly Csikszentmihalyi, Howard Gardner, John Falk and Lynn Dierking, as well as many others in twenty-five years of museum work, it was a revelation to read these papers in a concentrated span of time. It became clear that museum educators in particular have been focusing on teaching, not on learning, and that our teaching model was academe (courses, lectures, seminars, symposia, proseminars, discussion groups, preservice and in-service, hands-on, theoretical and practical).

For the museum visitors who actively participate in museum education programs and usually have graduate- and post-graduate-level education, the academic model has been a comfortable one which served them well in conveying a bounteous, one-way path of art historical and contextual information. For the majority of visitors, however, who may have less background or who determine their own learning paths, the academic paradigm fails. The irony is that while knowing that looking at original objects can bring enormous insight and enjoyment, we have relied on a teaching method that has little relationship to the way visitors really learn in a museum setting. Museum professionals extol the importance of looking at original objects, artifacts, and specimens but do not have a scientific understanding of how to create the optimal environment for this kind of learning. Typical museum evaluations assessing the effectiveness of education programs for visitors often fail to provide the kind of results that can be used to develop effective, less-structured ways of reaching the majority of the public in the galleries. Without research data it is difficult to characterize museums as educational institutions, or to know how to create authentic learning opportunities for the public. The article in the May/June 1995 issue of *Museum News* by Mihaly Csikszentmihalyi and Kim Hermanson attempts to translate theory into practice by characterizing the elements of intrinsic motivation to learn in a museum setting.[1] For example, museums need to know what people are attracted to, how visitors connect to objects and relate them to their lives, how to present multiple perspectives to stimulate intellectual discovery, and how to create opportunities for visitors to become deeply absorbed in the exhibitions. This article rightly points out that museum work will continue to be an art not a science until more research is carried out.

"Until we collect systematic knowledge on this topic, we shall have to proceed by trial and error, finding out which components of an exhibit are most attractive, for whom, under what conditions. In other words, museum work will continue to be an art rather than a science. Although this is not necessarily bad, a larger contribution of scientific knowledge would surely help." [2]

And so, the question remains, what does it mean in verifiable terms when art museum professionals say that learning in museums emanates from the works of art themselves? Most museum objects have been taken out of original context, displayed with like objects, and are presented with minimal information. Even the most ardent viewer can experience that numbness called 'museum fatigue' in a short period of time. But there are times when we have all had what Csikszentmihalyi has named *peak* and *flow* experiences with objects.

At the beginning of the Annapolis Conference participants were asked to present their best and worst personal museum-based experiences. I was most interested in the descriptions of experiences in art museums. We heard about peak experiences with Jan Vermeer's *Woman Reading a Letter* in Amsterdam's Rijksmuseum, a teenager's incredulous realization that he was looking at the original *American Gothic* by Grant Wood at the Art Institute of Chicago, and the transforming experience of seeing Masaccio's *Dead Christ* in Milan's Pinacoteca de Brera. We heard about a student field trip to the Philadelphia Museum of Art that opened up a new world, how museum-going helped bond a family, and the thrill of finding a grandfather's painting at the Metropolitan Museum of Art. We also heard about negative museum experiences, from intimidating architecture to unfriendly guards.

Given the high number of art museum examples, conference participants went on to consider what is magical about looking at original works of art. There is, they agreed, a suspension across time or to another place. There is a challenge to see intimately. There is an immediate understanding, as if what a viewer beholds is created by someone very familiar. One gets lost in an object. There is an excitement, and a wish that the connected moment will continue. The experience is memorable and is probably exaggerated with each telling. Why is this experienced prized by society. How can museum professionals understand it and enhance the possibility of its occurring for the majority of visitors? How do these experiences regularly help the learning process, alter attitudes, enhance values, change their lives? Are museum visitors different from nonmuseum visitors in the way they think, solve problems, value differences, and understand society? Most American museums were founded on the premise that looking at original objects of art or science, culture, or history, was educationally positive. What if museum professionals not only believed this, but could support that belief through research and apply it to enhance the museum environment for and with the public?

The first step in establishing museum learning as a genuine part of museological commitment is to demonstrate to museum colleagues what the value of learning research can be. To do that, each of us needs to create a strategy for introducing learning research in our museums. We can begin, for example, by formally recognizing a broad spectrum of learning styles and developing materials that meet various needs; carrying out small but critical learning research projects in the galleries such as interviews to determine attitudinal changes before and after a museum visit; establish longevity studies to determine how individuals learn in museums compared to other settings; and by observing visitors to determine how learning resources are used in galleries. The results of these studies can be generalized for use in other parts of the collections of in another exhibition.

Through their contact with the public, museum educators are well placed to carry out research. Cooperation with university researchers is needed for scientific gathering and analysis. The focus of the studies need to enhance the aesthetic experience, which is the single most recognized learning experience valued by art museum professionals and recognized by researchers.

Why are you concerned with learning theory when teaching is already carried out so well and visitor studies show high satisfaction with the National Gallery of Art? What does learning theory contribute to creating programs for the public? These were questions I received upon my departure to attend this conference.

A well-selected group of professionals at the conference, individuals already interested in museum learning and in most cases already applying research, convinced me of the importance of looking at the purpose of museums vis-a-vis the expectations of the visitors, the range of issues to be researched, the research methods to be selected and the ways museums can collaborate on research projects to determine similarities in learning and facilitate wide distribution of applicable results. While federal agencies, professional museum organizations, and academe are beginning to recognize and value museum learning, there is much that has to be done in preparing the groundwork with our own colleagues for research to be carried out.

Notes
1. Csikzentmihalyi, Mihaly and Hermanson, Kim, "Intrinsic Motivation in Museums: What Makes Visitors Want to Learn?", *Museum News*, vol. 74, no. 3, May/June 1995.
2. Ibid., p. 37.

Creating an Academic Home for Informal Science Education

Alan J. Friedman
New York Hall of Science

Two days of discussions at "Public Institutions for Personal Learning: Understanding the Long-Term Impact of Museums," demonstrated clearly that there are university and independent researchers, practitioners, and funders eager to create and carry out a research agenda for nonformal learning. The variety of compelling research questions proposed, the richness of the research methodologies suggested, the eagerness to use the results of that research, the interest of funders – all argue that there is a potential community that should get its act together and begin this important work.

The individuals who assembled in Annapolis, however, came from sectors that are normally separated, geographically and professionally. Most attendees had never met the majority of their fellow participants. Attendees belonged to sectors that do not share a common journal, professional organization, or specialized language of research and practice.

One reason for this isolation of professionals with a deeply shared interest is the lack of any academic center for informal (or nonformal) science learning. University departments traditionally support academic rigor, research teams, scholarly journals, symposia, and the other apparatuses that advance a research field. For informal science education to become a discipline it is probably necessary and certainly desirable to create at least one academic center. This function is not currently being filled by any university, at least in North America. A center for informal science learning could fill a serious void by providing the nexus for academic research and publications to sustain the rigorous study. The center could also serve to train leaders for the rapidly growing field of museums, science-technology centers, zoos, aquariums, community activity centers, and multimedia and mass-media educational enterprises. This paper describes the rationale and some of the essential characteristics of such a center.

Questions for a New Industry

Informal science learning is a billion-dollar industry. In North America alone there are more than a thousand science museums, natural history museums, zoos, aquariums, children's museums, and botanical gardens. Science, medicine, and natural history programs on television have crossed the boundary between noncommercial and commercial channels. You can get a scout merit badge in astronomy or ecology or geography. Science and math courses for families are offered in community centers around the United States.

But this kind of science learning opportunity differs from the formal school classroom in many ways. There are no grades and no tests. Frank Oppenheimer, founder of the Exploratorium in San Francisco, was fond of pointing out that nobody can flunk museum. Because there is no required attendance, participants must be attracted, lured into these learning experiences. Many informal learning experiences are flashy, exciting, advertised, and noisy.

How effective is the informal science education enterprise? Do the people who create and operate this enterprise know what they are doing? Do they have a theoretical base, or at least an agenda on the table, for examining what they are doing and why? Is there some training program for people in the field so that they start with a basic knowledge of what the field is, what it knows, and what it needs to learn?

The answers to all these questions are "we don't know" or "we are not sure" or simply "no." These are all issues that, in a field like physics or formal school-based education, would be handled by the academy. University programs have professors, postdocs, undergraduate and graduate students, books, peer-reviewed journals, research seminars, and dissertations. These mechanisms make sure that research and evaluation, theory, study agendas, vigorous debate, and a common knowledge base are pursued by an ongoing community with shared knowledge.

Is the Academy Ready to Help?

At least in North America, there is no academic home for informal science education. To be sure, there are a few dozen university faculty members, several of whom attended the Annapolis Conference, who are attempting to provide some of these components of a research establishment and who have been doing important work. In addition to the conference participants, Chandler Screven in Wisconsin, Stephen Bitgood in Alabama, and Ross Loomis in Colorado are among the important scholars in the field. But there is no center, no critical mass of activity sufficient to support, for example, a stable, refereed journal of informal science learning.

There are programs in science communications, reviewed recently by Lewenstein (1994). These programs are primarily targeted at journalists and writers and do not offer regular study of museums, zoos, botanic gardens, or science-technology centers. Museum studies programs exist at over a dozen universities in North America, but they are focused on art and history museums and on the collections aspects of natural history museums, not on the informal learning of science and technology.

For a few years in the 1970's an academic center for informal science learning did exist. It was at the University of California at Berkeley, and was called SESAME (Search for Excellence in Science and Mathematics Education). This interdisciplinary program, which offered a Ph.D., brought together faculty from science, engineering, cognitive psychology, and education; students were required to have strong backgrounds in science and technology. Dissertations included research in cognitive theory and evaluation, often in settings such as museums, zoos, and aquariums. There were exciting seminar series and, if not a refereed journal, at least a stream of articles published in various scholarly journals.

The program thrived for about ten years, a period during which several of the faculty were particularly interested in informal (rather than formal) science education. Those faculty have since retired or moved to other universities, and the program today is concentrated more traditionally in studies of cognition and formal education. But during the brief period when SESAME served as the academic home for informal science education, it and the nearby school of education at Berkeley produced perhaps half of the most often cited students of the field (Judy Diamond, John Falk, Jeff Gottfried, Cary Sneider, Mark St. John, and Sam Taylor, for example), including more than a dozen of the directors and senior staff of today's science museums and science-technology centers.

In the absence of an academic center, many of the dispersed scholars who pursue the field of informal science learning are attempting to produce and finance a journal and have held a half-dozen conferences, most recently in London and Albuquerque, devoted mostly to visitor studies. Thought-provoking papers do appear, but there is rarely a sustained debate that carries an issue long enough for consensus to emerge.

The Need for Research and Evaluation

The lack of a research center is holding back the entire field. Most informal science institutions have no ongoing research and do little summative evaluation. In response to demands by foundation funders, such as the National Science Foundation, institutions of informal learning may hire one of a dozen consultants to do a brief study at the end of the project. This contact is too casual and peripheral to establish a habit of reflection or rigorous self-questioning.

The need for research and evaluation in informal science education cannot be overemphasized. We do have excellent studies of the impact of individual informal science learning experiences. A recent publication edited by Crane (1994) provides the best available summary of these studies and what has been learned from them (Crane 1994). Yes, people do learn science from some of their experiences within museums, from watching films, and from participating in community activities. And we know how to improve the effectiveness of those experiences, whatever the relative effectiveness is at the beginning. Most impressive is how effectively informal science education projects have used formative evaluations. Any given aspect of a program can be and often is measurably improved. An exhibit at the new York Hall of Science is a case in point.

In the first prototype of a computer-based exhibit unit on the human immune system, the HIV virus, and AIDS, visitors navigated through sections on anatomy, invasion of the body by various forms of germs, and the body's elaborate defense mechanisms. Each section featured written and spoken text, colorful cartoon-style graphics, animation, and sound effects. A key goal of the exhibit unit was to address certain potentially fatal misconceptions about HIV, such as the notion that any form of birth control provides protection against infection. Once the biological characteristics of this virus's infection route are understood, it becomes apparent that only condoms or abstinence provide protection.

The exhibit designers wondered if the highly stylized representations of the human body, which had been used in an earlier, more general exhibit about the human immune system, would remain adequate for this very serious treatment and more focused exhibition. More realistic drawings might prove more effective, but might also draw visitor complaints.

Formative evaluation demonstrated that the new exhibit unit failed to make much of an impact on the widespread misconception about the ability of all contraceptives to prevent transmission of the disease. A more explicit depiction of intercourse was tried, and while still not approaching photographic realism, this version did significantly improve visitor understanding. Twice as many visitors left with the correct understanding of the relative efficacy of condoms versus other means of birth control in preventing the transmission of the virus. For example, correct answers to one question on condoms versus diaphragms rose from 22 percent to 45 percent of visitors tested (Falk and Weiss 1993).

While formative evaluation has repeatedly produced valuable results like these, the state of summative evaluation and generalizable results are much shakier. Even when the numbers of subjects are large, as in the audience for a television show or an exhibition, informal science education practitioners have been faced with the same problems of evaluation that bother formal education: the "treatment" experienced is not identical for every individual; the control audience can rarely be matched satisfactorily with the experimental audience; and in practice we measure only a tiny part of the potential effects, cognitive and affective, of a program.

A great deal of effort has been expended in such summative evaluation efforts as determining whether a planetarium or a classroom experience is the better communicator of astronomy. Yet it is not likely that comparative effectiveness questions can be posed in a way to yield any information of general utility.

So do participants in informal science learning become more effective and happier citizens, workers, and parents? We don't know. But then we don't know if formal education produces more effective and happier citizens, workers, or parents.

In understanding education, informal education in particular, we are in a state more comparable to astronomy in the days of Ptolemy than the days of Isaac Newton. We have lots of data on the individual entities (exhibit units, television shows, family math sessions), but no general rules that apply from one experience to the next or can be applied in devising a new program. Predicting the success or failure of an informal education project is a poorly practiced art. Even worse, we cannot learn much from our mistakes. We rarely build a second version of that exhibit or a remake of that film.

First we need to know what we do not know about this enterprise. Then we must decide what we need to know. For example, among the issues raised at the Annapolis Conference were:

• Who participates in each of the forms of informal science learning, who does not participate, and why?

• How do adults support and discourage learning by children in a museum?

• What elements of the museum experience occur regardless of the discipline presented?

• What do visitors expect when they come to a museum, and is learning one of those expectations?

• What is unique about museum-based learning?

• What is the cumulative effect of years of museum visits on an individual? on a community?

To begin to answer these questions, careful and sustained collection of anecdotal evidence and satisfaction surveys can be useful, especially for uncovering the critical questions to be asked. Then we need to expand our research and evaluation studies to cover a broader range of experiences, rather than the project-by-project, exhibit-by-exhibit, film-by-film studies that we have done to date.

Miller's (1991) ongoing longitudinal population studies are a start, even though informal education is treated only sketchily in his work. This type of study needs to be supported and extended to cover broader experiences and broader communities.

Does Informal Science Education Matter?

The goal of an institution like the New York Hall of Science is to change visitors. They should be different when the leave the museum. We would be happy if they learned something during their visit, but we would be even happier if we knew that they were more inclined to learn something after their visit.

Frank Oppenheimer liked to tell the story of a woman who called up to tell the Exploratorium that after a visit she had repaired a table lamp for the first time in her life. He explained that although there was not a single exhibit in the Exploratorium that would be directly relevant to repairing a table lamp, somehow experiencing the hands-on exhibits had given this visitor the confidence to try a technical task on her own_even if working with 110 volt wiring might not have been the safest apparatus for a beginner to try.

Affective changes can be measured. Television commercials, for example, are evaluated not merely by how many people watch them, or what viewers learn about the product, but by sales of the product in subsequent weeks. In the year after a temporary exhibit on insects is presented by the New York Hall of Science, is there a rise in the sales of books on insects at the Barnes and Noble chain? a rise in the number of visitors to the insect display at the zoo? an increase in the circulation of insect books at the New York Public Library? an increase in viewers for the insect film on NOVA? more girl scouts earning the insect merit badge? Of course there will be many confounding variables that will make any such changes based on the presence of one exhibit in one museum difficult to interpret. But if the study is broader, dealing with multiple topics treated by informal education programs in many cities, patterns may begin to emerge.

What does change the visitor or viewer or participant? The program itself may be only a small part of the experience. What about the social dimensions of the experiencëhow the visitor interacted with staff, gift shop items, or other visitors? Are all happy museum experiences alike in some ways? Are all unhappy museum experiences alike in some ways?

The long-term impact of informal science education should appear not only in continued informal learning but in such measures as enrollment in science courses in secondary and higher education. Successful experiences in informal science learning as children should be reflected in increased participation in lifelong learning opportunities at universities and continuing professional training in science and technology industries.

Devising a research agenda of sufficient scope is not going to be easy. There is the fear of failure and the subsequent drying up of funding not only for research but for the informal learning enterprise itself. There is the lack of research infrastructure: it is hard to sustain a research program without an academic center for such research, with its tireless graduate students, refereed journal, and provocative seminar series. But we cannot continue to sell informal science education to foundations and the public if we do not try. And our competitors who place entertainment first, and education a distant second, like Disney and the most of the mass media, have a long head start on us in understanding how to sell sizzle with the merest promise of nutritional benefit as an added bonus.

The Need for Leadership Training

Academic centers traditionally become the primary supply mechanism for leadership in a field. For those of us who administer informal science education institutions, the lack of a training center for leaders in the field is felt most keenly.

At the New York Hall of Science, which like many other science centers has been growing rapidly, we are in the process of recruiting several senior staff. To find well-prepared leaders who are familiar with the field, we will have to raid the staffs of other institutions. After all, in the past seven years our small staff has been raided several times, and at least two museum directors and the director of exhibits at a much larger institution have come from our tiny original staff. Beyond that, we know we will have to hire people with no familiarity of the world of science-technology centers people who must undertake the leadership of multimillion dollar projects and learn the context and details on the fly.

How serious is this lack of leadership training? In 1971, when the Association of Science-Technology Centers (ASTC) was formed, there were 17 North American institutions that qualified for membership. Today there are 240 institutional members, many created in the past decade, and there are 46 "developing" institutions, preparing to open their doors (ASTC 1992). In the most recent comprehensive survey of the 240 institutional members of ASTC, 179 institutions reported an aggregated full-time-equivalent staff of 14,530 (ASTC 1994).

A separate study (St. John and Grinell 1993) counted developing or recently opened science centers, natural history museums, zoos, botanic gardens, aquariums, and children's museums, and came up with 199 institutions. These institutions are in the process of finding directors, exhibit directors, education directors, project managers, evaluators, and fund raisers. If half of these institutions eventually reach the average 81.2 full-time-equivalent staff members of the reporting ASTC institutions, the field will have grown by eight thousand new employees.

The concern for the preparation of staff for informal science education extends beyond the institutional employers themselves. The science research community views the low level of public understanding of science with alarm. If informal science education institutions continue to be the major source of learning outside of school, the staff of these institutions must set and maintain standards of quality and scientific integrity in their public programs. A source of staff trained in science and science communications becomes all the more necessary since economic trends in the informal education sector are encouraging recruitment of many staff from the entertainment and service marketing industry.

We look not only for experienced, qualified staff; we would like to find a diverse staff, representative of the broad public we would like to serve. Over 70 percent of the 160,000 school-age children who visit the New York Hall of Science each year are members of minority populations. Since the field is relative young and is growing rapidly, informal science education could be creating an industry with visible equal opportunity at every level, including the executive offices. But without a prescribed career route, without brochures advising young people of the exciting jobs available, without the top-notch training and placement service available at a university center, informal science education presents a subterranean profile, especially for minority students who may be the first generation in their family to attend college. A look at the directors of museums in the United States will reveal that racial and ethnic diversity is essentially nonexistent.

Descriptors of a Center for Informal Science Learning

What would an academic center fulfilling these needs for research and leadership training look like? Here are some key features:

• an interdisciplinary faculty with several full-time-equivalents, with expertise in science, psychology, and education and in addition regular participation from departments of business, journalism, economic development, and the arts, such as theater, film, and graphic art

• a respected base within the university structure. Schools of education should be significant partners, but their sometimes arm's-length relations with the "hard" science faculty and the poor reputation of K-12 science education today might mean that a program based solely in the school of education would have a harder time placing its graduates than would an interdisciplinary program within the division housing physics, chemistry, and biology research.

• degrees at the master's and doctorate level, and perhaps a minor at the undergraduate level. Strong preparation in fundamental science and technology must be co- or prerequisite at all levels.

• intimate ties with informal science education institutions, including several close enough to provide daily research settings and part-time employment for students in the program. "Real world" experience, through practicums, internships, and thesis work in these institutions will greatly enhance the employment opportunities for students.

• sufficient seed funding to support visiting professorships, seminar series, publication, conferences, and travel for faculty. Once the program is under way and producing leadership for the field, the opportunities to place students, the demand for admissions, the grants from the National Science Foundation and private foundations, and the requests for consulting contracts will make the program one of the more self-supporting interdisciplinary efforts of the home university. But it will require a couple of years and incubation funding to launch the program.

Outline for Curriculum

A curriculum for research and leadership staff development for informal science education should include courses in cognitive psychology, science education, museum studies, and exemplary practice in the science center field. The outline which follows was developed from discussions with leaders in existing museum studies programs, schools of education, and informal science education institutions.

• cognitive and learning theory and criticism: Piaget, Brunner, Karplus learning cycle, naive theories, Gardner

• information theory: signals and noise, Shannon, Wiener

• research and evaluation methodology: qualitative and quantitative research design and methodologies, front-end, formative and summative strategies and practical techniques

• history and practice of informal science education: museums, science-technology centers, film, mass media, electronic media, community-operated programs like Scouts, 4-H, Girls Inc.

• relations with formal education: teacher preparation and professional development, K–12 curriculum development, enrichment programs, American Association for the Advancement of Science's Project 2061, National Science Foundation's systemic initiatives

• nonprofit institution funding and administration, including board and government relations

n project development and management, including ethics and intellectual property issues

• sector-specific skills, such as exhibition planning and design, multimedia production, and on-line technology

• interdisciplinary skills: the role of the arts, humanities, and sciences in creating public programs in science

• practicum or internship at an informal learning institution or related enterprise

Coming Soon to a Campus Near You?

Several universities are considering programs like the one described in this paper. There are in many places tenured, mid- and late-career faculty in need of a new field in which they can be reinvigorated and can excel. Universities just below the top tier in their realm are seeking programs in which they can be the world leaders. Even if those programs are relatively modest in size, moving up the university-prestige ladder means having undisputed leadership in several areas, and the well-established fields like physics and literature are hard to crack.

What will be needed are a few academic "stars" to give the new venture respectability from the start and a few angels or powerful senior administrators to fund the start-up costs. There are no assurances of success, but there is a new industry in search of leadership. There are important questions to be answered in how democracy can prepare its participants for an age of science and technology. And somebody will get to be the Newton of informal science learning.

Acknowledgments

The author would like to thank Pam Abdur, Jack Crow, Flora Kaplan, Sid Katz, and Cecily Selby for their helpful discussions and critiques on this issue. This paper was first presented by the author at a ses-

sion of the American Association for the
Advancement of Science meeting in San Francisco,
February 1994, and was presented in modified form
at the symposium "When Science Becomes Culture"
in Montréal, April 1994.

References

ASTC. 1992. *Membership Report.* Washington: Association of
Science-Technology Centers.

ASTC. 1994. *Directory.* Washington: Association of Science-
Technology Centers.

Crane, Valerie, ed. 1994. *Informal science learning/What the
research says about television, science museums, and community-based projects.* Dedham, MA: Research Communications
Inc.

Falk, John H. and Martin Weiss. 1933. Utilizing museums to
promote public understanding of science: early adolescent misconceptions about AIDS prevention. In *Visitor
Studies: Theory, Research and Practice, Vol. 6,* pp. 98-105.
Jacksonville, AL: Visitor Studies Association.

Lewenstein, Bruce V. 1994. A survey of activities in public
communication of science and technology in the United
States. In *When science becomes culture,* ed. Bernard
Schiele, pp. 119-178. Québec: Université du Québec à
Montréal, Centre Jacques-Cartier, and University of
Ottawa Press.

Miller, Jon. 1991. Public scientific literacy and attitudes
towards science and technology. In *Science & Engineering
Indicators — 1991,* ed. National Science Board, pp. 165-
191. Washington: US Government Printing Office.

St. John, Mark, and Sheila Grinell. 1993. *Vision to reality: critical dimensions in science center development.* Washington:
Association of Science-Technology Centers.

Notes on Contributors

Mihaly Csikszentmihaly is a professor of human development at the University of Chicago, and is the author of ten books and more than 150 scholarly articles. His research on the optimal experience of "flow" has helped several museums enhance the effectivenesss of their exhibits.

Lynn D. Dierking is Associate Director, Science Learning inc. (Sli), an Annapolis, Maryland-based non-profit educational research and development company which specializes in helping museums and other organizations better serve their publics. She is recognized for her research on family learning in museums and, with John H. Falk, is author of *The Museum Experience* (Whalesback Books, 1992) as well as numerous scholarly articles. Dr. Dierking has consulted with a wide range of institutions in the areas of interpretive planning, exhibition development and evauation, education program development and evaluation, audience assessment and long range planning.

Linda Downs is Head of Education at the National Gallery of Art in Washington, D.C. She has served as a board member of the American Association of Museums/International Council of Museums; is a board member of the American Federation of Arts; serves on the College Art Association Education Committee and Museum Committee and has been a consultant on museum education to foundations and museums in the United States, Australia, and Mexico.

Deborah Edward is Executive Director of the Austin Children's Museum. She received her Ph.D. in Educational Psychology from the University of Texas at Austin and has worked in elementary education, evaluation, and community-based informal education. As founding director of a ten-year old participatory museum, Edward is interested in exhibit design, program evaluation and research. She is currently Vice President for Programs of the Association of Youth Museums and she has published articles in Association of Youth Museum's *Hand-to-Hand* journal as well as AAM's Technical Reports. Her recent study of youth volunteer programs in museums, reflecting information from over 200 museums, has been published as a handbook for designing youth programs.

Gary W. Evans is Professor of Design and Environmental Analysis at Cornell University. He is an environmental psychologist whose primary areas of scholarly interest are in environmental stress and research methodology in human-environment relations. A Fulbright Research Fellow and an International Fellow of the Swedish Work Environment Fund, Professor Evans has authored or co-authored four books and over 100 scholarly publications. Among his recent works is *Environment, cognition and action* with T. Garling (Oxford University Press, 1991).

John H. Falk is Executive Director of Science Learning, inc. (Sli) , an Annapolis, Maryland-based non-profit educational research and development company which specializes in helping museums and other organizations to better serve their publics. Best known for his research on understanding museum visitor learning and behavior, Dr. Falk is the author of over fifty scholarly articles in the areas of learning, biology, and education as well as numerous educational materials and books. Recent publications include *Leisure Decisions Influencing African American Use of Museums* (American Association of Museums, 1993) and, with Dr. Lynn Dierking, *The Museum Experience*.

Alan J. Friedman is the Director of the New York Hall of Science, New York City's public science-technology center, a leading center with special recognition for its work in encouraging new technologies, in creating new models for teacher training, and in evluating the effectiveness of informal science learning. Before coming to New York, Dr. Friedman served as Conseiller Scientific et Muséologique for the Cité des

Sciences et de l'Industrie, Paris, and was the Director of Astronomy amd Physics at the Lawrence Hall of Science, University of California, Berkeley for 12 years. He is co-author, with Carol C. Donley, of *Einstein.as Myth and Muse* (Cambridge University Press, 1985). Dr. Friedman received his Ph.D. in Physics from Florida State University and his B.S. in Physics from the Georgia Institute of Technology.

Alan Hedge directs the Human Factors and Ergonomics program in the Department of Design and Environmental Analysis at Cornell University. His research focuses on indoor environment design issues that affect the comfort, health, and performance of people. This work includes studies of lighting, air quality, physical layout, and equipment design. He has published numerous research articles on indoor environment ergonomics. He is actively involved in both national and international professional ergonomics societies.

Kim Hermanson will receive her Ph.D. from the University of Chicago Graduate School of Education in March 1996. Her research examines learning in the formal and informal institutions of everyday life.

Douglas Herrman obtained a M.S. and a Ph.D. in Experimental Psychology at the University of Delaware, followed by postdoctoral study on mathematical modelling of conceptual processes at Stanford University. His research and writings on memory are well known among pyschologists in his field. For more than a decade Dr. Herrman has focused on investigating ways to improve or rehabilitate memory capabilities. He is a Fellow of the American Psychological Association and the American Psychological Society.

Dana G. Holland was a Research Associate for Science Learning, inc. for three years. She holds a Masters of Applied Anthropology from the University of Maryland, College Park. Her interests are in ethnographic/qualitiative research. She is currently traveling in Asia.

Eugene Matusov received his Ph.D. in pyschology from the University of California at Santa Cruz in 1994. He is currently a visiting researcher at the University of California, Santa Cruz and Research Fellow of the McDonnell Foundation. Dr. Matusov's areas of interest are the study of cognitive processes (such as planning, problem solving, resolving interpersonal conflicts, and organizing guidance and collaboration) in institutional contexts, especially schools. He is co-author, with J. Baker-Sennett and B. Rogoff of the chapter Sociocultural processes of creative planning in children's playcrafting in *Context and*

Cognition: Ways of Learning and Knowing. P. Light and G. Butterworth, eds. (Harvester-Wheatsheaf, Hertfordshire, U.K., 1992).

John U. Ogbu received his B.A., M.A., and Ph.D. in social anthropology from the University of California, Berkeley. He is Alumni Distinguished Professor of Anthropology at the University of California, Berkeley. His special field is Education and Culture, in which he has conducted several studies and published extensively. He is a member of the National Academy of Education and a former Chairman of the UNESCO Committee of Experts on Transfer of Knowledge.

Dana J. Plude is an Associate Professor of Pyschology at the University of Maryland where he has taught since 1984. He received his Ph.D. at Syracuse University and spent three years as a Postdoctoral Fellow at the highly regarded Mental Performance and Aging Laboratory of the Boston Veterans Administration Medical Center. Dr. Plude has published numerous articles and book chapters on the topic of memory, attention, and aging. Currently he is investigating how different methods of audio-visual presentation may be used in memory improvement training of the elderly.

Barbara Rogoff received her Ph.D. from Harvard University and is currently UC Santa Cruz Foundation Professor of Psychology at the University of California, Santa Cruz, an Osher Fellow of the Exploratorium in San Francisco, and an advisor to the Children's Discovery Museum of San Jose. Dr. Rogoff is Editor of *Human Development* and received the Scribner Award from the American Educational Research Association for her book *Apprenticeship in Thinking* (Oxford University Press, 1990). She is interested in how children and families, schools, and informal institutions manage learning and instruction, in differing communities. This topic is also dealt with in B. Rogoff, J. J. Mistry, and C. Mosier (1993), Guided participation in cultural activity by toddlers and caregivers, in Monographs of the Society for research in Child Development 58:7, Serial No. 236.

Jeremy Roschelle, formerly of the University of Massachusetts at Dartmouth, is Senior Software Designer and Co-Principal Investigator for the SimClac Project. His current research and software development is focussed on the use of computer graphics to enable all students to gain access to calculus. He is most interested in how visualization and imagery can enable students to develop complex concepts in science and mathematics. Roschelle has a Ph.D. in Education: Math, Science and Tecnology from the University of California, Berkeley.

Conference Participants

_Attendees at the conference "Public Institutions for Personal Learning:
Understanding the Long-Term Impact of Museums"
Annapolis, Maryland, August 1994_

Name	Institution
John Balling	Dickinson College
Minda Borun	Franklin Institute
Barbara Butler	National Science Foundation
Valerie Crane	Research Communications Ltd.
Mihalyi Czikszentmihalyi	University of Chicago
Rebecca Danvers	Institute of Museum Services
David Davis-Vanatta	Howard Hughes Medical Institute
Raylene Decatur	Maryland Science Center
Lynn Dierking	Science Learning, inc.
Linda Downs	National Gallery of Art
Amina Dickerson	The Chicago Hisorical Society
Sara Dubberly	American Association of Museums
Sally Duensing	The Exploratorium
John Durel	Baltimore City Life Museums
Deborah Edward	Austin Children's Museum
Carol Enseki	The Brooklyn Children's Museum
Gary Evans	Cornell University
John Falk	Science Learning, inc.
Alan Friedman	New York Hall of Science
Ellen Giusti	Amer. Mus. of Nat. Hist.
Jeff Hayward	People, Places & Design Research
Alan Hedge	Cornell University
George Hein	Lesley College
Douglas Herrmann	National Center for Health Statistics
Kim Igoe	American Association of Museums
Thomas Krakauer	Museum of Life and Science
Karen Leutjen	The Valentine Museum

Name	Institution
Margie Marino	Denver Mus. of Nat. Hist.
Ann Mintz	Orlando Science Center
Martha Morris	National Museum of American History
Mary Ellen Munley	New York State Museum
Ann Muscat	California Museum of Science & Industry
John Ogbu	University of California, Berkeley
Wendy Pollock	Association of Science-Technology Centers
Lisa Roberts	Chicago Botanic Garden
Barbara Rogoff	University of California, Santa Cruz
Jeremy Roschelle	SimCalc Project, San Francisco
Bob Russell	Informal Science Review(observer)
Judith Segal	U.S. Department of Education
Marsha Semmel	National Endowment for the Humanities
Karen Sensenig	The Annenberg/CPB Math and Science Project
John Shane	Museum of Science (Boston)
Ruth Shelly	Stephen Birch Aquarium-Museum, Scripps
Michael Spock	The Field Museum
A.T. Stephens	Fairfax County Park Authority
Mac West	Informal Science Review(observer)
Karen Wizevich	Liberty Science Center
John Wright	Henry Ford Museum & Greenfield Village